Contemporary Political Ideologies

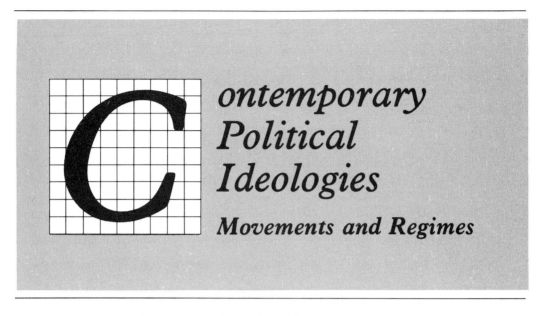

Contemporary Political Ideologies

Movements and Regimes

Second Edition

Roy C. Macridis

Brandeis University

Little, Brown and Company   Boston   Toronto

Library of Congress Cataloging in Publication Data

Macridis, Roy C.
  Contemporary political ideologies.

  Includes bibliographies and index.
  1. Political science--History. 2. Comparative
government. I. Title.
JA81.M316 1983   320.5   82-4653
ISBN 0-316-54281-4

Library of Congress Catalog Card No. 82-4653

ISBN 0-316-54281-4

9 8 7 6 5 4 3 2 1

BP

Published simultaneously in Canada by Little, Brown & Company (Canada) Limited

Printed in the United States of America

This book is dedicated to the memory of my late son, Peter.

Preface to the Second Edition

This second, revised edition, only three years after the appearance of the first book, is an acknowledgment of its good reception and wide use among many students in a great number of colleges and universities, in many different courses, and at different levels—from introductory to advanced. It all goes to show how variegated the appeals of ideology can be!

I used the opportunity to overhaul three chapters. I broadened my introductory chapter to include some remarks on the theory of ideology and to indicate what I call the basic building blocks of major political ideologies and movements. I expanded the chapter on the New Left to give a broad overview of revolutionary ideologies—anarchism, populism, guerrilla revolutionary warfare—that bring into focus the Iranian Revolution, guerrilla warfare in Central America, and, even if indirectly, terrorism. In my last chapter, I return in more detail to what I continue to claim to be one of the most enduring attachments of men and women everywhere—nationalism.

A number of people helped me with advice. Professor John Gunnel of the State University of New York-Albany urged me to rework my first chapter and made many welcome suggestions about it; Professor Eric Nordlinger of Brown University read the three overhauled chapters, and his many excellent comments saved me from many errors and hasty interpretative statements; Professor John George of Oklahoma State University had the kindness to write to me about one error and some discrepancies he had found; Geraldyn Spaulding retyped, fast and accurately, almost the whole manuscript. Finally, Little, Brown and Will Ethridge, the political science editor, exercised their newly acquired proprietary rights over the book with great tact and civility. I thank warmly each and all of them.

Roy C. Macridis
Waltham, Mass.

July 1, 1982

Preface to the First Edition

This book is in a sense an acknowledgment of the vitality of political ideologies and the need to know them and understand them better. Without ideology we are almost without a conscience, without law and order, without an anchor and a port. But also, without ideology we can have no vision of the other worlds we want to sail to. Ideologies fashion our motivations, our attitudes, and the political regimes under which we live. They shape our values.

A number of colleagues have helped me at various stages of the writing of this book. Professors David Schmitt of Northeastern University and Professor Fred von der Mehden of Rice University read the manuscript twice and made valuable suggestions with regard to emphasis, organization, and substance. I am deeply indebted to both, and, as they can see, I followed their suggestions in a great number of instances. Professor George J. Graham, Jr. of Vanderbilt University went through the first draft, and his many careful comments and observations helped me clarify my presentation and correct quite a few errors. Professor Robert McHenry of Montgomery College read the sections on democracy and communism, and his vigorous reactions, even if positive, made me realize how easy it is to appear "ideological" in discussing political ideologies. I have tried to avoid it. Marc Posner, a graduate student in politics at Brandeis, checked a number of references, supplied many others, and helped me with the bibliographical and biographical material and sketches. Needless to say, I am responsible for all mistakes and interpretative statements.

Some authors and their books were of particular value to me and they should be singled out. Bogdan B. Denitch's *The Legitimization of Revolution: The Yugoslav Case* (New Haven, Conn.: Yale U.P., 1976) is excellent. K. Dietrich Bracher's *The German Dictatorship* (New York: Praeger, 1970) is, to my best knowledge, the most thoughtful and sober account of the Hitler movement and Nazi regime. I found Edward R. Tannebaum's *The*

Fascist Experience (New York: Basic Books, 1972) very helpful, and the same is true for Herman Finer's *Mussolini's Italy* (New York: Henry Holt, 1935), which, though written in the late 1930s, retains a remarkable freshness. James R. Townsend's *Politics in China* (Boston: Little, Brown, 1974) sets high standards of analysis and interpretation. If these authors find that I have followed some of their observations even when I fail, inadvertently, to cite them, I hope they will accept this acknowledgment of my thankful appreciation.

Barbara Nagy, Geraldyn Spaulding and Zina Goldman—all women who keep Brandeis going—typed various versions of the manuscript and they have my warmest thanks. Acknowledgments and thanks go also to my wife for her great help with the early stages of the book.

Last but not least, my friend James Murray III, President of Winthrop Publishers, has been, as in the past, a constant source of encouragement and support.

This book is dedicated to my late son, Peter, who turned out to have been the only "ideologue" in the family. He drowned in the Columbia River on March 11, 1978, while trying to realize a youthful dream with his friend, Tim Black—crossing the United States from West to East by canoe.

Roy C. Macridis
Waltham, Mass.

February 1, 1979

Contents

One person with a belief is a social power equal to ninety-nine who have only interests.

JOHN STUART MILL Representative Government

1 | Political Ideologies: Introduction

*Every . . . state is a species of association, and . . .
all associations are instituted for the purpose of
attaining some good. . . . We may therefore
hold . . . that the particular association [the State]
which . . . includes all the rest will pursue this aim
most. . . .*

ARISTOTLE Politics

*. . . Aspirations, passion, hope, volition and choice
. . . belong inalienably to the life of mind and the
spirit. Without them . . . we languish, we perish. We
must not allow ourselves to be paralyzed by thought;
rather we must use it. We dare not forever stand and
wait. It is late and there is a world at stake.*

HENRY AIKEN Ideology—A Debate

All of us, whether we know it or not, have an ideology, even those who claim
openly that they do not. All of us believe in certain things. All of us value
something — property, friends, the law, freedom, or authority. All of us
have prejudices, even those who claim to be free of them. We all look at the
world in one way or another — we have "ideas" about it — and we try to
make sense out of what is going on in it. Also, we all are attracted to those
with similar values and ideas, who like the same things we do, who have
prejudices similar to ours, and who, in general, look upon the world in the
same way we do. In fact, we talk of "like-minded" people, individuals who
share certain beliefs and tend to congregate — in clubs, churches, political
parties and movements, various associations, and so on. Lastly, no matter
how independent we claim to be, we all are influenced by ideas. We are
sensitive, in varying degrees and ways, to appeals made — to our honor,
patriotism, family, religion, pocketbook, race, or class — and we can all be
manipulated and aroused. We are creators and creatures of ideas — of
ideologies — and through them we manipulate others or are ourselves manipulated.

Ideologies are very much a part of our lives; they are not dead and they
are not on the decline anywhere, as some authors have argued.

Ah, but a man's reach should exceed his grasp,
Or what's a Heaven for?

wrote Browning in 1885. Almost a century later, a strong upsurge in ideological and utopian movements made powerful governments totter as many sought their own vision of heaven on earth. "Be rational; think of the impossible" was one of the slogans of intellectuals and students in the late 1960s.

Not only are ideologies surviving, their all-embracing importance is again being recognized. "Neo-Marxists" now agree that a drastic revolutionary overhaul of the society, if there is to be one, must be above all a moral and intellectual revolution: a revolution in the *ideology* of society. It must create its own "counter-consciousness," its own "counterculture" — a new set of beliefs and values and a new style of life that will eat, like a worm, into the core of prevailing liberal-capitalist orthodoxy. Only with its ideological core gone can the old society be changed and replaced. The socialization of the means of production, economic planning, communism, and the abolition of income inequalities — none of these have a chance of success until and unless the ideas that people have about society and about their relations with each other change.

What Is an Ideology?

Ideology has been defined as "a set of closely related beliefs, or ideas, or even attitudes, characteristic of a group or community."[1] Similarly a *political* ideology is "a set of ideas and beliefs" that people hold about their political regime and its institutions and about their own position and role in it. Political ideology accordingly appears synonymous with "political culture" or "political tradition." The British or the Americans or the French or the Russians pattern their political life on the basis of different sets of interrelated ideas, beliefs, and attitudes.

Various groups, however, within one and the same political community may, and often do, at given times and under given conditions, challenge the prevailing ideology. Interests, classes, and various political and religious associations may develop a "counter-ideology" or even a "counterculture" that questions the status quo and attempts to modify it. They advocate change rather than order; they criticize, to the point of rejecting, the political regime and the existing social and economic arrangements; they advance schemes for the restructuring and the reordering of the society; and they spawn political movements that in one way or another attempt to gain power to bring about the changes they advocate. In this sense, a political ideology moves people into action to bring about changes in their way of life and to modify the existing political, social, and economic relations. In discussing ideologies — all ideologies — we must always bear in mind these two all-important characteristics: a given political ideology rationalizes the status quo, whereas other, competing ideologies and movements challenge it.

1. Plamenatz, *Ideology*. New York: Praeger, 1970, p. 15.

Philosophy, Theory, and Ideology

A distinction should be made between philosophy or theory on the one hand, and ideology on the other. "Philosophy" means literally love of wisdom — the detached and often solitary contemplation and search for truth. In the strictest meaning of the term, "theory" is the formulation of propositions that causally link variables to account for or explain a phenomenon. Such linkages should be, again in the strict sense, empirically verifiable. But this is so primarily in the natural sciences; in social sciences it is very difficult to come up with empirical verifications. What separates theory or philosophy from ideology is that while the first two involve contemplation, organization of ideas, and whenever possible, demonstration, ideology incites people to action. It shapes beliefs that move people into action. Men and women organize to *impose* certain philosophies or theories and to realize them in a given society. Ideology thus involves action and collective effort. Even when they originate (as they often do) in philosophy or theory, ideologies are inevitably highly simplified, and even distorted, versions of the original doctrines. It is always interesting to know the philosophy or the theory from which an ideology originates. But it is at least as important to understand ideology as a distinct and separate entity to be studied in terms of its own logic and dynamics, rather than in terms of the theory from which it stems or the closeness of its resemblance to it.

It is difficult to understand when and under what circumstances a theory or a philosophy becomes transformed into an ideology — that is, into an action-oriented movement. Important theories and philosophic doctrines remain unnoticed and untouched for generations before they are "discovered." History may be compared to a freezer where ideas and theories are stored to be used at a later time. Different works of Plato, for example, have been at various times the origin of different ideological movements. Similarly, whereas a powerful ideological movement developed from the major works of Karl Marx, it is his early works today — the "early Marx" or the "young Marx" — that have been adapted to suit some contemporary movements and tastes. There is a dialectic between ideas, as such, and social needs, and both are needed in order to have an ideology. Heartfelt demands arising from the social body may fail for the lack of ideas; and ideas may go begging for a long time for the lack of relevance to social needs.

Philosophy and Political Ideology: Major Themes

The debt most political ideologies owe to political speculation and philosophy is quite obvious when we look at some of the major themes that political ideologies address: (1) the role and the nature of the individual (human nature); (2) the nature of truth and how it can be discovered; (3) the relationship between the individual and the group, be it the tribe, the small city-state, or the contemporary state as we know it; (4) the characteristics of

Plato (c. 427–347 B.C.)

Plato was a Greek philosopher, a disciple of Socrates, and the founder of philosophic idealism, according to which ideas exist in themselves and by themselves, forming a perfect and harmonious universe. As a political philosopher, Plato wrote *The Republic,* an ideal state with a strict class structure ruled by philosopher-kings who divested themselves of property and family ties in order to rule for the common good. Plato's description of a more practical state can be found in his *Laws.*

political authority — its source and limits, if any; (5) the goals and the mechanics of economic organization and (6) the much-debated issue of material and economic equality as it relates to individual freedom. Normative judgments about each and all of the themes mentioned above and many more are the very "stuff" of contemporary political ideologies. Some have been hotly debated over many centuries and will continue to be debated.

The Individual

Political ideologies are addressed to each one of us; they all begin with one preconception or another about us — about human nature. Some believe that we are the creatures of history and the environment, that our nature and characteristics are interwoven with the material conditions of life and ultimately shaped by them. Human nature is plastic and everchanging and with the proper "social engineering" — another word for education — it can be shaped into a pattern. Many ideologies assume that with the proper changes in our environment and the proper inculcation of new values, "new" men and women can be created. There is nothing sacrosanct, therefore, in our present institutions and values; on the contrary, many of them are downright bad. On the other hand, many well-known philosophers, especially those in the period of the Enlightenment and in the eighteenth century, have presented a different notion of human nature. People have some innate characteristics: we are born with traits of sociability, goodness, and rationality. We are also endowed with rights, such as life, liberty, and property. Institutions are but a reflection of these human traits and rights, and a political organization must respect them; indeed, it must provide the best means for protecting them. Therefore, the State that protects these rights cannot invade them — the State is limited. Finally, other political philosophers have argued that human nature is "greedy," "selfish," and "bellicose" and that it is the duty of the State to curb our ignoble drives. Political power and coercion are what make social life possible and safe.

The Nature of Truth

Is there one truth that can be imposed? Or is truth progressively discovered as many ideas and points of view compete with each other — every generation adding something to it? The notion that there is one truth revealed only to some or perceived authoritatively by them requires us to submit to it. We must hew as closely as possible to what is given, and obey those who speak for it. Human beings are thus deprived of the freedom to seek truth, to experiment with new ideas, to confront each other with different points of view, and to live in a system that tolerates different ways.

On the other hand, there are those for whom a constant exploration of the universe by human beings and a constant inquiry into the foundations and condition of life is the only way to discover truth. "Such is the nature of the understanding that it cannot be compelled to the belief of anything by outside force," wrote John Locke. People who hold this view favor competition of ideas, advocate tolerance for all points of view, and want to assure the conditions of freedom that are indispensable for ongoing inquiry. This is what we call pluralism. If one Absolute Truth did exist, pluralists would be the first to reject it for fear that it would deprive human beings of the challenge of discovering it!

The Individual and Society

For some social scientists there is no such entity as an "individual." The individuals are perceived as part of a herd or a group whose protection and survival require cooperation. The individual is considered helpless outside the group or the State. The group or the State then makes the rules of conduct and establishes the relationship between rulers and ruled. The individual is a "social being" — first and last!

The other point of view stresses the opposite — the primacy of individuals. They are perceived as having originally lived in the state of nature and endowed with reason and natural rights. To protect themselves and their belongings, these individuals contrive to create a political society that protects their lives and their property. The political system — the State — is made up of individuals, by the individuals, and for the individuals. It is the result of a contract — freely entered upon.

As with theories about human nature, the manner in which we view the relationship between the individual and the society often determines our political ideology. Those who give primacy to the group show an inclination to emphasize the "organic" nature of society and of the political system: it is a whole, like our body, and the individuals may be viewed like the cells of our organism. They are only parts that fit into the whole; they have no freedoms and rights. The "organic" theory puts the accent on the whole and the close interdependence of the parts that is required to make it function. This theory, therefore, does not make room for *change,* since any change unbalances the existing relationships among the parts and hence endangers the whole — the society. It is also totalitarian in the name of society's overriding purpose to which all parts and individuals remain subservient.

Those who assume the primacy of the individual reach diametrically opposite conclusions. *The individual is all that counts.* Individuals make the political society in which they live, and they can change it. Political life is an act of will and political authority is based on consent. The society consists of a maze of overlapping, cooperating, or conflicting wills and units — both individuals and groups — participating in the political system. The preservation of the individual and of individual freedom is a value greater than the survival of the whole.

Political Authority

Basic divisions on the nature and the organization of political authority derive from theories discussed above about the nature of truth and about the relationship between the individual and the group. Belief in one overriding truth leads almost always to an authoritarian position. It is *elitist.* It assumes that a small group "knows" and is capable of governing on the basis of certain qualities. For Plato these qualities were *intellectual:* the philosopher-king; for some they are *religious:* the priesthood; for others they are *prescriptive:* based on inheritance. The qualities deemed necessary for governing could also be *charismatic:* appeal and personality, or *class* — either the property owners or the working class — having a historical mission of ruling or transforming the society.

On the other hand, those who postulate that political authority derives from the will of individuals favor limiting political authority in order to allow for participation and open deliberation. They advocate freedom of thought and expression, respect for individual freedoms, and freedom from associations, political parties, and all other organizations. *No claims to rule based on birth, heredity, wealth, intellectual superiority, or prescriptive titles are accepted.* No "monopoly of truth" is conceded — to anybody.

Equality and Property

Many of the most important political ideologies can be distinguished in terms of the answers they try to provide to the following questions: *Who produces and what is produced? Who gets what and how much?* The answers are very complex and all the more so since the very concepts and questions, let alone the answers, are laden with emotions and values; they are steeped in ideology.

The central issue remains that of equality. For the early liberals, equality was interpreted narrowly to mean equality before the law, or equality of all to vote and participate in the choice of political leaders. Yet, unless people have equal access to education and to material, even if minimal, living standards, equality before the law is a fiction. Throughout the twentieth century, as we shall see, those who advocated political or legal equality above all clashed with the proponents of material equality. There is a constant tension between material and economic equality on the one hand and formal legal and political equality on the other.

Liberal democracies have emphasized freedoms and property rights — even when they have been forced to qualify them for the sake of greater material equality. Socialism and communism on the other hand have tended to stress material equality. But throughout the twentieth century, as we shall see, virtually all political regimes and all political ideologies have come to terms with the need for providing for greater material opportunities and equality. There has been, as a result, a corresponding change in our concepts of property and of property relations.

Property is no longer defined only in terms of land or the real estate one owns or even in terms of liquid wealth and high salaries. These still remain important. But for the majority of the people in most societies, "property" has become "public" in the sense that it consists of claims against the State that individuals have for services and benefits to which they are entitled. Education, health, housing, transportation, old age pensions, unemployment benefits, and special assistance programs have become rights —

"entitlements" — and they are just as important as property rights. Whatever the justification or the adequacy of such "entitlements," they have changed significantly the distribution of material benefits and the nature of property in most all societies. Claims for such services and benefits have, as long as they remain secure, given a cushion to many that is just as important as ownership. They provide at least for a degree of material equality.

Notions about human nature, truth, political authority, freedom, property and equality, and the production and the distribution of goods and services are present in each and every ideology we shall study. They are the major building blocks of all contemporary ideologies and movements. Men and women organize behind their respective visions of a just and better world or barricade themselves to defend their own visions of justice — of their own world. Political philosophy gives us all a chance to contemplate these notions in a detached and objective way; political ideologies and movements often transform them into a battle cry.

The Uses of Political Ideology

An ideology, then, is a set of ideas and beliefs held by a number of people. It spells out what is valued and what is not, what must be maintained and what must be changed, and it shapes accordingly the attitudes of those who share it. In contrast to philosophy and theory, which are concerned with knowledge and understanding, ideologies relate to social and political behavior and action. They incite people to political action and provide the basic framework for political action.

Legitimization

One of the most important functions of a political ideology is, as we already pointed out, to give value to a political regime and its institutions. It shapes the "operative ideas" that make a political regime work. Political ideology provides for the basic categories in terms of which the people know the political regime, abide by the rules, and participate in one manner or another in it. To perform this all-important role, a political ideology must provide for a *coherent set of rules* and it must set them forth as clearly as possible. A constitution is a political document, generally speaking, that embodies these rules, but to function well it must be valued by the people. A political ideology shapes these values and beliefs about the constitution and lets the people know their role and position within the political regime in which they live.

Solidarity and Mobilization

A common sharing of ideas integrates individuals into the community, a group, a party, or a movement. Ideas, commonly held, define the things that are acceptable and the tasks to be accomplished, excluding all others.

Ideologies play the same role that totems and taboos play in primitive tribes, defining what is common to the members and what is alien. The Soviet Communist ideology, for instance, unifies those who adhere to it by branding the outside world of capitalism as the enemy. All ideologies perform this function of unifying, integrating, and giving a sense of identity to those who share it, but they do so with varying degrees of success. Nationalism as an ideology, for instance, has provided the unifying and integrating force that has made it possible for nation-states to emerge and retain their positions. The greater the integration sought and the stronger the solidarity to be maintained, the greater the emphasis on unifying symbolisms.

Leadership and Manipulation

Ideologies incite people to action, as we have pointed out, but to what kind of action, and for what purpose, depends very much on the content and substance of an ideology — of the ideologies we shall discuss in this book. Manipulation of ideas, a special case, often involves the conscious and deliberate formulation of propositions that incite people to action for ends that are clearly perceived only by those in power or attempting to get political power. They may promise peace in order to make war, freedom in order to establish an authoritarian system, socialism in order to consolidate the position and privileges of the property holders, and so on.

Ideology often becomes, under certain circumstances, a powerful instrument of manipulation. Usually in times of social distress and anxiety, or when society seems divided into warring groups and frustration warps daily life, simple propositions and promises on how to remove the evils besetting society fall upon receptive ears and minds. The demagogue, the leader, the self-professed savior is lurking somewhere in all societies in such times to spread his or her message and to manipulate those who seem to have nowhere else to turn.

Communication

A coherent set of ideas — an ideology — shared by a given number of people makes communication among them much easier. It provides a *common, highly simplified special language,* like shorthand. Words have special meaning — "the Reds," "the bleeding-heart liberals," "the pigs," "the Establishment," "fat cats," "the power elite," "the chosen people," or "communist conspiracy." These are terms easily understood by those who belong to a given group, and they help others to place them within a given ideological family. They are, of course, very crude terms, and ideologies usually provide more sophisticated ones. "The last stage of capitalism," "neo-colonialism," "avant-garde of the working class," "democratic centralism," "democratic pluralism," "human rights," and "gradual change" are commonly understood by those who use them in their own respective political group or party. These terms can help the outsider to identify the ideological family to which the speaker belongs. A common ideology simplifies communication and makes common effort easier for all those who accept it.

Communication is also made easier because people with a common ideology look upon the outside world with the same preconceptions. They all have the same binoculars! People receive messages from the world outside and have to put these messages into some kind of order — into concepts. These concepts, in terms of which messages for the outside world are sorted out, depend on ideology. For some, the condition of the poor calls for study and concern; for others, it is a bore — the situation of the poor is attributed to innate laziness. This, however, is an extreme case. More frequent are cases of interpretation or evaluation, where the same event is seen from a different viewpoint — a different ideological perspective. The assassination of a political leader is applauded by some and regretted by others. Any Soviet move anywhere in the world is an indication of the Communist expansionist conspiracy for some; for others, it is an inevitable reaction to American provocation! People may also reject messages because of their ideology. A mystic is blind to the world outside; for a scientist, the world is a constant source of wonder to be studied and explained.

Expression

Ideology provides a vehicle to express our wants, our interests, and our hopes, and even our personal drives and anxieties. Some have argued that the primary function of an ideology is to rationalize and protect material interests or to provide for a powerful medium for their fulfillment. Thus, liberal democracy has been viewed as the rationalization of the interests of the rich and the relatively well-to-do, while revolutionary Marxism is an instrument for the satisfaction of the demands of the propertyless, the workers, and the poor.

But it is not only interest that spawns an ideology. Emotional drives and personality traits are expressed through different ideologies. It has been argued, for instance, that there is a distinct "authoritarian personality" which finds expression and fulfillment through being subject to rank and authority. In this manner, any ideology can provide a form of expression, and usually brings like-minded people together. The Anti-Vivisection League, environmentalists, anti- and pro-abortionists, proponents or opponents of the Equal Rights Amendment, as well as democrats, communists, and fascists, all may give vent to their personality, interests, and emotions through their particular ideology.

Ideology then, provides for *emotional attachments*. People are proud of their ideas and proud of each other and all those who share them. They belong to the group that espouses them just as people belong to their families. They relate to it, and help each other in a common search of realization. A person who has an ideology that is shared within a group of people is likely to be happy and secure, basking in the togetherness of the common endeavor. Identifying with it, he or she is never alone.

Criticism and Utopia

Ideologies often embody *social criticism.* Criticism confronts existing beliefs and attempts through argument and persuasion to challenge and change them. Critical examination of social and political beliefs has also played an important role in the development of new ideologies and the rejection of others. Many beliefs have yielded to it, to be replaced by others. Institutions like slavery, property, hereditary monarchy, bureaucratic centralization, and many others have been critically challenged and accordingly abandoned or qualified.

In certain instances, criticism may be pushed to extremes. Certain ideologies are like a *dream,* an impossible and unrealizable quest. An "ideological" person is one who criticizes and rejects the existing order of things while dreaming of other and better worlds: world government, perfect equality, abundance for all, elimination of force, and abolition of war. Many political ideologies have something of this quality, but those that have it in an exaggerated form are called *utopias,* a word derived from the Greek for "nowhere." If we give this particular meaning to the term, we are implying that an "ideologue" is either naive or dangerous or a little bit crazy, ignoring Shakespeare's pithy remark that dreams are the stuff that life is made of!

Ideology and Political Action

Above all, ideology *moves* people into concerted action. Sometimes it moves a whole nation; sometimes it is a group, a class or a political party that unite behind certain principles to express their interests, demands, and beliefs. In France today, socialism is for many the vindication of a long-standing quest for equality — material equality. In the United States, on the other hand, it is political and economic liberalism — the freedom to produce, consume, think, and worship — that seem to be the major rallying point for many political movements. An example of a single-issue organization motivated by ideology to take political action is the "environmentalists," who, both in the United States and elsewhere, seek to put an end to the despoliation of our physical environment; they share many of the same objectives with the various "No Nuke" organizations. Other powerful single groups want to reintroduce religious teaching and prayers in the schools, while still others mount a fierce campaign against abortion. "Welfare liberals" continue to reconcile freedoms with state intervention and welfare legislation to mitigate the harshness of economic competition. Communism — whether adopted by a nation, a movement, or a party that challenges the existing political order — is an ideology that projects a vision of abundance, equality, and peace. Most of the Communist movements view the Soviet Union as the legitimate advocate of a new social order that will replace the existing one. "Action-oriented" ideologies are everywhere in the air!

The dynamics of politics, therefore, lie in the ideas people develop. But the same is true with political institutions, movements, social groups, and political parties. We have to focus on the ideologies they represent, and the beliefs they propagate and legitimize. The same is true for political attitudes. They, too, are fashioned by political ideologies. It is in terms of different constellations of attitudes that major political movements and ideologies can be identified and described. Liberals share common attitudes with regard to race relations, economic policy, prayers in the school, the United Nations, taxes, the draft, nuclear weapons, food stamps, social security, and so on. Conservatives can be identified in terms of a set of different attitudes with regard to some of the same issues; so can socialists or communists.

In studying political ideologies, therefore, we are studying the dynamics of political systems — the type of political regime, its constitution and institutions — the degree to which the regime is accepted, the existing conflicts within the regime, and the manner in which conflicts can be resolved. Compatibility of ideological outlooks makes for stability and acceptance; incompatibility always presages conflict, instabilities, and possibly revolutions.

Types of Political Ideologies

Political ideologies address themselves to values: the quality of life, the distribution of goods and services, freedom and equality. If there were agreement on each and all there would be one single ideology shared by all. But there is no agreement within any society nor, needless to say, among the various political societies of the world. People hold different views; nations project different values and beliefs.

It is precisely here that we see the role of political ideologies: they mobilize men and women into action in favor of one point of view or another, and in favor of one movement or party or another. Their aim is invariably either the preservation of a given point of view or the overhaul of the existing state of things, including the political system itself. The British squire who defended his privilege and his property; the workers who formed trade unions or parties to defend their interests; the American conservatives — all have had a common set of ideas which united them into a common posture. The same is true for the small terrorist bands who seize planes. They want to destroy what they despise most — the complacency of an orderly society interested in material satisfaction.

We may divide political ideologies into three broad categories.

1. Those that defend and rationalize the existing economic, social, and political order at any given time in any given society, which we call *status quo* ideologies.
2. Ideologies that advocate far-reaching changes in the existing social, economic, and political order, which we call *radical* or *revolutionary* ideologies.
3. In between there is, of course, a large gray area favoring gradual changes. We may call these the *reformist* ideologies.

One way to state the difference between *status quo, reformist* and *revolutionary* ideologies is to think of maps and mapmaking. Someone who diligently learns to read a map and to travel by following given routes and signals may be considered to represent a status quo mentality or ideology: he or she simply follows the rules and the signs and is guided by them. On the other hand, a person who attempts to trace his or her own route and to change the signals, but not the destination, is a reformist. There is an agreement that the means must change, not the end. But a revolutionary changes both the map and the destination.

This typology is only a formal one. Ideologies shift and change in content, but also in the particular functions and roles they perform. A revolutionary ideology, for instance, may become transformed into one of status quo when it succeeds in imposing its own values and beliefs. Similarly, the same ideology may be a status quo ideology, protecting the existing order of things in a given place at a given time, and a revolutionary one in a different place or at a different time. Soviet communism in the Soviet Union is a status quo political ideology, while in other countries communism is considered to be a revolutionary one. While workers in the nineteenth century were rising in the name of socialism against Western European liberalism which had become a status quo ideology, liberalism was very much a revolutionary ideology in the eyes of many in Central Europe and in Russia.

Status quo, reformist, and revolutionary ideologies can also be distinguished by the tactics they use to realize their goals. They relate to persuasion, organization, and force. Few, if any, ideologies rely exclusively upon one to the exclusion of the others. Most use, in different proportions, all three. The more fundamental and comprehensive the goals are and the more an ideology and a political movement challenge the status quo, the greater the chances that it will resort to organized force, without, of course, neglecting organization and persuasion. A political ideology, on the other hand, that has limited and incremental goals, as is the case with reformist ideologies, is more likely to resort to political organization and persuasion, but without, however, excluding the use of force.

In general, political ideologies and movements that challenge the status quo are more likely to use force at the time when they confront it. This was the case with Liberalism before it overthrew the aristocratic and monarchical regimes in the eighteenth century and after, and with the Communist and other revolutionary movements first in Russia and later in other countries. Yet, when such political ideologies succeed — when they have been transformed into political regimes and have implemented their major goals and consolidated their position, persuasion and organization is likely to take the place of force.

There is one qualification to these generalizations. According to some analysts there are some political ideologies for which force is a necessary and permanent characteristic. And there are others for which persuasion and political organization, rather than force, is an inherent characteristic. Some authoritarian systems — and communist regimes are included — institutionalize the use of force in order to bring about and maintain compliance. On the other hand, liberal and democratic regimes, committed to political competition and to pluralism, eschew the use of force. If it is to be used, it is only as a last resort.

The Major Political Ideologies: Criteria of Choice

If we look at the spread of contemporary political ideological movements, we have a rich choice of subjects: liberalism, capitalism, democratic socialism, socialism, communism, national communism, consociationalism, corporatism, Eurocommunism, anarchism, Gaullism, Stalinism and post-Stalinism, communalism, self-determination in industry, Titoism, Maoism, welfarism, to say nothing of variations that come from the Third World under various labels. Which ones shall we discuss, and why? We obviously need some criteria to help, and I suggest four: *coherence, pervasiveness, extensiveness,* and *intensiveness.*

Coherence By coherence I have in mind the overall scope of an ideology, along with its internal logic and structure. Is it complete? Does it spell clearly a set of goals and the means to bring them about? Do its various propositions about social, economic, and political life hang together? Is there an organization — a movement or a party — to promote the means of action envisaged? Are the goals varied and many, or is there a single overriding goal?

Pervasiveness Pervasiveness refers to the length of time during which an ideology has been "operative." Some ideologies may show decline over a period of time, only to reappear. Others have been operative over a long period, despite variations and qualifications. Whatever the case, the basic test is the length of time during which an ideology has been shared by people, has affected their lives, and shaped their attitudes and actions.

Extensiveness This refers simply to a crude numerical test. How many people share a given ideology? One can draw a crude "ideological map" showing the number of people sharing, by and large, common political ideologies. The larger the "population space" of a given ideology, the greater its extensiveness. How many people are influenced today by communism? By liberalism? By socialism? By anarchism? An estimate of numbers will answer the question of extensiveness.

Intensiveness Finally, by intensiveness I mean the degree and the intensity of the appeal of an ideology — irrespective of whether it satisfied any of the other three criteria. Does it evoke a spirit of total loyalty and action? "Interest is sluggish," wrote John Stuart Mill. Ideas are not! They are like weapons that in the hands of even a small minority may have a far greater impact on society than widely shared interests. Intensiveness implies emotional commitment, total loyalty, and unequivocal determination to act even at the risk of one's life. It was this kind of intensiveness that Lenin managed to impart to his Bolsheviks, to the Communist party.

Ideally, we should choose among various ideologies only those that satisfy *all* the criteria set forth here — coherence, pervasiveness, extensiveness, and intensiveness. However, this would fail to do justice to some ideologies that have played or are playing an important role in political life, even though they may satisfy only one or two of these criteria, and I intend to take some such movements into account.

For each ideology to be discussed, I shall begin by examining the basic theoretical formulations to which it owes a major debt, and describe its transformation into a political movement and, in some cases, into a political regime. We should never lose sight of the fact that we are dealing with ideas that become political movements and lead people to political action; that their "influence" can be assessed in terms of the strength of the movements and parties through which ideas become readied and armed for a struggle for supremacy. Ideologies are not disembodied entities; they are not abstractions. They exist because men and women share them and adopt them as part of their own lives. Ideologies are weapons when men and women make them so; but they are also havens that produce companionship, cooperation, and fulfillment.

One last remark is in order. If there are so many ideologies and if all of us share different ideologies to help us "know" the outside world and prompt us to act in one way or another, which one of them is "correct"? If all ideologies provide us with different perceptions of the world and views about the world, how do we know what the world is really like? How can we tell about the landscape if we use different binoculars? This is the nagging question throughout the book — the question of the validity of a given ideology. When it comes to the political ideologies that we shall study in this book there is really no authoritative test to produce definitive proof of validity. We can only present the various political ideologies in terms of their internal logic, their coherence, and their relevance to the outside world.

This book does not ask, therefore, which ideologies are "true" and which are "false," even if it criticizes and passes judgment on them. Rather, our approach will be expository: Where does an ideology come from? What does it posit? What does it purport to achieve? What have been its accomplishments or failures?

Bibliography

Apter, David (ed.). *Ideology and Its Discontents.* Englewood Cliffs, N.J.: Prentice-Hall, 1964.

Aristotle. *Politics.* Translated by Ernest Barker. New York: Oxford U.P., 1962.

Aron, Raymond. *The Opium of the Intellectuals.* New York: Norton, 1962.

Bell, Daniel. *The End of Ideology.* Rev. ed. New York: Free Press, 1965.

Bluhm, William T. *Ideologies and Attitudes: Modern Political Culture*. Englewood Cliffs, N.J.: Prentice-Hall, 1974.

Brown, L. B. *Ideology*. New York: Penguin, 1973.

Cox, Richard H. *Ideology, Politics and Political Theory*. Belmont, Calif.: Wadsworth, 1968.

Grimes, Alan, and Horowitz, Robert (eds.). *Modern Political Ideologies*. New York: Oxford U.P., 1959.

Hartz, Louis. *The Liberal Tradition in America*, New York: Harcourt, Brace, 1955.

Lerner, Max. *Ideas Are Weapons: The History and Uses of Ideas*. New York: Viking, 1939.

Lichtheim, George. *The Concept of Ideology and Other Essays*. New York: Random House, 1967.

Mannheim, Karl. *Ideology and Utopia*. New York: Harcourt Brace and World, 1955.

Oakeshott, Michael. *The Social and Political Doctrines of Contemporary Europe*. New York: Cambridge U.P., 1942.

Plamenatz, John. *Ideology*. New York: Praeger, 1970.

Wolin, Sheldon. *Politics and Vision*. Boston: Little, Brown, 1960.

Part One

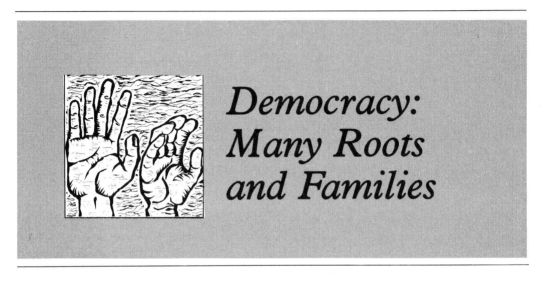

Democracy: Many Roots and Families

Our constitution is called a democracy because power is in the hands not of the few but of the many.

THUCYDIDES   Funeral Oration of Pericles

Democracy literally means "the government of the people." It comes from the Greek word *demos,* people, and *kratos,* government or power. The concept developed first in the small Greek city-states, and the Athenian democracy (roughly between 450 B.C. and 350 B.C.) is what we always go back to as the principal early example. Pericles, the great Athenian statesman, speaking in 431 B.C., defined it in the following terms:

> Our constitution is named a democracy, because it is in the hands not of the few but of the many. But our laws secure equal justice for all in their private disputes and our public opinion welcomes and honors talent in every branch of achievement . . . on grounds of excellence alone. . . . Our citizens attend both to public and private duties and do not allow absorption in their various affairs to interfere with their knowledge of the city's. . . . We decide or debate, carefully and in person all matters of policy, holding . . . that acts are foredoomed to failure when undertaken undiscussed.[1]

In this classic formulation Pericles identifies the following characteristics of a democracy:

1. Government by the people with the full and direct participation of the people.

1. Thucydides. *The History of the Peloponnesian War.* Edited and translated by Sir Richard Livingston. New York: Oxford U.P., "The World's Classics," 1951, pp. 111–13.

19

2. Equality before the law.
3. Pluralism — that is, respect for all talents, pursuits, and viewpoints.
4. Respect for a separate and private (as opposed to public) domain for fulfillment and expression of an individual's personality.

Participation, equality before the law, pluralism and individualism for everyone (except for women and also the many slaves): these were the cornerstones of early democracy, before it disappeared from Greece and the then known world after a relatively short, and unsuccessful, revival in Rome.

Contemporary Democracy: Major Phases

Contemporary democratic thought goes back to the sixteenth century and earlier. It has many roots: feudal practices and institutions, theories about natural law and natural rights, the religious wars and the demand for toleration, the assertion of property rights and freedom to pursue individual economic ventures, the notion of limitations upon political authority — to name only some of them. The basic landmark is provided by the English philosopher John Locke who, writing in the latter part of the seventeenth century, developed in some detail four of the cardinal concepts of democracy: *equality, individual freedom, government based upon consent of the governed,* and *limitations upon the State.* Locke's theories led to the development of representative and parliamentary government.

The second historical landmark in the emergence of liberal democracy are the works of Adam Smith, especially his *Wealth of Nations* (1776), and of a new school of radical philosophers known as the utilitarians who developed in detail the theory of the "economic man" who is driven by the twin impulses to satisfy pleasure and to avoid pain. In line with Adam Smith, they constructed theoretically a limited State that would allow individuals freedom to pursue their own interests. The utilitarians became the exponents of economic liberalism and individualism between 1790 and 1850.

Throughout the nineteenth century Locke's theory of consent and representative government was broadened, but economic liberalism and economic individualism came constantly under scrutiny and criticism. The works of the French philosopher Jean Jacques Rousseau, especially his *Social Contract* (1762), were used to broaden the theory of participation so as to include everybody. The role of the State was reassessed to favor more intervention in economic and social matters for the better protection of the poor, the unemployed, the old, the young, and other disadvantaged groups. For the first time the notion of a *Positive State* — one that acts to provide social services and to guarantee rights — appeared.

Finally, beginning in the twentieth century and extending well into the present, socialists and a growing number of democrats have begun to broaden the notion of a Positive State. They ask for sweeping reforms of the economic system so that the State assumes the obligation of providing an ever-increasing number of services. This is the *Welfare State.*

Socialists question economic individualism and wish to replace it with a system in which productive resources are owned and managed by the State itself. The economy is to be run by the State, no longer for the purpose of profit, but to further social and community needs. Many of the socialist parties today are committed to this, and they represent a synthesis that combines democratic political and individual rights with massive state intervention in the economy and socialization of major units of production.

Thus, in discussing democracy as an ideology, we are dealing with a very rich and comprehensive body of thought and action — one that has undergone shifts and changes in the last three centuries and has produced a great variety of political movements. We shall look at the liberal phase of democracy first, and then its growing welfarist, socialist, or collectivist orientation.

2 | *Democracy and Liberalism*

Laissez-faire, laissez-passer

The individual — his or her experiences and interests — is the basic concept associated with the origin and growth of liberalism and of liberal societies. Knowledge and truth are derived from the judgment of the individual, which in turn is formed by the associations his or her senses make of the outside world — from experience. There is no established truth, nor any transcendental values. Individual experience becomes the supreme value in itself, and the joining of many individual experiences in deliberation is the best possible way for a community to make decisions.

Liberalism is a pure and simple individualistic ethic. In its earliest phase, individualism is cast in terms of natural rights — freedom and equality. It is steeped in moral and religious thought, but already the first signs of a psychology that considers material interests and their satisfaction to be important in the motivation of the individual appear. In its second phase it is based on a psychological theory according to which the realization of interest is the major force that motivates individuals.

Interest, in turn, is related to satisfaction of pleasure. Liberalism is anchored on this simple proposition: men and women strive to maximize pleasure and to minimize pain. But it is not up to the collectivity to impose it; it is not up to a philosopher or a political party to determine it. On the contrary, it is up to individuals to pursue it and in so doing fulfill themselves. Knowledge that stems from experience and education will presumably set limits beyond which pleasure-maximization will not be pushed.

The propositions of early liberalism were directed against eighteenth century absolutism and the many feudal practices that lingered on. Absolutism, supported by a landed aristocracy, stifled human activity while maintaining the feudal privileges of the nobility at a time when the growth of manufacturing and commerce (even if ever so gradual) had begun to open up new vistas of individual effort, exploration, wealth, and change. Yet nations were divided internally into many jurisdictions with different laws, different standards, different tariffs, different regulations, and different weights and measures, all of which impeded communication, trade, and individual freedoms. The famous expression *laissez-faire, laissez-passer* was the battle cry of the burghers, the tradesmen, the moneylenders, the small manufacturers. "Let us do; let us pass" was the motto of the new middle classes. This liberalism was a challenge to the existing order, for laissez-faire capitalism, as we still call it, was the ideology that expressed the interests of the middle class; it stood against absolutism, and especially against political and economic constraints.

Liberals proclaimed individualism and individual freedoms — especially freedom of movement and trade; they borrowed from the past to develop what gradually became a comprehensive theory of individual rights to challenge and to limit absolute political power; they appealed to and represented the rising new classes and the new forms of wealth that began to appear in Western Europe. They also received the support of the peasants, against the landed aristocracy, and the workingmen, who became attracted by the promise of freedoms and equality. As a political ideology, liberalism appealed to large sectors of the society, while being opposed by the monarchy, the landed aristocracy, and the Church.

The Three Cores of Liberalism

There are three elements within liberalism. One is *moral,* the second is *political,* and the third is *economic.* The moral core contains an affirmation of basic values and rights attributable to the "nature" of a human being — freedom, dignity, and life — subordinating everything else to their implementation. The political core includes primarily political rights — the right to vote, to participate, to decide what kind of government to elect, and what kind of policies to follow. It is associated with representative democracy. The economic core has to do with economic and property rights. It is still referred to as "economic individualism," the "free enterprise system," or "capitalism," and pertains to the rights and freedoms of individuals to produce and to consume, to enter into contractual relations, to buy and sell through a market economy, to satisfy their wants in their own way, and to dispose of their own property and labor as they decide. Its cornerstones have been private property and a market economy that is free from State controls and regulations.

The Moral Core

Long before Christianity, the notion had developed that the individual human being has innate qualities and potentialities commanding the highest respect. With a spark of divine will or reason, each and every individual should be protected, respected, and given freedom to seek fulfillment.

The Stoics and the Epicureans put individuals — their freedom, their detachment, their personal life — above all considerations of social utility or political expediency. Early Christians went a step further to determine that all individuals are the children of God, that we are all brothers and sisters, that our duty is to God above all, and that salvation is the ultimate fulfillment. Temporal powers cannot impinge on this, but even if they did (in order, for example, to collect taxes or to maintain order) there were still many things that belonged *only* to God.

A number of inferences stem from this notion of the moral and rational nature of the individual. Many of them have been institutionalized in the practice of liberalism and continue to be essential to it. Recent proclamations supporting human rights in the United Nations and elsewhere, represent one of the oldest battle cries of liberalism.

Personal Liberty   Personal liberty consists of all those rights guaranteeing the individual protection against government. It is the requirement that men and women live under a known law with known procedures. Locke wrote: "Freedom is . . . to have a standing rule to live by, common to everyone of that society and made by the legislative power erected in it."[1] Such a law protects all and restrains the rulers. It corresponds to individual "freedoms" — freedom to think, talk, and worship. No policeman will enter one's home at night without due authority; no individual, even the poorest or lowest, will be thrown into prison without a chance to hear the charges and argue before a judge; nobody will have to discover one Sunday morning that his or her church is closed, or that their son or daughter has disappeared, and so forth. To American students such freedoms appear self-evident and naturally due. Unfortunately this is not quite so, for in fact, they exist, even today, in but a small number of countries.

Civil Liberty   While personal liberties in general define a set of protections, civil liberties indicate the free and positive channels and areas of human activity and participation. They are, in the liberal ideology and practice, equally valued. Basic to the liberal faith is the concept of freedom of thought. The only way to define this positively is to state it as the right of individuals to think their own thoughts and learn in their own ways from experience with nobody impeding the process. Freedom of thought is closely associated with freedom of expression, freedom of speech, freedom to write, freedom to publish and disseminate one's thoughts, freedom to discuss things with others, and freedom to associate with others in the peaceful expression of ideas. We find these freedoms enshrined in the First Amendment of the United States Constitution, and also in many solemn documents in British and European political history — the Bill of Rights, the Petition of Rights, the Declaration of the Rights of Man, and so on.

The achievement and implementation of full civil liberties in the societies of Western Europe and the United States took time. Until the end of the nineteenth century, there were countries where people were excluded from political participation because of their ideas — religious or other. Censoring

---

1. Locke. *Second Treatise on Civil Government.* Chapter 4.

of books, pamphlets, and the press was a common practice long after Milton wrote his famous pamphlet against censorship, *The Areopagitica,* in 1644. Freedom of the press had a particularly shaky existence until the end of the nineteenth century, and freedom of association — to form clubs, groups of like-minded people, political parties, trade unions, and religious sects — was hedged and qualified until almost the same time.

What is more, at no time could civil liberties be taken for granted. There were and still are constant exceptions and setbacks. There is always an inclination on the part of certain groups to deny to others what they do not like, and there is a pervasive suspicion on the part of political authorities of nonconformist and dissenting groups.

Social Liberty Freedom of thought and expression, protections against government in the form of personal and civil rights, have little value if the individuals are not given a proper recognition so that they can work and live in accordance with their talents and capabilities. Social liberty corresponds to what we refer to today as opportunities for advancement or social mobility. It is the right of all individuals, irrespective of race and creed and irrespective of the position of their parents, to be given every opportunity to attain a position in society commensurate with their capabilities. Personal liberties may become an empty or purely formal prescription if they impose discrimination. There is little hope in the life of a Mexican peon, or a black, or the poor, if they know that they and their children will always remain tied down to the same occupation, status, education, and income. Only when equal opportunities are seen to be provided for all can all forms of discrimination be abolished.

Emphasis upon legal rights characterized the liberal movement at its early stages. Material rights, as part of the broader discussion of economic rights, became the major preoccupation of liberalism in the twentieth century.

The Economic Core

As already pointed out, liberalism was the ideology of the middle classes rising to replace the old landed aristocracy. Their purpose was to liberate individual economic activity, to establish large trading areas that corresponded to the nation-state and if possible the world, and to do away with all obstacles to the transportation and the trading of goods. It was their aim to reorganize the economy, introduce new methods (the market), and to invest capital in factories and machines.

Economic liberties, and in general the economic core of liberalism, assumed at least as great an importance, as what we have called the moral core. The right to property, the right of inheritance, the right to accumulate wealth and capital, freedom to produce, sell, and buy — all contractual freedoms — became an essential part of the new social order. Emphasis was put on the voluntary character of the relations between various economic factors, whether the employer, the worker, the lender, the producer, or the consumer. Freedom of contract was more valued than freedom of speech. The pattern of social life, according to which people were born and belonged in certain social categories and groups, was shattered, and the individuals became free to shape their own situation by voluntary acts and contractual relations with others. One great British historian, Sir Henry Maine, claimed that the essence of liberalism lay precisely in this transition from "status" (fixed group relations) to "contract" (individual self-determination).

The meeting point of various individual wills, where contractual relations were made, is the market. Here the individual — the famous "economic man" — propelled by self-interest, buys and sells, hires laborers, borrows or loans money, invests in joint-stock companies or maritime ventures, and finds employment. The market reflects the supply and demand for goods, and this in turn determines their prices. The market is the best barometer to register economic activity, for demand obviously pushes prices up, and hence incites production until the demand is met and prices begin to level off. Since the market does not sanction the incompetent and the inefficient, goods produced that do not meet a demand or are not widely desirable fall in price, until the producer is driven out of business, and replaced by a shrewder one.

Thousands of individual entrepreneurs face not only millions of consumers, who compare quality and prices, but also each other. If a given product sells well and fast, other manufacturers will produce it, increasing the supply and thus bringing prices down. The system is supposed to be both sensitive to consumer demand as well as entirely open, allowing for entry of new competitors and the exit of unsuccessful ones. Prices faithfully register the volume of demand and supply adjusted to it.

It is a system that at least in theory favors the consumer: prices cannot be fixed, the volume of production cannot be controlled, competition makes monopolies or cartels impossible. But the advantages for the producers are also great; they can take advantage of the same law of supply and demand in hiring or dismissing workers, in settling on the wages to be paid, and in setting the prices of new products. It is a system that provides the best mechanism for production and the satisfaction of wants, and its classic formulation was provided by Adam Smith.

Adam Smith and *The Wealth of Nations* The bible of liberal economic theory was, and still remains, Adam Smith's *The Wealth of Nations*. Smith's purpose was to open the channels of free individual economic effort and to defend the free market economy as the best instrument for the growth of wealth — individual, national, and world-wide. Each person, he assumes, is the best judge of his or her actions and interests. If people are allowed a free hand to pursue these interests they will, and by so doing will improve the wealth of the society and the nation as a whole. What counts above all is to give free rein to individual action and to limit the role of the State to the simple maintenance of order and defense.

Adam Smith rose against every conceivable state intervention in commerce, agriculture, and manufacturing. He was against not only tariffs, trade

Adam Smith (1723–1790)

Adam Smith was a social philosopher and political economist, best known for his major work, *An Inquiry into the Nature and Causes of the Wealth of Nations* (1776), in which he developed his theories of economic liberalism, competition, and free trade. His major plea was to release human activity from all State administrative and economic controls, allowing the individuals to seek individual profit and the satisfaction of wants. Adam Smith claimed that there were fundamental economic laws, such as the law of supply and demand, that provided for the self-regulation of the economy. He is the father of economic liberalism.

associations and combinations, labor unions and state regulations, but also monopolies and almost any form of public enterprise. He favored free contractual relations. The State had to keep its hands and agents off.

Though Adam Smith spoke of the "Divine hand of Providence" bringing order and wealth out of the myriads of individual wills and interests that compete with each other in trying to satisfy their respective interests, his faith was not in divine providence. Rather he believed that a social and economic harmony would result from the free competition and interplay of economic interests and forces. In his words, natural order would be promoted in every country by the natural inclinations of the individuals if political institutions had never thwarted those natural inclinations. If all systems of restraint were completely taken away, the system of natural liberty would establish itself. Or as one of Smith's followers put the matter even more succinctly:

> As soon as a need becomes the object of public service the individual loses part of his freedom, becomes less progressive and less man. He becomes prone to moral inertia which spreads out to all citizens.[2]

Jeremy Bentham and Utilitarianism   But the real father of philosophic and political liberalism was Jeremy Bentham. His philosophy, followed also by James Mill and John Stuart Mill, is known as *utilitarianism*, from the term utility. Its basic elements can be summarized as follows:

1. Every object has a utility — that is, every object can satisfy a want.
2. Utility, as the attribute of an object, is subjective. It is what we like or do not like. It is amenable only to some crude quantifiable criteria that relate to the duration, the intensity, and the proximity of the pleasure that a given object can provide. There are no qualitative criteria that can be established by anybody but the user. For some a poem has a greater "utility" than a hot dog. For others the hot dog comes first. The market ultimately registers utility as it reflects the volume of goods in demand.
3. The purpose of our lives is to satisfy pleasure (that is, to use goods that have utility for each one of us) and to avoid pain. This is the *hedonistic* or the *felicific calculus* that applies not just in economic life but also in any other aspect of an individual's existence.

In order to work, this utilitarian model must be allowed to operate freely. If every man and woman were free to maximize pleasure and avoid pain, "the greatest happiness for the greatest number" would result. More people would be happy than unhappy!

The concept of utility and the utilitarian ethic is not restricted to the economy. It applies to everything. Social institutions, artistic works, education, philosophy — all must meet the test of utility and provide pleasure, in varying degrees, to some, or conversely result in pain if they are absent. *Utility* as a criterion of social, political, and economic life replaces moral and natural *rights*.

2. Cited by Harold Laski. *The Rise of European Liberalism*, p. 203.

THE BETTMANN ARCHIVE, INC.

Jeremy Bentham (1748–1831)

Jeremy Bentham was the founder of the utilitarian school, according to which pleasure-maximizing, pain-avoiding (the so-called *felicific calculus*) is the source of human motivation. His various works, such as *Fragment on Government* and *Defense of Usury*, and most particularly his *Introduction to the Principles of Morals and Legislation*, expounded the theories of individualism and economic freedom. Benthamite liberals were extremely influential through the nineteenth century in England in pushing for administrative, criminal law, taxation, and economic reforms.

Bentham had no great respect for abstract moral rights, yet in a peculiar way he defends, *in terms of utility*, many of the freedoms and rights that were defended previously, in terms of a natural law, or that which stemmed from what we have called the moral core of liberalism. Bentham defended freedoms on the basis of their utility. It is more pleasurable (or less painful), for instance, for a greater number of people in a system to freely express their ideas, worship God in their chosen way, and to read what they please. Conversely, it would be painful if there were censorship and lack of freedom of expression and worship.

Thus millions of individuals armed with small calculators, so to speak, constantly sift the pleasurable in a given society from the painful, maximizing the first and minimizing the second. The calculations are always directly related to self-interest, but they are not necessarily simple. The individual will have to balance a number of requirements — for example, the immediate utility an object may have compared to the far greater utility it may represent in five or ten years; the possibility of suffering deprivation and even pain *now* in order to enjoy pleasure later on; the pain that may be suffered in order to derive pleasure from protecting loved ones; the intensity of a given pleasure as opposed to its duration; and finally, overall considerations of peace and tranquility at home and national defense against outside enemies. They too represent a utility, no matter what the immediate pain of providing for them may be.

These considerations show that while self-interest and the pleasure-maximizing calculations are the motivating force for all of us, a point comes when considerations other than their pure and simple realization enter into the equation of social, political, and economic life. Self-interest gives way to *enlightened* self-interest.

John Stuart Mill and Enlightened Self-Interest   Enlightened self-interest becomes an important criterion to guide the individual. For instance, someone who foregoes an immediate pleasure in order to derive a greater one later on shows enlightenment. Accepting a lesser pleasure in order to maintain a *fairly* pleasurable existence, rather than insisting on the maximum pleasure possible and in the process risking the loss of everything, is also "enlightenment." The same criteria apply to groups or to classes of people. If they act in terms of enlightened self-interest, they may consider concessions to other social groups or classes rather than risk the loss of all they have.

John Stuart Mill came to grips with this problem by redefining utility. He introduces qualitative standards and establishes a hierarchy of pleasures on the basis of criteria that are *not* subjective. Some pleasures are better than others because of their intrinsic quality, not because of the particular pleasure they give to an individual. A poem has more utility than a hot dog!

There is, therefore, a necessary gradation in the utility of different goods. Some have a higher value even if they give pleasure to only few; others may, in the long run, prove to be painful even if they give pleasure to many. What then? Shall we introduce a dictator or a philosopher-king who will impose his hierarchy of pleasures upon society and make it produce goods and services that correspond to it? Or should we expect individuals to make the right choice?

The question is not speculative. It is right before us. Driving a car is pleasurable, but by depleting our energy resources American drivers weaken the country to the point where it may be unable to defend many of the values that are equally pleasurable to us — our freedoms, for instance. A com-

THE BETTMAN ARCHIVE, INC.

John Stuart Mill (1806–1873)

John Stuart Mill was an English philosopher, who had studied under the strict tutelage of his father, a foremost utilitarian, James Mill. John Stuart Mill considerably modified utilitarian thought to abandon the simple pleasure-maximizing, pain-avoiding formula and to seek qualitative criteria to evaluate human behavior and motivation. In his essay *On Liberty* he developed the theory of moral (as opposed simply to economic) individualism and linked it to requirements of education and enlightenment. Although he argued against state intervention he was forced to introduce collective and social considerations and thus had to allow, contrary to what he seemed to profess, for state intervention. Many consider Mill, because of this, to be one of the precursors of socialism. He is known primarily, however, for *On Liberty* (1859), in which he appears a strong advocate of individualism.

prehensive scheme of public transportation would be preferable to private ownership of cars. But how can the people be led to make the right decision?

The utilitarians, and particularly John Stuart Mill, put their hopes in education, and in the wisdom and self-restraint of the middle classes. It was the obligation of the State to establish education, and it was the function of education to *enlighten* self-interest in terms of collective, group, social, and national interests and considerations. Education would transform an essentially hedonistic society into a body of civic-minded citizens — that in the last analysis would choose public transportation! They would put the general good above their own particular pleasure.

The Political Core

Four basic principles make up the political core of liberalism: individual consent; representation and representative government; constitutionalism; and popular sovereignty.

Individual Consent As we have already noted, "status" had been giving place to "contract." Contractual theories became the basis of political authority. Men and women simply consent to bind themselves in a political system and to accept its decisions. The Mayflower Compact of 1629, when the Pilgrims wrote a "constitution," is the best illustration.

It was John Locke who developed the theory of consent in detail. Men and women, he pointed out, live in the state of nature with certain natural rights: life, liberty, and property. At a given time they discover that it is difficult to safeguard these rights without a common authority committed to them and to their protection. They agree to set up a political society consisting of a common legislature, a common judge, and a common executive. The first will interpret and safeguard the natural rights, the second will adjudicate conflicts about these rights, and the third will provide for enforcement. The contract is made by all individuals, and those who do not agree are not bound by it. They can leave! *The source of political authority and the powers of the State over those who stay is their consent.* The purpose of the State is the better preservation of the natural rights of life, liberty, and property.

Representation But who can make decisions within this system? According to Locke it is the legislature elected by the people (at the time, to be sure, on a very limited franchise). However, the legislature must accept certain restraints, all of them implicit or explicit in the original contract setting up the political system. It cannot deprive individuals of their natural rights, cannot abolish their freedom, and cannot do away with their lives or take away their property. The political authority — the legislature — is restrained by the very nature of the compact that originally established it.

Locke's idea of representative government, then, is based on the notion that political authority derives from people. But moral, civil, and economic or property individual rights cannot be transgressed. The majority and its

John Locke (1632–1704)

John Locke was an English philosopher generally considered one of the founders of empiricism. His principle works include *Letters on Toleration* (1689–92), *Essay Concerning Human Understanding* (1960), and *Thoughts on Education* (1693). As a political philosopher Locke developed in his *Two Treatises on Government* the "contract: theory of the State, according to which the State is the custodian of natural rights and is founded upon the consent of the governed in order to protect these rights — specifically, the rights of life, liberty, and property. It led to the elaboration of institutions of a limited State and a limited government.

elected representatives can make all and any decisions, but the original contract and the good sense of the people who made it, as well as of their representatives, restrain it from violating the people's natural rights. Thus, the British tradition established parliamentary sovereignty and majority rule, rather than the checks and balances and judicial review that have been the case in the United States.

It should be noted, however, that while Locke gave to the legislature the right to make decisions without any limitations, his theory of representation and representative government applied only to a small number — those who held property. They represented the middle classes and the landed aristocracy. It was only much later, when the franchise was expanded to most citizens (and ultimately to all) that the problem of how to limit the majority — who might decide to take away the property of the few — assumed particular importance.

Theories of representation and representative government also stemmed directly from utilitarian premises that led ultimately to the "one man, one vote" principle. At first the utilitarians attacked the vested interests, the aristocracy, the landowners, the Church, and the well-to-do, and discarded the notion that these groups, more than others, had a special stake in the country and hence had a special right to represent the community and govern it. Mill argued that the best individual protection was to allow each and all to select their representatives. "Human beings," he pointed out, "are only secure from evil at the hands of others in proportion to their ability to protect themselves,"[3] and he considered representation was the best protection.

However, John Stuart Mill did not quite accept the notion of the supremacy of the representatives — the legislature — and with it the right of the majority to govern. He and many other liberals feared that if all the people were given the right to vote and to elect their own representatives, and if decisions in the representative assembly were to be made by majority vote, then the poor would use their numerical strength to take care of *their* interests at the expense of the middle classes and all others. There were, therefore, a number of direct and indirect restraints. One was the proposition that representative government could function well only when the educational level of the voters had improved. Citizens should learn to think of the "general prosperity and the general good" rather than of their own immediate interest; in other words, the system could work well only when people as a whole acted according to their enlightened interest. Mill wrote:

> The positive evils and dangers of representative government can
> be reduced to two: general ignorance and incapacity, and the
> danger of its being under the influence of interests not identical
> with the general welfare of the community.[4]

3. J. S. Mill. "Considerations on Representative Government" in *Utilitarianism*. Chapter 3, p. 43.
4. Ibid., Chapter 6, p. 86.

He mentioned specifically the "body of unskilled laborers" who were ignorant and likely to act at the expense of the general welfare.

Mill had also an aversion to the development of large national political parties which could mobilize the vote and capture a majority through the organization and discipline of its members. He was, moreover, not against property and age qualifications. He favored these at least for the candidates for election, who in this way would come from the middle classes and would have the proper level of maturity and moderation. He also favored giving a great weight — more votes — to people with education. Finally, he was in favor of a second chamber, the House of Lords, representing "personal merit" and acting as a "moral center of resistance" against the decisions of a popularly elected assembly — that is, against the majority.

Despite their insistence on representation and elections, the liberals hedged and hemmed the power of the legislature and the right of the majority to decide. They did not have enough confidence in the people. Yet, notwithstanding their fears of the poor, the ignorant and "the many," the utilitarian premises led gradually to universal suffrage. Representation and representative government gradually spread, and with it majoritarianism, the right for the majority to form a government and make decisions for all, gained legitimacy.

Constitutionalism   The notion of restraints on political authority, as proposed by Locke, influenced the framers of the United States Constitution. They feared arbitrary and absolute power so much that they rejected a concentration of power in the hands of any one body, whether it be the legislature, or even the majority of the people. While stressing the idea of natural rights, of individual freedoms, and the derivation of authority from the people, they wanted to find a way to make it impossible for any single organ of government to become truly sovereign and overwhelm the others. Their emphasis was more on how to restrain political power, even when it was based on the will of the people, than on how to make it effective.

The answer was a written Constitution which limits power, sets explicit restraints (including the ten amendments) on the national government and on the individual states, and which institutionalizes the separation of powers in such a manner that one power checks another. At no time would it be possible for one branch — executive, legislative, or judicial — to overwhelm and subordinate the others. Having accepted the idea of fully representative government through periodic elections, the founders of the American Constitution put heavy restraints upon it.

This is essentially what we mean by constitutionalism. Constitutionalism provides solid guarantees for the individual by explicitly limiting government; it also provides ruling procedures for the implementation of the government's functions. In many cases it establishes a watchdog, in the form of a judicial body, to safeguard the Constitution and all the restraints written into it. In addition, it provides procedures through which the responsibility of the governors to the governed is maintained by periodic elections.

The government is both *limited* and *responsible*. But the idea of limitations is far more important than that of popular sovereignty. The United States Constitution established a republic, not a democracy.

Popular Sovereignty   It was Jean Jacques Rousseau who set up the model of a popular democracy before the French Revolution of 1789. He, too, found the source of political authority in the people. They were sovereign, and their sovereignty was "inalienable, infallible, and indestructible."[5] In contrast to those who favored representation and representative government, Rousseau believed in direct government by the people. There were to be no restraints on the popular will. He called it "the general will" and claimed that under certain conditions it was always right, and that representation would only distort it. In the last analysis, he argued, nobody could really represent anybody else. Something like town meetings in small communities would be the only appropriate instruments for the expression of the general will.

Rousseau's affirmation of the absolute power of the general will, that many interpreted to be the will of the people, had revolutionary implications. It pitted an extreme doctrine of popular sovereignty against absolutism, which was current in France and many other continental countries in the eighteenth century. But it also antagonized liberals who believed in representative government with restraints and were particularly reluctant to see all the people participate directly or indirectly in decisions.

Consent, representation, popular sovereignty leading to majority rule, and constitutional restraints upon the state and its government (even upon a majority) obviously emphasize different forms of liberal thought and put the accent on different values. They inevitably lead to different political institutions. Emphasis upon constitutional restraints and the protection of individual and minority rights — economic rights at first — led to the type of liberalism, still very much in evidence in the United States, that restricts the majority and allows the judiciary to act as the supreme umpire. On the other hand, emphasis upon the Rousseauian idea of popular sovereignty leads to unrestricted majority rule, either directly by the people or by their representatives. In between these two extremes liberals and liberal institutions attempted, not always successfully, to find a solution that reconciled the idea of majoritarianism with the notion of restraints. Limitation upon representative assemblies, various voting qualifications, a bicameral legislature in which one chamber is not directly elected by the people but represents wealth or birth or some other attribute of "moderation," the veto of the monarch or a president were the devices most often used to deny a numerical majority the power to make decisions.

Throughout the nineteenth century the main stresses within the political core of liberalism lay in the conflict between those who, in line with Locke and some of the utilitarians, advocated restraints upon the legislature and the majority, and those who, in line with Rousseau's theory of popular sovereignty, pressed for uninhibited majority rule.

5. Rousseau. *The Social Contract*. Book 2.

THE BETTMANN ARCHIVE, INC.

Jean Jacques Rousseau (1712–1778)

Jean Jacques Rousseau was a French philosopher who, in contrast
to the rationalism of the French eighteenth-century philosophers
(the Encyclopedists), stressed the role of sentiments and emotions, thus becoming the precursor of many nineteenth-century
romantics. He wrote widely on a number of subjects, but his two
most important works are on education (*Emile*, 1762) and on politics (*The Social Contract*, 1762). In the latter he argued for the
sovereignty of the people, claiming that the "general will"
emanating from them is absolute and infallible. It was the combination of this theory of general will and his emphasis on feeling
and emotion that led him to glorify nationalism as an all-embracing myth that creates unity and solidarity among a people. The
best exposition of his theory of nationalism can be found in his
Considerations on the Government of Poland, written in 1770.

The State and the Individual

Liberalism was an anti-State philosophy and remains one in the sense that, all other things being more or less equal, it values the individual and his or her initiative more than the State and its intervention. Nowhere has this position been better set forth than in John Stuart Mill's essay *On Liberty,* published in 1859. To approach it, let us set forth two models, the totalitarian and the liberal. According to the first, the individual and the civil society (i.e., the family, economic organizations, school and universities, and so on) are controlled by the State. It is the State, therefore, that shapes the social institutions on the basis of a predetermined scheme of values. The State exacts conformity and obedience.

The liberal model presents an entirely different order of things. Individuals and their social institutions are separate from the State. Strictly speaking, they constitute two different spheres of life and action. But when the two spheres do intersect, the intersection should cover only a limited and recognized area. Spontaneity, creativity, experimentation, and the search for truth are within the domain of individuals and their social institutions. It is at best and at most the function of the State to maintain order, to see that nobody in his or her relations with others uses force, to protect civil liberties and personal freedom, and at the same time to maintain the economic freedom of the individual. In other words, the role of the State is to protect the individual.

In his essay *On Liberty* Mill summarizes this by asserting:

1. That every restraint imposed by the State is bad.
2. That even if the individual cannot do certain things well, the State should not do them for fear that it might undermine the individual's independence and initiative.
3. That any increase in the powers of the State is automatically bad and prejudicial to individual freedoms: it decreases individual freedom.

Thus Mill views the State on the one hand, and society and the individual on the other, in a mechanical and antithetical kind of relationship. The increase of the powers of the state necessarily involves the decrease of powers of individuals. While it is highly desirable to strengthen the power of the individual correspondingly, people must be extremely vigilant not to allow an increase in the power of the State.

The most crucial problem for liberal thought has been the identification of exactly where the lines separating the State, on the one hand, and society and individuals, on the other, intersect. One might develop an elastic concept, allowing a fairly wide area within the intersecting lines, in which the State can intervene (numbers 2 and 3 in Figure 2-1). Or, in line with the thinking of early liberals, one might allow for the minimum area of intersection in which the State can intervene (number 1 in Figure 2-1). Here the intersection would encompass only order and protection. In this latter case, the State becomes something like a police officer or a "night watchman" making sure that the factory does not burn down and no thieves break in and otherwise allowing full autonomy within the factory, or the university, or the

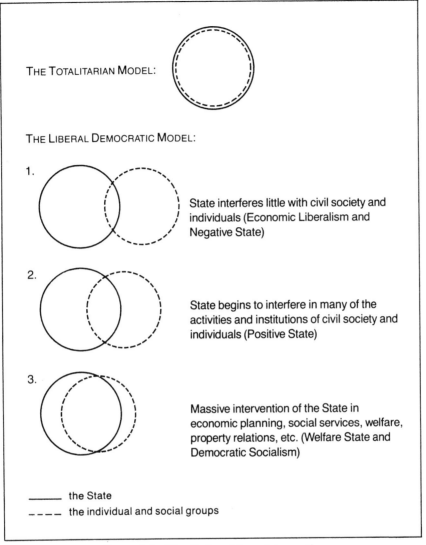

THE TOTALITARIAN MODEL:

THE LIBERAL DEMOCRATIC MODEL:

1.

State interferes little with civil society and individuals (Economic Liberalism and Negative State)

2.

State begins to interfere in many of the activities and institutions of civil society and individuals (Positive State)

3.

Massive intervention of the State in economic planning, social services, welfare, property relations, etc. (Welfare State and Democratic Socialism)

——— the State

– – – – the individual and social groups

FIGURE 2-1   The limits of State intervention

home, or the school. The smaller the area included within the intersecting lines of Figure 2-1 the closer we are to laissez-faire liberalism: the larger the area the more we move in the direction of the *Positive State* or the *Welfare State,* perhaps even getting close to socialism.

Self-regarding and Other-regarding Acts

Different periods in the history of liberalism tell us where the lines have been drawn. War, for example, necessitates State intervention. But this was considered to be an exception, since there is an understanding that with the passing of such a national emergency the situation would revert to the original liberal model. John Stuart Mill provided us with a criterion in terms of which we can draw the lines. For Mill, all individual acts that concern the individual — *self-regarding acts,* as he called them — are acts that cannot be controlled or regulated by the State. However, acts that concern and affect others — *other-regarding acts* — can and should come under the control and regulation of the State. Thus, the area within our intersecting circles should include the other-regarding acts.

But "concern" provides no clean standard. Is smoking self-regarding or other-regarding? Is the use of drugs self-regarding or other-regarding? What about alcoholism? What about pornographic literature? Violence on television? The manufacture of drugs? The administration and the high cost of hospitals? The additives put in our foods? Ownership and use of private cars? Nuclear energy? This is just the first set of questions that comes to mind.

The second set of questions is more complex, and relates to exactly *when* the State should bring into its purview other-regarding acts (if we have managed to define exactly what they are). Can it do so only after an act is *shown* to affect others, or can it control it because it *might* affect others? The first would provide a very strict and limiting criterion. The State could regulate the manufacturing of drugs only when it is shown that they have caused cancer. The second interpretation, however, provides a very generous criterion whereby the State can intervene. It would do so every time there is some doubt about the consequences certain drugs can have upon individuals. Drugs that *might* cause cancer should be taken off the market. Whenever certain acts *might* affect others, they should be regulated and controlled.

Mill did not have to answer these questions explicitly, because of the way he defined self-regarding and other-regarding acts. *All individual acts, he claimed, are self-regarding except those that cause harm to others. The criterion in terms of which other-regarding acts are defined is that of harm. Only if harm is done can the State intervene.* Commerce, production, consumption are self-regarding.[6] The State should not intervene. But so, of course, are freedom of thought and expression and freedom of association. The State should not intervene here, either. So, in the last analysis, the individual has the right to get drunk and to use drugs. However, your actions become other-regarding, and hence invite State intervention, when they cause harm to others. You can stay in your attic drinking beer as long as you want; you are free to indulge in this self-regarding act. But when you open the window and start throwing the empty cans out you endanger passersby, and the act becomes other-regarding.

However, the moment we give a more relaxed definition of what is other-regarding, and introduce the concept of *effect* or *influence* rather than *harm,* then we move in the opposite direction to favor State intervention and regulation. The police officer may try to save you from too much beer, even if you have not harmed anybody!

6. J. S. Mill. "Of the Limits of the Authority of Society over the Individual" in *Utilitarianism.* Chapter 4.

Liberalism and Pluralism

The liberal ethic and the liberal ideology we discussed are intensely individualistic. "Group" liberalism would appear to be a self-contradictory term, and perhaps it is. However, liberalism is used also to refer to the rights and freedoms not only of individuals, but of groups. Replace the "individual" with the group to which he or she belongs and you have group liberalism or pluralism. Groups demand and expect the same treatment in regard to tolerance, representation, and participation that the individuals have. With the breakdown of rigid class and religious or ethnic solidarities in many modern systems, thousands of groups have mushroomed. Groups organize; they make their demands. Public policy, it is expected, will then be made in response to their demands. As Professor Apter writes, "The notion of individual competitions is replaced [under pluralism] by a network of organizational competition, influence, accountability and information in which groups can organize and, by exercising rights, realize interests to affect policy outcomes."[7]

But groups may make claims that go beyond the mere satisfaction of interest. They may claim the same autonomy that the individuals claim. These are claims for ethnic, racial, local, functional, occupational, and economic autonomy. Their implementation requires a great deal of decentralization of the Democratic State. Very often demands on the part of certain groups even go beyond decentralization to assert separation and independence from the State. Sometimes pluralism is used to justify economic democracy — that is, the rights of certain groups and organizations to decide by themselves on the economic activities in which they are engaged without any intervention from the State.

As long as there is a basic agreement in the political society on the rules that determine political competition, and as long as there is economic growth, pluralism and liberalism may coexist. But the moment the State is challenged by some groups in the name of group autonomy and independence, or the moment economic growth falters, liberalism is in danger. In the first case, demands for autonomy will undermine the political community and its unity; in the second case, groups competing for scarce resources will find no satisfaction, or at least they will not get what they expect. Finally, and perhaps more significantly, for group pluralism to exist side by side with liberalism, groups, as with the individuals in the liberal theory, should remain more or less equal. The moment a group or a combination of groups subordinate others, they will dominate not only the society but also the members of the group — the individuals. The early liberal theorists had feared group dominance and had tried in one way or another to make it difficult for groups to develop and to supplant the individuals. They argued that a group is not a moral entity like the individual. It overshadows the individual and subordinates him or her to the imperative of group solidarity. Groups coerce the individual, and group pluralism may subvert individual freedoms.

7. Apter. *Introduction to Political Analysis.* Cambridge, Mass.: Winthrop, 1978. pp. 314–315.

Achievements:
The Expansion of Liberalism

If we take a fairly thick brush and paint onto the canvas of the nineteenth century all the liberal achievements in the realm of economic rights, civil liberties, and political rights, the picture that emerges is breathtaking. The liberals and the liberal movements and parties changed the economic, social, and political structure of Europe, and drastically modified the international community as well. Some of the major achievements are listed here.

Slavery was outlawed. In the United States it continued until the Civil War, but the importation of slaves after 1808 had been declared illegal. In England the slave trade was banned in 1807, and slavery was abolished in the British Empire in 1833. France followed in 1848; the Netherlands in 1869; Argentina in 1853; Portugal in 1858; Brazil in 1888. Serfdom was abolished in Russia in 1861.

Gradually *religious disabilities* against holding political or other offices were abandoned virtually everywhere. Catholics, Protestants, Jews, Quakers, and nonconformist religious minorities were allowed full participation by the end of the nineteenth century.

After bitter controversies, *toleration* was granted and the Church and the State were separated in many countries. Religious affiliations and worship became a personal right.

Freedom of press, speech, and association were granted. By the end of the nineteenth century, in Western Europe, Britain and its dominions, and the United States, rare were the cases where people could not express their views or were penalized for the views they did express, no matter how heretical or subversive.

The State began to provide *education* and to require children to attend school up to the age of ten, twelve, or fourteen.

The vote was gradually extended to all males first, and to women only after World War I. There was universal suffrage in England by 1884; in France in 1848; in Italy by the end of the century; in Russia in 1905 (but not for long); and in Germany and the Scandinavian countries in varying degrees by the end of the century. In the United States, male universal suffrage (limited to whites) was established in the 1820s. Property qualifications for voters and candidates were eliminated, but some other qualifications — literacy, age, or residence — remained. All in all, the prediction of Lord Macaulay that "universal suffrage is utterly incompatible with the existence of civilization" proved quite wrong!

Nothing illustrates the force of liberalism better than the reforms undertaken in France after the revolution of 1830. The second chamber was changed from a hereditary one to one in which members sat for life; the electorate was broadened by lowering the age qualifications to twenty-five instead of thirty; property qualifications were reduced from three hundred francs to two hundred. Candidates for office were to be thirty years old instead of forty, censorship was abolished, extraordinary tribunals were eliminated, schools were set up in every commune by the State and the control of the Church over them was put to an end. These reforms were modest; indeed, they stopped far short of what democrats wanted to accomplish. But they were moving in the direction of democracy. It took, for example, just eighteen years (after another revolution) before universal suffrage was introduced to France, in 1848.

Similarly, the liberal Reform Act of 1832 in England provided for a property qualification of ten pounds a year, thus excluding the poor and the workers from voting but allowing the middle classes to do so. The act increased the electorate to about 750,000 out of a total population of about 13.5 million. Further extension in 1867 and 1884 followed, bringing the workers into the political system.

Constitutions, constitution-making, and constitutionalism were everywhere in the air. Even where a constitution had only symbolic character it still echoed the aspiration of citizens to limit government and to establish the rules that made the holders of power responsible to the people or their representatives.

In Russia a movement for a constitution which would limit the powers of the Tsar emerged in 1824; in Greece liberal constitutions were promulgated in 1827 and again in 1843; in Germany a liberal constitution was prepared by a convention that met in Frankfurt in 1848; in France liberal constitutions were promulgated (after the failure of the ones established during the French Revolution) in 1830, 1848, and 1871. In Spain, Portugal, Italy, and in many Latin American republics, constitutional documents came into force by the end of the nineteenth century and often earlier. Even Poland, the Austro-Hungarian Empire, and the Turkish Empire experienced liberal reforms that were embodied in constitutional documents or charters.

These reforms were not granted easily; occasionally they were granted only to be withdrawn. Frequently liberal political movements were repressed, but the overall impact was the same — broadening and safeguarding civil liberties, and extending political participation to an ever-growing number of people in every political system. Above all, they imposed responsibility and restraints, no matter how fragile and temporary, upon the holders of political power. This in itself helped to erode the claims of absolutism.

Representative government became increasingly accepted throughout Europe and in the English-speaking countries. With the exception of Russia (with a notable interval between 1905 and 1914), there was hardly a political system in the nineteenth century which did not introduce representative assemblies and did not give them some (often considerable) power over decisions. In many cases, the assembly was given the power to censure the government and force it out of office. Representative assemblies participated in the formulation of laws and decided on taxation and expenditures. Within limits (and sometimes without any restriction) debate was free and representatives were not liable for their words and actions in the legislature.

As the suffrage expanded to new groups, *political parties* began to emerge, seeking the vote in order to govern on the basis of pledges they offered to the electorate. They became transmission belts between the people and the government, making the latter increasingly responsive to popular demands and aspirations, and helping translate demands and wants into policy and action. Parties emerged, at first in the United States where male universal suffrage was introduced as early as 1824, with platforms, leadership, organization, and ideological loyalties. In England they gradually evolved from factions and cliques, manipulated and controlled by the king and the landed gentry, into national organizations representing the new towns and the middle classes. The Liberals and Conservatives, the two large parties, established national headquarters, designated candidates, prepared their platforms, solicited membership, and vied for office against each other after the middle of the nineteenth century. The Conservatives followed the logic of liberalism and enacted legislation enfranchising new groups by lowering property qualifications. Their leader, Disraeli, spoke of the union between "the cottage and the throne," an expression that symbolized the reconciliation of the aristocracy with the principles of democracy and the needs of the common man.

In France the nobility continued to influence the vote and political parties were numerous, badly organized, regional rather than national, and without clear-cut platforms. Until 1880 their differences were about the political regime: some favoring the Republic, others a return to the Monarchy, and still others aspiring to Bonapartism. It was only by the very end of the nineteenth century that the socialists became unified into one party; the centrist groups — republican, anticlerical, and liberal — formed the Radical-Socialist party.

In Germany the powerful Social Democratic Party had the best organization and the largest membership and became revisionist and reformist rather than a revolutionary party. It was opposed by the Center Party (liberal but appealing to Catholic groups), the Liberals (a middle-class party) and the Conservatives.

Almost everywhere the development of political parties strengthened the liberal-democratic principles and institutions. It allowed the people to opt directly for candidates and policies and brought the governments that emerged from elections closer to their control.

Liberalism had, of course, a profound impact on *economic life*. Freedom of movement (a simple right in our eyes) became a reality for the first time. A journeyman, a merchant, a manufacturer, or a farmer could move not only their produce and goods but themselves without any prior restraint and prior permission. They could dispose of their property and do as they pleased with it. Individuals became free to change professions just as easily as they could change their domiciles; they could enter into partnership or agree to provide their services on the basis of mutually binding agreements.

Not only their home but also their property became a "castle" against intervention, regulation, and confiscation by an arbitrary ruler. There was (though not everywhere) a *trend against all forms of tariffs* and all indirect restrictions on the movement of goods — first, against internal tariffs that allowed cities, municipalities, or regional authorities to tax goods at the point of their entry or exit. But even more, a great movement got under way, spearheaded by British industrial and trading groups, to reduce and even to eliminate all external tariffs that taxed goods coming into or moving out of a state. It favored worldwide free trade. As one of Adam Smith's disciples wrote in 1846:

> There is no human event that has happened in the world more calculated to promote the enduring interests of humanity than the establishment of the principle of free trade.[8]

Despite their aversion to state intervention in social and economic matters, liberals were forced to consider *limited interventions.* "Poor laws" were introduced to keep the destitute from starvation. As unemployment assumed menacing proportions in the 1840s, public work-shops were established in France and at one time they employed as many as a quarter of a million people. Child labor legislation gradually began to prohibit the employment of children under certain ages, and required them to go to school. A ten-hour working day was decreed in England in 1846. Factory laws began to provide for the safety of workers. They were to receive compensation for accidents caused in their work. By the end of the century many of these measures had been expanded to provide added protection, including the first steps in the direction of health insurance.

In the name of liberalism a vast movement in favor of *national self-determination* and national independence spread all over Europe. It culminated in the Wilsonian principles of self-determination. Throughout the nineteenth century, dynasties disintegrated and new nations came into being. Greece (1827), Norway (1830), and Belgium (1830) became independent. A Polish liberal national uprising in favor of independence took place in 1831. Italy became a unified national state in 1870, and Germany followed in 1871. The Ottoman Empire, encompassing the Balkans, Turkey, and the Middle East, cracked wide open, allowing for the emergence of a number of independent states, some late in the nineteenth century and the beginning of the twentieth. Bulgaria, Rumania, part of Yugoslavia, and Albania became new national states. The same is the case with the Austro-Hungarian Empire from which came Hungary, Serbia, and ultimately Czechoslovakia. Powerful liberal independence movements manifested themselves within the Tsarist Empire. Most of these new states undertook, in the name of liberalism, constitutional reforms providing for individual rights, election and popular participation, and restraints upon the government.

Conclusion

In overall terms, nineteenth century liberalism shows a remarkable record in bringing forth and institutionalizing civil rights, political rights, and economic freedoms. It was equally potent in causing a profound reconsideration of the position of the aristocracy, the Church, and many unreconstructed traditionalists. But the century was also remarkable for the growth and the

---

8. Cited by Donald Read. *Cobden and Bright.* London: St. Martin's Press, 1968, p. 65.

unprecedented development of technology and production. This, despite the many miseries that continued to afflict the workers, gave credence to some of the assertions of Adam Smith and the utilitarians. Economies grew; world population began a rapid climb; water and rail communications were established, bringing people closer together in their national community as well as in the world; new cities developed rapidly while many old ones were literally torn apart and rebuilt; currency in gold or paper money and new banking practices facilitated exchange while savings were channeled into new investments. Nations mushroomed in the name of self-determination. The best eulogy on the spirit of innovation and modernity that bourgeois liberalism exemplified was given by its greatest critic, Karl Marx, in the *Communist Manifesto*.

> Constant revolutionizing of production, uninterrupted disturbance of all social relations, everlasting uncertainty and agitation, distinguish the bourgeois epoch from all earlier times. All fixed, fast-frozen relationships, with their train of venerable ideas and opinions, are swept away, all new-formed ones become obsolete before they can ossify. All that is solid melts into air, all that is holy is profaned. . . .

At the end of the century a new factor was injected into the liberal philosophy — social justice. It was needed to support individuals in one form or another when their self-reliance and initiative could no longer provide them with protection, or when the market did not show the flexibility or the sensitivity it was supposed to show in satisfying basic wants. A new spirit of mutual aid, cooperation, and service began to develop. It became stronger with the coming of the twentieth century.

Bibliography

Black, Eugene (ed.). *Posture of Europe, 1815–1940*. Homewood, Ill.: The Dorsey Press, 1964.

———. *Victorians: Culture and Society*. New York: Harper and Row, 1973.

Briggs, Asa. *The Age of Improvement*. London: Longmans, 1959.

Clark, G. Kitson. *An Expanding Society: Britain 1830–1900*. New York: Cambridge U.P., 1967.

"Declaration of the Rights of Man and of the Citizen," in Paul H. Beik. *The French Revolution*. New York: Harper and Row, 1970.

Dicey, A. V. *Lectures on the Relationship Between Law and Public Opinion in England During the 19th Century*. New York: Macmillan, 1952.

Friedman, Milton. *Capitalism and Freedom*. Chicago: University of Chicago Press, 1963.

Hamilton, Alexander; Madison, James; and Jay, John. *The Federalist Papers*. New York: New American Library, 1961.

Hartz, Louis. *The Liberal Tradition in America*. New York: Harcourt, Brace and World, 1962.

Hayek, Friedrich A. *The Road to Serfdom*. Chicago: University of Chicago Press, 1944.

Hobhouse, L. T. *Liberalism*. New York: Oxford U.P., 1964.

Jefferson, Thomas. *Drafts of the Declaration of Independence*. Washington, D.C.: Acropolis, 1963.

Laski, Harold J. *The Rise of European Liberalism*. Atlantic Highlands, N.J.: Humanities Press, 1962.

Locke, John. *Two Treatises on Government*. Edited by Peter Laslett. New York: New American Library, 1965.

MacPherson, C. B. *The Political Theory of Possessive Individualism*. New York: Oxford U.P., 1962.

McIlwain, Charles H. *Constitutionalism: Ancient and Modern*. Ithaca, N.Y.: Cornell U.P., 1958.

Mill, John Stuart. *Consideration on Representative Government*. New York: Bobbs-Merrill, Library of Liberal Arts, 1958.

————. *On Liberty*. 1956.

————. *Utilitarianism*. 1957.

Palmer, R. R. *The Age of the Democratic Revolution*. 2 volumes. Princeton, N.J.: Princeton U.P., 1959.

Palmer, R. R. and Colton, Joel. *A History of the Modern World Since 1815*. New York: Knopf, 1971.

Pinson, K. S. *Modern Germany, Its History and Civilization*. 2nd ed. New York: Macmillan, 1966.

Rousseau, Jean Jacques. *The Social Contract and Discourse on Inequality*. New York: Washington Square Press, 1967.

Rugiero, E. *The History of European Liberalism*. Boston: Beacon Press, 1959.

Smith, Adam. *The Wealth of Nations: Representative Selections*. New York: Bobbs-Merrill, 1961.

Tawney, R. H. *Religion and the Rise of Capitalism*. New York: New American Library, 1954.

Thomson, David. *Europe Since 1815*. 2nd rev. ed. New York: Knopf, 1957.

————. *Democracy in France Since 1870*. 4th ed. New York: Oxford U.P., 1964.

————. *France: Empire and Republic, 1850–1940*. New York: Walker and Co., 1968.

Weber, Max. *The Protestant Ethic and the Spirit of Capitalism*. New York: Charles Scribner's Sons, 1958.

3 | *Democracy and Socialism*

But man in society not only lives his individual life:
he also modifies the form of social institutions in the
direction indicated by reason — in such a manner . . .
that will render them more efficient for securing
freedom . . .
SYDNEY OLIVER   The Fabian Essays in Socialism

Using the three basic cores of the liberal democratic ideology as a guide, it is relatively easy to map out its evolution and to assess its present position.

The year 1848 represents the watershed of European liberalism. From it powerful and divergent currents began to flow. From Paris to Palermo, from Frankfurt and London to Budapest, Vienna, and Madrid, the poor, the workers, and the peasants, who had left the countryside for the urban centers, rose to take power away from the propertied classes in the name of *radical democracy* and *socialism*. Writing in the same year, John Stuart Mill commented on the industrial and technological achievements of the period and pointed out that they had improved the living standard of the middle classes only. "They have not as yet," he added, "begun to effect those great changes in human destiny, which it is their nature and in their futurity to accomplish."[1]

The middle classes found themselves wavering. Some sided with radical democrats and the socialists and joined forces with them in an alliance that could not last. Others backed conservative groups — the nobility, the Church, the landowners — that had resisted liberalism.

Radical Democrats

Radical democrats accepted the moral core of liberalism and its civil rights, individual freedoms, freedom of press, religion, and association (though they insisted on the secularization of many of the functions that the Church pro-

1. Cited by Asa Briggs. *The Age of Improvement.* London: Longmans, 1959, p. 303.

vided, such as education, and favored outright expropriation of its landed domains). They also supported the political core but interpreted it in Rousseauian terms: all political power should come directly from the people and a majority could make all decisions directly or through sovereign representative assemblies. They were against all voting qualifications and against any restraints on the exercise of popular will. They also began to express fundamental reservations about the economic core.

Radical Democrats in England and France

A strong radical democratic movement developed in England roughly between 1830 and 1850. This was *Chartism,* a movement of middle class reformers with working-class support. Their program (the Charter) seemed to be primarily political, calling for universal manhood franchise, equal electorate districts, "one man, one vote," annual parliaments, elimination of all property qualifications, and the secret ballot. The leaders, Feargus O'Connor, Francis Place, and William Lovett, attempted time after time to pressure Parliament into passing legislation in accordance with Charter, but without success.

But in addition to political reform, a strong group among the Chartists urged for social and economic reform. Sometimes they came close to the socialist ideas that were circulating in England and the Continent at the time. They demanded the regulation of hours of work and wages, and the need for social benefits for the workers.

> Eight hours to work; eight hours to play
> Eight hours to sleep; eight bob [shillings] a day

was one among many Chartist slogans. Some of the Chartist leaders openly advocated socialist measures:

> It is the duty of the Government to appropriate its present surplus revenue, and the proceeds of national and public property, to the purchasing of lands, and the location thereon of the unemployed poor. . . .

> The gradual resumption by the State . . . of its ancient, undoubted, inalienable domain, and sole proprietorship over all the lands, mines, tributaries, fisheries, &c., of the United Kingdom and our Colonies; for the same to be held by the State, as trustee in perpetuity, for the entire people . . .

> It is the recognized duty of the State to support all those of its subjects, who, from incapacity or misfortune, are unable to procure their own subsistence.[2]

2. Cited in G. D. H. Cole and A. W. Filson. *Working Class Movements: Selected Documents.* New York: St. Martin's Press, 1965, p. 79.

In France during the same period, radical democracy took a more extreme form. Louis Blanqui, one of the early social reformers, moved very close to revolutionary socialism and led a number of armed uprisings against the governmental authorities. Louis Blanc, another social reformer, came closer to the Chartist position. He believed political reforms were essential, but it was the duty of the State to safeguard the "right to work." He urged the government to set up national workshops to employ workers, and he believed that such workshops would compete successfully with privately owned firms. As time went on radical democracy in France increasingly moved in the direction of economic and social reforms — especially after 1848 when universal manhood suffrage, one of the major demands, was adopted. It raised the electorate overnight from a quarter million to nine million voters!

Thus, many radical democrats parted company with liberals on the definition of the economic core. They questioned the laissez-faire model of capitalism as it had been portrayed by Adam Smith. They were in favor of using the State in order to correct some of the evils and the uncertainties of the market, but they went beyond the mere search for corrective measures. They emphasized the importance of social and collective goals that could best be implemented by collective (i.e., State) action. They favored extensive State regulation not simply through legislation but through direct action and performance. Not just laws regulating child labor, but inspection and enforcement was demanded; not only poor laws providing for relief, but the actual operation of State workshops to provide employment to the poor. They demanded that the provision of social services be implemented directly by the public authorities.

Most radical democrats, however, did not advocate socialism. Their position was that the State should act and intervene where major social services and needs were involved without reaching out to expropriate property or to directly take over economic activities such as production and trade. They favored wide regulations and occasional direct controls but not the socialization of the means of production.

Thus, if we situate the radical democrats in terms of our basic cores of liberalism, we shall find them strong on the political core (leaning all the way to majoritarianism and popular sovereignty), strong on the moral core, but faithful to only a few of the basic principles defined as the economic core of early liberalism. In 1869, the French politician Jules Gambetta summed up the *political* program of radical democrats everywhere in his Belleville Manifesto, and intimated at the same time the need for economic reform:

> ". . . I think that there is no other sovereign but the people and that universal suffrage, the instrument of this sovereignty, has no value and basis unless it be radically free."

He asked for:

> . . . the most radical application of universal suffrage; . . . individual liberty to be . . . protected by law; . . . trial by jury for every kind of political offense; complete freedom of the Press;

. . . freedom of meeting . . . with liberty to discuss all religious, philosophical, political, and social affairs; . . . complete freedom of association . . . separation of church and state; free, compulsory, secular primary education; . . . suppression of standing armies; . . . abolition of privileges and monopolies.[3]

Liberal and Radical Democrats: Reconciliation

With the exception of a few who remained attached to the economic philosophy of Adam Smith, most liberals, and what we have called radical democrats, came gradually to terms. Liberals accepted the full logic of democracy. The franchise has been extended to cover all citizens, male and female, above eighteen. All of the many qualifications for voting based on literacy, age, residence, income, and so on, have been eliminated. Restraints upon representative assemblies have been virtually lifted except in cases where the chief executive is also elected directly by the people. In all existing constitutional monarchies the monarch has become a mere figurehead.

The people were mobilized in large mass parties and these parties, in many countries, exercise a controlling influence over their representatives. In some instances provisions for referenda give the people an additional measure of direct democracy. Popular democracy and majority rule expressed through direct elections for or against the members and candidates of large national political parties has been accepted by all liberals and democrats to be the major source of policymaking. At the same time the moral core of liberalism in the form of individual and minority rights has been reaffirmed.

There has also been a similar reconciliation between radical democrats and liberals with regard to economic matters. Liberal, as well as many other parties, even when they call themselves conservative, have found themselves increasingly in agreement. State intervention to support economic activities, in the form of price and other controls is deemed acceptable; State intervention through direct or indirect means to stimulate economic activity is again deemed desirable; State regulation of a growing number of economic activities is viewed as indispensable; State direct involvement in providing for unemployment assistance and State indirect and direct action to provide for employment is now taken for granted in most democracies. Thus, the functions of the State are viewed not only as supportive or regulatory; they have actually become complementary to the private sector.

The Socialist Impulse

Socialism as a philosophy of life and as a scheme for the organization of society is as old as (perhaps older than) democracy or any other form of social,

3. Cited in David Thomson. *Democracy in France Since 1870.* 5th ed. New York: Oxford U.P., 1969, pp. 315–16.

economic, or political organization. Some consider it, in fact, to have been prevalent among primitive societies where it has been suggested that land was collectively owned.

Socialism also represents an ethic diametrically opposed to that of private ownership and private profit and the inequalities that these systems may lead to. It is an ethic of an egalitarian and free society, from which the words "mine" and "yours" are eliminated.

Utopian Socialism

Utopian socialists, beginning with Thomas More (1478–1535), through Francis Bacon (1561–1621), and Tommaso Campanella (1568–1639), down to some of the most important French and British utopian socialists of the nineteenth century, shared a set of common ideas.

1. They had an aversion to private property and the exploitation of the poor by those who owned the wealth, whether landed, commercial, or industrial. "Property is theft" was the curt aphorism of the French socialist Proudhon. The Romantic poet Shelley voiced these early nineteenth century socialist beliefs:

> The seed ye sow, another reaps,
> The wealth ye find, another keeps,
> The robes ye weave, another wears,
> The arms ye forge, another bears.

2. A passionate commitment to collectivism — the common ownership of wealth — was partly based on notions about primitive communism, and partly on ideas of mutual cooperation and social solidarity. Thus, socialism was seen as the way to extirpate strife, antagonisms, and selfishness. Utopian socialists shared the nostalgic vision of the Roman poet Virgil about bygone happy ages:

> No fences parted fields, nor marks nor bounds
> Divided acres of litigious grounds,
> But all was common.

In a famous passage, Rousseau expressed similar thoughts:

> The first man, who after enclosing a piece of ground, took it into his head to say, *this is mine,* and found people simple enough to believe him, was the real founder of civil society. How many crimes, how many wars, how many murders, how many misfortunes and horrors, would that man have saved the human species, who pulling up the stakes or filling up the ditches should have cried to his fellows: Beware of listening to this impostor; you are lost, if you forget that the fruits of the earth belong equally to us all, and the earth itself to nobody![4]

4. Rousseau. *The Social Contract and Discourse on the Origins of Inequality.* Book 1.

3. A passionate belief in what might be called "social collectivism," emphasized the interdependence and solidarity of social life — the "social nature" of men and women, as opposed to the individualistic or utilitarian ethic. Communitarianism was the supreme value; individualism, competition, and self-interest were detested.

4. There were many divergences among the early utopian socialists on *how* to bring socialism about. Some believed in violence and revolution, but did not spell out any details; others believed in persuasion and example. For instance, the British socialist Robert Owen (1771–1856) set up a model textile factory in East Lanark, Scotland, where such features as the good working conditions and wages, and the participation of the workers in some of the profits were to become a model to convince other businessmen that it was in their own interests to follow the same pattern. Most utopian socialists, however, believed in education. If men and women were properly educated they would opt for socialism, and it was the task of the intellectuals to provide this kind of education.

5. Many, especially among the French utopian socialists, were what we would call today social engineers. Society would be controlled and manipulated so that under proper conditions and with the proper social organization, human beings could attain perfection — both moral and material.

6. Most of the utopian socialists were not democrats. They paid lip service to the moral core of liberalism but argued that liberal political and economic principles and practices could not bring it about. A "new ideology" had to be imposed first, or inculcated through education.

Utopian socialists never managed to form a party or even a political movement, but their writings had a profound influence upon the development of socialist thought.

Democratic Socialism

We have already noted that by the end of the nineteenth century there developed a gradual reconciliation between the proponents of liberalism and the radical democrats, in the form of political democracy. A similar reconciliation was also beginning to take place — one that developed throughout the twentieth century, and accounts for what is generally called today democratic socialism.

Nineteenth century democrats endorsed popular sovereignty and majoritarianism while accepting the individual and civil rights that we have discussed as the moral core of liberalism. This set the tone for state intervention to regulate the market, to correct malfunctioning, and to provide social service. But socialism, as first propounded by Marx and some Utopian socialists, rejected the political core of liberalism. Thus, even if for a short period of time, socialism appeared to be directly opposed to basic democratic principles and practices.

However, revolutionary Marxism gave place by the end of the nineteenth century to "revisionism." In France, in Germany, especially in

England, but also in Belgium, Holland, and the Scandinavian countries, socialist parties began increasingly to accept the logic and the techniques of democracy. Their goal was modified to bringing about social change through peaceful political means and established democratic procedures, and they became attached to the moral core of liberalism and its stress on individual and civil rights. Socialists began to consider these ideals as ends in themselves rather than as means to be used for the conquest of power. They became increasingly attracted to electoral politics, especially when socialist candidates won appreciable numbers of votes at the polls. They began to see the proper instrument for change in democracy, and that they could substitute democratic process for revolution and force.

The Fabians In England at this time a number of intellectuals were expounding upon socialism. Most important were the Fabians (who took their name from the Roman general Fabius, whose defensive "wait and see" tactics gradually weakened Hannibal's invading forces until they were defeated). The Fabians and the Fabian Society, which they established in 1884, relied upon three forces: *time*, which meant that socialism would come about gradually; *education*, to persuade the elites and the people that socialism was a superior system, morally and economically, to capitalism; and *political action in the context of democratic and parliamentary institutions*. This meant the formation of a Socialist party that would present its socialist doctrine to the people for their approval. There was not even a mention of the use of force, and nothing about a dictatorship: in fact, many of their socialist principles were inspired by the Bible. British socialism was steeped in moral, egalitarian, and humanistic values, seeking human dignity and freedom in a society from which profit and selfishness had been removed.

The philosophic foundations of Fabian socialism were set forth in *The Fabian Essays*, published in 1889. Wrote George Bernard Shaw, one of the movement's leaders:

> It was in 1885, that the Fabian Society . . . set . . . two definite tasks; first, to provide a parliamentary program for a Prime Minister converted to Socialism . . . and second, to make it as easy and matter-of-course for the ordinary respectable Englishman to be a Socialist . . .[5]

The Fabians favored socialization of the means of production, state controls, and broad welfare measures to bring about as much social equality as possible. They had no regard whatsoever for the economic core of liberalism and advocated drastic overhaul of the economy; in doing so they went way beyond the simple regulation of social legislation advocated by radical democrats (and increasingly acquiesced in by liberals). They favored the abolition of property and of the free enterprise system. Socialism was

---

5. Shaw (ed.). *The Fabian Essays in Socialism.* London: Allen & Unwin, 1958, p. 33. (1st ed. 1889.)

THE BETTMANN ARCHIVE, INC.

Sidney and Beatrice Webb

Sidney Webb (1859–1947), an Englishman of petit bourgeois background, spent over ten years in the service of the Colonial Office. In 1885, the year he joined the bar, he also joined the Fabian Society, a group of British socialists dedicated to the education of the British people in socialist principles. In 1889, Webb, along with other notable Fabians such as George Bernard Shaw and Graham Wallas, issued *The Fabian Essays in Socialism*, a book which was to become a classic of non-Marxist socialist thought. In 1887, Sidney Webb was married to Beatrice Potter (1858–1943), a woman of similar views. Both were actively concerned with social issues, and were active in the formation of the British Labour Party. Sidney drafted its manifesto — *Labour and the New Social Order* — which served as the party's platform in the elections of 1918, 1922, and 1924.

declared, however, to be an advanced form of individualism: "Socialism is merely individualism rationalised, organised, clothed, and in its right mind."[6]

6. Ibid., p. 99.

TABLE 3-1   The Rise of the Labour Party Vote

GENERAL ELECTION	SEATS CONTESTED	MEMBERS RETURNED	LABOUR VOTE
1900	15	2	62,698
1906	50	29	323,195
1910 (Jan.)	78	40	505,690
1910 (Dec.)	56	42	370,802
1918	361	57	2,244,945
1922	414	142	4,236,733
1923	427	191	4,348,379
1924	514	151	5,487,620
1945	**640**	**393**	**11,632,891**

At the beginning of this century, in 1901, the Fabians and the leaders of the major British trade unions formed the Labour party, and by 1906 were running their own independent candidates for election. They won 323,195 votes and secured twenty-nine seats in the House of Commons. Socialism began to gain the respectability that the Fabians wanted to give it (Table 3-1).

In 1918, Fabian intellectuals provided a definitive platform for the Labour Party. The party declared the need for

> . . . the gradual building up of a new social order based, not on internecine conflict, inequality of riches, and dominion over subject classes, subject races, or a subject sex, but on the deliberately planned cooperation in production and distribution, the sympathetic approach to a healthy equality, the widest possible participation in power, both economic and political, and the general consciousness of consent which characterise a true democracy.[7]

Socialism was explicitly and proudly endorsed by the Labour party, in order

> to secure for the producers by hand or by brain the full fruits of their industry, and the most equitable distribution thereof that may be possible, *upon the basis of the common ownership of the means of production* and the best obtainable system of popular administration and control of each industry and service.[8] [Emphasis added.]

European Revisionism   In Western Europe it was revolutionary Marxism that remained the dominant intellectual force and inspiration of working-class socialist movements, but in the latter part of the nineteenth century, democratic socialism (in the name of "revisionism") began to gain the upper hand.

---

7. Cited in G. D. H. Cole. *A History of the Labour Party Since 1914*. London: Routledge and Kegan Paul, 1948, p. 65.
8. Ibid., p. 72.

Revisionism became a distinct ideological movement, based on the works of Eduard Bernstein, a German socialist who produced the most comprehensive criticism of Marx and Marxism. He pointed out that:

1. The liberal capitalist system was not about to collapse, as Marx had anticipated.

2. The number of capitalists and property owners was increasing absolutely rather than decreasing, as Marxist theory stipulated it would. Thanks to the corporations and the stock exchange, a greater number of people began to "own" property in the form of stocks.

3. The capitalistic economy was generating an ever-increasing number of jobs as production became more specialized. The middle classes were, in fact, growing in number and changing in character. They no longer consisted of people who owned property, as in the past, but of new salaried personnel: technicians, engineers, white-collar workers, service personnel, civil servants, those in the liberal professions, teachers, and so on. Thus, instead of a pyramid with a huge base and sharp apex, the changing class structure under liberal capitalism was beginning to resemble a stepped pyramid in which blocks of decreasing width were superimposed upon each other.

According to Bernstein, class structure could be schematized, as shown on the left in Figure 3-1, as a stepped pyramid made up of many intermediate layers. This was contrary to Marx's view (to the right), which represents society as a smooth-sided pyramid, with the capitalist class at the apex.

4. As societies democratized, allowing for equal and universal franchise, associational freedoms, and the formation of political parties, strong working-class parties would be able to assume political power against the capitalist class and use the State as an instrument for their own protection and to secure a better allocation of goods and services. This would be accomplished through legislation and nationalizations. Bernstein felt that Marx had seriously underestimated the capabilities of the democratic state to intervene in favor of the workers and the underprivileged.

In the light of these observations, Bernstein concluded that *Evolutionary Socialism* (the title of his book, published in 1899 — ten years after

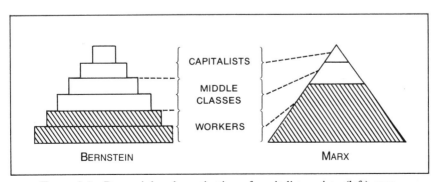

FIGURE 3-1 Bernstein's schematization of capitalist society (left) compared to Marx's (right).

The Fabian Essays were published) and not revolutionary socialism was to gain ascendancy. It was step-by-step and stage-by-stage development of socialism that would gradually replace capitalism. Bernstein's influence was profound. Revisionism was gradually adopted by the socialist parties, and revolutionary socialism and its tactics were abandoned. Socialism became synonymous with *democratic socialism*. It accepted parliamentary government and elections, and emphasized, almost exclusively, political activity within the framework of bourgeois legality and democracy. It signified the abandonment of revolutionary class struggle.

The workers were to devote themselves to improving their working conditions, their pension benefits, and their wages within the capitalistic economy, and to see to it that a larger share of the national wealth went to them and their families. The trade unions and democratic political action were to become the instruments for the realization of such tasks.

The socialist movements and parties in Europe began to move, therefore, close to the position of the British Labour party. They, too, accepted the logic of democracy and began to rely more and more on elections, votes, and the conquest of political power through elections. In so doing, they endorsed fully both the moral and the political cores of liberalism but remained hostile to private property and the market economy, promising to socialize the means of production when they achieved full power. But, as with the British Labour party, their approach became gradualistic, even eclectic and pragmatic. Socialists on the Continent and the Labour party in England began to propose only specific and selective measures, dealing primarily with the major industries. Small shopkeepers, manufacturers, farmers, and also many large industrial firms and groups, would be allowed to operate on their own.

What revisionism accomplished was to mobilize a strong percentage of the workers in favor of democratic change and to convince them (not always completely) that they could promote and defend their interests within the democratic political institutions. Socialism, as such, remained the ultimate end, and strong socialist parties, supported by the vote of the workers, were expected to press for or undertake comprehensive measures for the welfare and well-being of the workers. Even if socialist parties did not gain a majority, they could still carry great weight within representative assemblies and could directly influence governments to adopt measures favoring the working class. Broad educational reforms, health, accident, and unemployment insurances, retirement benefits, paid holidays, the reduction of the hours of work, paid vacations, collective bargaining, retirement pensions, welfare measures for the poor and the incapacitated, public works, reform in tax policies favoring low income groups, and progressively increasing taxes on middle and higher incomes — these were essential and beneficial measures to ameliorate the conditions of the workers within the broad framework of both capitalism and democracy. The dismantling of capitalism, in the form of widespread nationalizations, could wait or be selectively undertaken under propitious political and economic circumstances.

The Great Synthesis: Democratic Socialism

Ultimately, this was the general posture assumed by European socialist parties (and the Socialist party of the United States) at the end of World War I. Ever since, socialist parties have been advocating the cause of socialism in a democratic setting with full respect for democratic institutions. In so doing, they have been extending the pact between liberals and radical democrats further into what, in effect, has become a liberal-radical and democratic-socialist synthesis or, better, *democratic socialism.*

The concept of the triple core of liberalism will again help us identify the consensus that has evolved over the last fifty years. Democrats *and* socialists now fully accept *both* the moral core and the political core. In fact, the political and moral cores have expanded. Freedoms have been maintained and extended — for workers, the underprivileged, and minorities. It is not only political parties but, even more so, the various interest groups and associations that make their demands known and that participate in policymaking.

Differences continue to exist when it comes to the economic core but they are no longer sharp or irreconcilable. In many cases agreement on the content of policies to be pursued by far overshadows ideological or policy differences. Reconsideration by democrats of the validity and the efficacy of laissez-faire economics and equally significant, second thoughts on the part of socialists on the efficacy and wisdom of nationalizations and state controls, have helped bridge and reconcile differences.

Today, in many democracies, an appreciable part of the industrial production is in the hands of the State. The State also indirectly controls a substantial part of economic activity — investment, income, exports, imports, economic growth, prices, and so on. In other words, many democracies have moved increasingly in the direction of socialism.

The U.S.A.: Is There a Synthesis?

As for the United States, major social and economic reforms were undertaken by the Democrats under Roosevelt's New Deal in the 1930s. There were no nationalizations and no direct public ownership and operation except for the Tennessee Valley Authority (TVA), a public corporation that provided for electricity in the southeastern region of the country. But massive federally supported public works programs gave employment to millions. The federal government began to regulate credit; it provided low interest loans to homeowners and small businesspeople; it established controls on the production of agricultural commodities; it regulated hours of work for the first time and set minimum wages; it promoted collective bargaining and introduced a comprehensive social security system which was to be broadened with the passing of time, to provide for unemployment and retirement benefits. Many of the federal controls were indirect, but welfare measures also provided for direct supports to those in need. For the first time virtually all aspects of an individual's life came within the purview of federal jurisdiction.

Most of these measures were expanded with the passage of time, while civil rights legislation, affirmative action laws, and federal legislation on voters' registration provided fuller participation of all minority groups in the political process and insured them against any discrimination in employment and education. Massive aid to education, through direct supports, grants-in-aid, federal scholarships, and interest-free or low interest loans, provided for an unprecedented expansion in educational facilities and opportunities. Out of a total budget of $760 billion, $79 billion go for health care, $270 billion for income benefit, and $27 billion for Education and Social Service — at least 45% of the federal budget!

Democrats and Republicans differ only in details about the overall trend and direction of welfare and State controls. Better and broader medical supports, health care for the aged, higher welfare payments for mothers with children, and increased social security benefits have been enacted or expanded by both Republicans and Democratic administrations.

Yet the United States has not reached, and may well never reach, the democratic-socialist synthesis we have discussed. First of all, the American Socialist party has been attracting only very small support from workers and

The Great Depression of 1929 heralded to many, even within the United States, the decline of capitalism. Here is a typical picture of the unemployed in the 1930s, in one of what became known as the "Hoovervilles," a shanty town for the unemployed. (*Photo by Lewis Hines, from the International Museum of Photography at George Eastman House*)

voters. Secondly, economic liberalism was extremely successful until the Great Depression of 1929, and witnessed a spectacular revival in providing for economic growth, higher wages, and a better standard of living for American families since World War II. A strong body of American "liberals" therefore remained opposed to many of the policies of Roosevelt's New Deal. In fact, liberalism split into two groups. The first espoused, and continues to espouse, State controls and regulation, social legislation, and welfare measures. The second group held fast to the fundamental tenets of nineteenth-century economic liberalism. It still relies on the efficiency and sufficiency of the market economy to provide goods and values.

Democracy and Socialism: Current Trends

Democracy, liberalism, radical democracy, democratic socialism — in successive waves through the nineteenth century and into the twentieth, these movements have shaped the "great synthesis." Its major feature is the reconciliation of individual and political rights and freedoms with massive State intervention in the economy — an intervention that in some countries has gone so far as socialization of some of the means of production. It is a synthesis that in varying degrees can be found in most contemporary democracies.

Where do we stand today? Early liberalism stressed personal rights and civil rights — the moral core. This was retained by democracy, which also expanded the political core of liberalism by institutionalizing majoritarianism, organizing political parties, eliminating voter qualifications, and minimizing restraints upon the power of the representative assemblies. It also urged the regulation and control of economic life. Socialism maintained respect for individual and civil rights (the moral core), accepted the political core, and squarely introduced the question of comprehensive economic controls and welfare measures. It favored collectivization of the means of production gradually and selectively, with many qualifications and hesitations, over the last two decades.

Liberals, democrats, and socialists find themselves in agreement on many policy issues confronting modern democracies, or at least their disagreements appear to divide them less. There is an ideological convergence and a synthesis of points of view — indicating an attachment to the principles of democracy, and only secondary differences with regard to the running of the economy.

The Crisis of Democracy

Today, looking at the map of the world, we find democracy and democratic institutions implanted in the whole of Western Europe, North America, Australia, and New Zealand. It seems to have gained some roots in India and even more so in Japan. Democracy has become "operational" for more than a billion people if India is counted. Many of them have a standard of living that ranks among the highest, and they live under conditions of "modernity." Indeed, if we were to exclude India, we can say that they represent the countries with the highest per capita income in the world.

It would be downright silly, however, to assume or to pretend that the democratic synthesis we have outlined is complete and that it has been successful and widely accepted everywhere. Democracies face serious internal problems. Democratic systems and ideologies have not gained new recruits especially in the Third World nations where the label is often used but it has a very different meaning. Finally, all contemporary democracies — liberal or socialist — face some immediate and urgent challenges. There are many strains and stresses. Some people, in fact, talk of a "crisis of democracy."[9]

The Crisis of Ideology

The crisis of democracy everywhere lies in its lack of a transcendental ideology. There are no absolutes associated with it, except the moral autonomy of the individual. Democracy consists of a set of procedures to preserve and to promote this profoundly individualist ethic. But otherwise as an ideology — to use Marx's phrase — democracy does not "grip the masses." It offers no easy solution to many of our predicaments and it promises no blue horizons except the ones that we shall open up through our own exertions. It is not geared to a scheme of history that tells us that a democratic development is inevitable and just. On the contrary, it tells us that we make our history and that in the process we may make mistakes. It sets no unifying themes. On the contrary, it tells us that we are all different from each other and that we rightfully should follow our own drummer; we are not meant to "march in step." In short, there is no vision to guide us all. There are no "true believers" among real democrats — only skeptics!

How do democracies define the "public good"? It is not ordained by divine word; it is not decreed by a ruling governing body; it is not identified with that of a class — though the bourgeoisie claimed to be its spokesman for a long time. The public good is the sum total of the thousands of interests that compete with each other (although some may argue that it is not even that). It lies in the existence of procedures that allow for competition. It is the procedures, then, that have value in themselves — the Constitution, parliamentary government, party and economic competition, and so on. Procedures, however, are only forms — ways of doing things; they are not easily converted to substantive values to which people become passionately attached. Democracy provides the means, the instruments, and the processes of political life; it does not, like so many ideologies, tell us what life is all about. We are free to find out — or to give up and have somebody tell us!

9. M. J. Crozier, S. P. Huntington, and J. Watanuki. *The Crisis of Democracy*. New York: New York U.P., 1975. I have summarized some of the arguments of the authors.

Everybody is familiar with the term "the revolution of rising expectations." It is common not only among poor nations which have recently gained their independence and are underdeveloped, but also among the peoples of the rich countries in Western Europe and the United States. The most characteristic manifestation of the "revolution" is that all people want *more of everything* — more wealth, a higher standard of living, better education, greater security, better health care, more participation in decision making, more leisure, and greater equality. The speed with which these expectations have escalated and have converged has created serious problems.

The crisis of modern democratic regimes is primarily caused by the disparity between ideology and institutional capabilities. Ideology conjures up a world of plenty and immediate fulfillment. It shapes the new moral imperatives of equality and of equal sharing in opportunities and of benefits. Institutions are slow to respond to the pressure, and as a result, democratic regimes are faced with the prospect of instability.

It is simply difficult to meet all the rising demands, not only because resources are limited, but because structural and institutional changes are needed in order to meet them. New services are required and new institutional mechanisms must be put in place. Even the most open and responsive systems experience a time lag between demands being made and registered and developing new mechanisms to respond to them — let alone satisfy them.

The intensity and number of demands from minorities, professional organizations, trade unions, student groups, cultural associations, and so on (many couched in sharp ideological terms) threaten to overwhelm the existing democratic institutions. This is a *revolutionary prospect,* for it is likely to cause upheavals in the institutional framework of democratic societies. But it is also conceivable that democratic elites may have to resort to repressive measures in order to curb demands and stifle the rising expectations. This is the *authoritarian prospect.* There is, of course, the possibility that some democratic societies may "muddle through" by adjusting their institutions to meet the new demands, constantly experiencing temporary dislocations but capable of reforms.

The Crisis of Institutions

Representative institutions, either in parliamentary or presidential systems, face a double crisis in performance and legitimacy. Gone are the days when the radical democrats believed that universal manhood, suffrage, and representative government would solve all social and economic evils. Only a small number believes now that representative assemblies really represent the people. Few think that, out of the welter of interests represented in the representative assemblies, a common purpose and common policies for society as a whole can evolve. There is a crisis of democratic representative institutions.

If the representative assemblies are no longer viewed as being truly representative, new institutions must be sought to safeguard the interests of the people at large. One such proposal is direct participation. This is the demand for direct participation in decision making by all those who are affected. The corollary is decentralization of the decision-making mechanism; the virtual dismantling of the bureaucratic apparatus of the State into small and manageable units such as the city, the locality, the particular administrative services, the neighborhood. Thus the citizen can participate, and the recipients or beneficiaries of services may have a direct say and direct supervision of them. Questions about urban renewal or new housing construction should be decided by those living in the particular areas concerned, and welfare service should be decentralized in a manner to allow for the recipients' direct control and management. The accent is put on "community control," on "neighborhood city halls," and "direct democracy" in the economy. Grass-roots politics, parochial and local "nationalisms" are beginning to develop. Small towns, localities, and neighborhoods are beginning to claim precedence over national representative organs.

The Crisis of Authority

Institutional weakness, real or imaginary, seems to parallel a profound moral crisis — a crisis of the authority of the democratic State. It is translated into a widespread decline in the consensus democracies enjoyed in the past. Many of the traditional authority structures have weakened: for instance, the Church, the family, the social elites, and more recently the trade unions and fraternal associations. Similarly, highly valued organizations like the army or the university have declined in importance. None of them play the role they played in the past, serving to structure demands, to slow down the urge for immediate fulfillment, and to inculcate respect for existing institutions. These agencies no longer play the role of intermediary between the State and the public at large to sustain its authority and to secure agreement on its decisions. On the contrary, particularisms have begun to assert their primacy — special interests, particular ethnic groups, special localities, different religious bodies; they all assert their virtual autonomy. This further undermines consensus to a democratic policy and makes compliance with the decisions of the democratic State uncertain.

The Crisis of Legitimacy

These are the words of a noted sociologist.

> Democracy, as the sorry history of Europe has shown, is a fragile system . . . [it may collapse] when political parties or social movements can successfully establish "private armies" whose resort to violence — street fighting, bombings, the breakup of their opponent's meetings or simply intimidation — cannot be con-

trolled by the elected authorities, and whose use of violence is justified or made legitimate by the respectable elements in society.[10]

Daniel Bell is, of course, referring here to the Nazi and fascist movements and their counterparts in Central Europe that we shall discuss in Chapter 9, but today both the legacy of guerrilla war and the growth of terrorism pose the same dangers for contemporary democracies.

Guerrilla warfare occurred widely after World War II as the various colonies attempted to oust the colonial power. It took the form of both political organization and military confrontation. At first, small detachments with makeshift arms would begin to harass the colonial administration and the forces allied to it. At the same time a large network of political support was being built to support the guerrillas. Under a leadership and a party, the indigenous population was organized to give its total support to the fighting forces.

Guerrilla warfare and terrorism in advanced democracies, in the form of urban guerrillas such as Italy's Red Brigades, or Germany's Baader-Meinhof group, have been responsible for the assassinations of top political leaders. Here and in other democratic societies, extremist groups advocating revolution, separatism, or anarchism approximate the model of guerrilla warfare. A prerequisite to this activity is the organization of a group of faithful supporters who will support the terrorists, urban guerrillas, and revolutionaries. How can democracy defend itself?

The most pressing danger is that democratic societies, faced with dissent and acts of violence by terrorist organizations, may seek counterrevolutionary policies which will force them to jettison democratic principles and practices. Repressive measures, serious qualifications of political and individual freedoms, special forms of control and police surveillance may be introduced, indeed *have* been introduced, in the name of counterterrorism. Democracy remains fragile indeed, and never more so than when multiple and conflicting ideological movements begin to undermine the support it needs.

Socialism:
Crisis and Future Perspectives

Socialism, as an ideology and movement, offered suggestions about social and economic organization and the role of the State and also advocated measures to end inequalities in opportunities and income. Socialist governments, with adequate support to implement their ideology and programs, have been relatively few in the post-World War II period. One example, however, is the Labour party in English government from 1945–1951, 1964–1970, and again from 1974–1979. In Germany, the Social Democratic party — only in coali-

10. Daniel Bell (ed.). *The Radical Right.* New York: Doubleday, 1963, p. 33.

tion with the Liberals — was in office between 1973 and 1982. In Sweden, Socialists have been in government for about half a century with two short interruptions. In Austria, they have had an uninterrupted rule since the end of World War II.

Both the British Labour party and the German Social Democrats had to qualify considerably one of the major tenets of socialism — the nationalization of the economy. After the first nationalization effort of the Labour party (1945–1951) during which the coal mines, railroads, electrical, gas, iron, and steel were nationalized, the emphasis was put on welfare legislation, an equitable incomes policy, and efforts to meet the demands of the trade unions and to arrest inflation. Reconstruction of the economy, in order to maintain Great Britain's competitive position in the world economy, became a primary target. In 1979 the Labour government gave place to the Conservatives who seemed determined to restrict the role of the State in economic matters.

Today, the Labour party is badly divided, with some left-wing socialists moving in a doctrinaire fashion once again toward comprehensive nationalizations and the imposition of State controls. But the moderates have seceded from the Labour party, and have formed a reformist Social-democratic party that may cooperate closely with the Liberals.

In Germany the Social-Democrats, in effect, abandoned their commitment to socialization as early as 1959 in the Bad Godesberg Congress with the slogan "the State whenever necessary; freedom whenever possible." In office since the early 1970s, the German Social Democrats have undertaken no major structural reforms of the economy. However, they introduced welfare legislation and maintained a wage policy that favored the workers — something that was made possible by the remarkable strength and competitiveness of the German industry. But the party, as the Labour party in England, faces internal splits with some of the left-wing groups advocating a different foreign policy and drastic economic and structural reforms.

It is only in Sweden and in Austria that "socialism" has fared well, but again, with some serious qualifications. Sweden, during a long socialist party rule, did not undertake nationalizations of the economy. The private sector is stronger by far than the public one. There are institutions that provide for bargaining and compromise between the State, the strong cooperatives, the trade unions, and the private sector. The State is, in effect, a redistributive agency that attempts to equalize incomes through welfare legislation and public services. But in Sweden, too, the Socialist party was defeated in 1976 in the face of rising demands for greater economic and social freedoms. It was returned to office, however, in 1982.

The disarray of the Labour party, the difficulties of the Socialists in Sweden, and the virtual complete acceptance of free enterprise by the German Social Democrats all seemed to spell the decline of socialism. Social democratic and reformist policies meant greater tolerance for a free economy and private incentive rather than socialism. Many nationalizations, in fact, involved bankrupt industries and monopolies. The State took them over at the expense of the taxpayer. Their management was not superior to that of the private sector. In fact in some countries — notably in Italy — the bureaucratization of the economy because of nationalizations resulted in low productivity and inefficiency at high cost to the consumer. Many political leaders, even those from the left, have since urged that management again be returned to the private sector.

In England, Germany, and other countries, socialism had been supported by a strong working class organized in powerful trade unions, and the socialist parties had been its spokesmen. But Karl Kautsky, one of the fathers of the German social democracy, had noted that as socialist parties became transformed from parties of the working class to "parties of the people," their militancy and ideology underwent profound changes. Socialist parties and governments had to represent the nation; they became the representatives of many socioeconomic groups — especially the new white-collar workers and the new middle classes. The Socialist parties had to compromise and use the State to arbitrate rather than to impose a given point of view or follow a given economic or social blueprint. Their ideology became more comprehensive and more diffuse. Socialist parties became like all other parties, and as the magic of nationalizations began to wane, socialists, too, came to terms with capitalist structures and practices — notably the market. Their commitment to democracy made it impossible for them to *impose* their program, as the Marxist would have done, and as they had in fact done in the Soviet Union and in Eastern Europe.

By the middle 1970s it appeared that socialism had run its course. It had served well the working classes, the underprivileged, and the society as a whole: the need of economic equality became increasingly accepted; it had "legitimized" the State even in the eyes of the workers and had shown them that it was no instrument of a class, as the Marxists had argued, but an institution capable of arbitrating among groups and classes to provide for service on the basis of need; it had developed a body of legislation that in effect mitigated the hardships of economic conflict and poverty in the form of programs in health insurance, retirement policies, family care, housing, full employment, and free education. On the other hand, socialism had not provided a solution to economic growth, higher productivity, and economic well-being. Above all it had not managed to reconcile the principle of individual freedom with that of equality. Too much individualism led to inequalities; but too much emphasis upon equality appeared to be an invasion of individual freedoms — a steamroller that wiped out initiative, thwarted experimentation, and discouraged effort. Lastly, socialism had not even attempted to give an answer to international problems. The building of a transnational and supranational community of free peoples remained out of reach and sight. In fact, socialism, like communism elsewhere, continued to be associated with nationalism.

Socialism in the 1980s: The Case of France

Contrary to all expectations, socialism, with new suggestions for reforming the economy and the society, received a new lease on life with the victory of the Socialist party in France. The Socialists elected the president of the

Republic in May 1981 and in the legislative elections in June 1981 they won an absolute majority of the seats in Parliament. It was the first time that an all-socialist government was formed in the history of France and it was a victory that was bound to have repercussions in the whole of Europe. Within six months the elections in Greece — October 18, 1981 — brought a Socialist majority into office. In Italy, Spain, and Portugal socialism and the Socialist parties received a new boost. What were the major characteristics of French socialism?

Marxism had produced two competing parties in Europe and France whose fortunes knew many ups and downs — the Soviet-oriented Communist party and the democratic and reformist Socialist party. In France, until almost 1980, the Communists were by far the stronger — receiving solid working-class support, controlling the most powerful trade union, and having the ability to mobilize the public and the electorate. However, beginning in the early 1970s a new Socialist leadership and a new program accounted for renewed strength. It began to catch up with the Communists.

The new Socialist party moved clearly to the left — cooperating with the Communists and advocating broad structural reforms and the nationalizations of about eleven key industries and virtually all banks. The party promised to expand social legislation, to provide for full employment, to impose higher taxes, and to narrow income disparities. It stood out as a party of the left, and while it appealed to all groups it sought the support of the workers. But the Socialists continued to stress their attachment to democracy — to the political freedoms that they had always respected. In contrast to the centralized and bureaucratic socialism from above — the Soviet-style state socialism — they promised to decentralize and to give autonomous powers to local units and firms. They favored what is known in France as *autogestion* — the organization of economic production and industrial activity (even within the nationalized industries) in a manner allowing for the participation and decision making of those working in them. They promised to take environmental measures to protect the citizen and to gear investment and industrial activities to qualitative considerations — to education, art, leisure, early retirement, better living conditions for the old, and greater opportunities for the young. Theirs was to be a socialism "au visage humain" — socialism with a "human face." To the impersonal bureaucratic socialist planning of the Soviet type, they suggested a people's socialism managed by the people in an economy and in which the public sector would operate side-by-side with the private sector; to the reformist democratic socialism of England, Germany, or Sweden, they offered important structural changes that would bring the economy directly under overall public supervision and control but not necessarily State management. To the inequalities of the market, and the risks associated with private economy and a free enterprise system, they offered solid welfare cushions to protect the individual.

The new Socialist party and its programs represented a synthesis of powerful intellectual and political currents that have run for many decades within the French noncommunist left. "Decentralization" went back to Proudhon's antistatism and his emphasis on voluntary associations to manage the economy. "Democracy" combined the thinking of the humanists among the socialists and also with that of a strong segment of liberal Catholics, who had insisted that good Catholics should move from the Church into the society so they could actively implement the gospel of social justice and freedom. Nationalizations borrowed from both the strong current of utopian socialism and social engineering, and also from the traditions of an efficient French civil service that had supervised and managed many sectors of the economy over a long period of time. Finally, the French socialists remained good patriots — their program for economic reform was linked to an effort to build a strong and independent France.

The French Socialist ideology, if successful, may inject new life into democratic socialism. It is an ideology that may appear very attractive to the Eastern European countries and may cast more doubts upon the centralized authoritarian control of the Soviet system. The success or failure of the French experiment, in other words, will affect the course of politics in the whole of Europe for many years to come.

Socialism and Democracy
in the Third World

While a number of the moral assumptions of liberal democracy — individual freedom, human dignity, religious freedoms — have been endorsed in the abstract by many of the leaders of the new nations in Asia and Africa, political and economic freedoms (what we have called the political and the economic core) and also the democratic institutions themselves, were given new interpretations. This has happened to such an extent that democracy has come to mean something very different from what it has meant in Western Europe or the United States. Basic principles like pluralism, and basic institutions like representative government and the political parties, which allow for dissent and competition, have been rejected. Instead, they have been superseded by the search for a "popular" or "communitarian" will, one that is often expressed by a single party or very often by a single leader. The terms "democracy" or "republic" are used even when in practice the system is a dictatorship — with powers concentrated in the hands of one leader or a military junta that claims to represent the community as a whole. "Democratic dictatorship," "guided democracy," "controlled democracy" are the expressions one finds frequently.[11]

Some of the reasons for this are historical. In almost all cases the emancipation of the colonies was the outcome of collective and communitarian effort. It called for complete mobilization and organization of the population. While the guerrillas had fought for independence the population had to be organized; their hearts and minds had to be conquered. This called for a highly disciplined political party, and the development of total control with an ideological and political conformity. This was seen as the only way to

11. Paul E. Sigmund, Jr. *The Ideologies of the Developing Nations.* New York: Praeger, 1964.

sustain the fighting men and women. In Mao's expression, the population was to the guerrillas what water is to fish. It sustained, sheltered, and nourished them; it provided them with a built-in hiding place. In Algeria, in Vietnam, and in some African colonies, efforts to build totalitarian control were made during the national liberation wars, and the party developed into a State within a State with its own schools, courts, tax collectors, and administrative apparatus. It sought conformity, discipline, and obedience to leadership.

It was this tight political organization and control that accounted, above all, for the ultimate victory of independence movements and the withdrawal of the colonial powers. But it carried its legacy after independence. The party remained a disciplined paramilitary force allowing no freedoms and competition. Its energy was now directed to other ends — national integration, economic development, the elimination of internal dissent and of "counter-revolutionary" forces, and the subjugation of traditional elites, whether religious, linguistic, tribal, or economic, that might obstruct its efforts. Total effort led to "total" regimes, after liberation.

In institutional terms this meant that competition and political pluralisms could not be accepted and representative assemblies could not be allowed to serve as the spokesmen of particular and competing interests. Instead, they should speak for a whole and united community from which they derived their mandate. If they would not, then the leader would become the spokesman for the new nation.

The one-party system has been defended as truly democratic. "Does democracy necessarily imply several parties?" asked Jomo Kenyatta (of Kenya). "We say no," he answers. Political parties, according to him, are a reflection of classes and economic interests, but when no diversity exists or is permitted to exist in terms of interests and classes, then many parties are not needed. One is enough. Many political parties would divide the people and give rise to rivalries that would disrupt national unity.

In the same vein the leader of Guinea, President Sekou Touré, has spoken of a "democratic dictatorship." "If the dictatorship exercised by the government apparatus emanates directly from the whole people, this dictatorship is popular in nature and the State is a democratic state . . ."[12] The late leader of Egypt, Gamal Abdel Nasser, rejected a multiparty system. The latter would serve the interests of the colonial powers by dividing the Egyptian people. His answer was the *National* Unity Party — a mass popular organization representing *all* the people.

Virtually none of the new nations has accepted economic liberalism. Many of them claim to be "socialist." Socialism is distinguished, however, from Marxism and communism, and though there is widespread admiration for the Soviet system, none of the new states has fully endorsed its model of economic organization. Generally the control of the State is accepted for the key economic activities and for investment. There is a public sector controlled and manned by the State. But there is also a private sector with a fairly

12. Ibid., pp. 162–63.

wide margin of initiative in commerce, farming, and manufacturing. Socialism is described as "democratic" but some speak of "democratic collectivism."[13]

Socialism, almost everywhere in Africa (but in parts of Asia too), is defined in "humanistic" terms. The African intellectual, Leopold Senghor, suggests that African socialism should develop in the form of a synthesis that brings together the works of Marx, the utopian socialists, trade unionism, and democratic socialism. It represents a reaction against both "capitalistic and Communist imperialism."[14] In many of the new nations, but especially in Africa, religious beliefs continue to play a more important role than material and economic considerations. Even more important, religions and religious values make the acceptance of Marxism difficult.

Thus, most of the new nations pay lip service to democracy but reject dissent, political competition, and pluralism and endorse the one-party system or personal authoritarian leadership. They strive to consolidate the unity they have acquired and wish to defend it against the outside interventions that internal divisions may invite.

Bibliography

Beer, Samuel H. *British Politics in the Collectivist Age.* New York: Vintage, 1969. Reedited under the title *Modern British Politics,* 1982.

Bell, Daniel, and Kristol, Irving (eds.). *Capitalism Today.* New York: New American Library, 1971.

Bernstein, Eduard. *Evolutionary Socialism.* New York: Charles Scribner's Sons, 1961.

Buber, Martin. *Paths in Utopia.* Boston: Beacon Press, 1958.

Cole, G. D. H. *A History of Socialist Thought.* (6 volumes) London: Macmillan, 1953–60.

Colton, Joel. *Leon Blum: Humanist in Politics.* Cambridge, Mass.: M.I.T. Press, 1974.

Crossman, R. H. S. (ed.). *The New Fabian Essays.* New York: Praeger, 1952.

_____. *The Politics of Socialism.* New York: Atheneum, 1965.

Cyr, Arthur I. *Liberal Party Politics in Britain.* New Brunswick, N.J.: Transaction Books, 1977.

Dahl, Robert A. *Democracy in the United States.* 3rd ed. Chicago: Rand McNally, 1976.

Desfosses, Helen and Levesque, Jacques (eds.). *Socialism in the Third World,* New York: Praeger, 1975.

Galbraith, John Kenneth. *American Capitalism: The Concept of Countervailing Power.* Rev. ed. Boston: Houghton Mifflin, 1956.

_____. *The New Industrial State.* Boston: Houghton Mifflin, 1967.

13. For the early manifestations of African socialism, see William H. Friedland and Carl G. Rosberg, Jr., (eds.). *African Socialism.* Stanford, Calif.: Stanford U.P., 1964.
14. Sigmund, op. cit., p. 245.

Gay, Peter. *The Dilemma of Democratic Socialism.* New York: Columbia U.P., 1952.

Girvetz, H. K. *From Wealth to Welfare: The Evolution of Liberalism.* Stanford, Calif.: Stanford U.P., 1950.

Goldberg, Harvey. *The Life of Jean Jaurés.* Madison: University of Wisconsin Press, 1962.

Halévy, Elie. *The Growth of Philosophic Radicalism.* Boston: Beacon Press, 1955.

Hancock, Donald M., and Sjoberg, Gideon (eds.). *Politics in the Post-Welfare State.* New York: Columbia U.P., 1972.

Harrington, Michael. *Socialism.* New York: Bantam Books, 1972.

Heilbroner, Robert L. *The Limits of American Capitalism.* New York: Harper and Row, 1967.

Huntington, Samuel *et al. The Crisis of Democracy,* New York: New York U.P., 1975.

Joll, James. *The Second International, 1889–1914.* New York: Praeger, 1956.

Lowi, Theodore J. *The End of Liberalism.* New York: Norton, 1969.

Manuel, Frank. *Utopian Thought in the Western World.* Cambridge, Mass.: Harvard U.P., 1979.

Mills, C. Wright. *The Power Elite.* New York: Oxford U.P., 1956.

Paterson, William E. and Campbell, Ian. *Social Democracy in Post-War Europe.* New York: St. Martin's Press, 1974.

Rawls, John. *A Theory of Justice.* Cambridge, Mass.: Harvard U.P., 1971.

Research Institute on International Change. *The Relevance of Liberalism.* Boulder, Colo.: Westview Press, 1977.

Schlesinger, Arthur, Jr. *The Age of Roosevelt,* vols. 1 and 2. Boston: Houghton Mifflin, 1957.

Schumpeter, Joseph A. *Capitalism, Socialism and Democracy.* New York: Harper & Row, 1950.

Shaw, George Bernard (ed.). *The Fabian Essays in Socialism.* Gloucester, Mass.: Smith, 1967. (Reprint of 1889 Edition)

4 | *Conservatism: England and the U.S.A.*

The good citizen is a law-abiding traditionalist.
RUSSELL KIRK   What Is Conservatism?

Conservatism is, perhaps, more a state of mind than a political ideology. In order to be conservative one must have something to conserve — property, status, power, a way of life. Conservatives are therefore likely to be those who have power or wealth or status, and who simply want to keep things the way they are. Also, a significant number of people — mostly among rural groups, those who live in small towns, the old and the uneducated — cannot imagine something different, or are afraid of change. They, too, want to keep their way of life the way it is.

Even if we were, however, to define conservatism simply as the defense of the status quo and the rationalization and the legitimization of a given order of things — in other words as a "situational ideology" — we would find that conservative ideology has its own logic.[1] Conservative movements always and everywhere borrow from some of the same principles, irrespective of the particular situation they face at a particular time. They are the following:

1. "Liberty" is more important to conservatives than "equality."
2. They have a pronounced allergy for political power — and are against its concentration in the hands of anybody, especially the people.
3. They insist on an organic theory of the society involving a hierarchy of groups and classes and a cooperation among them — the community and its interests are always above the individual.
4. They have a respect for tradition and "inheritance" — that which is bequeathed to us from our ancestors.

---

1. In a penetrating article, Samuel Huntington indicates that conservatism can be viewed as (1) an ideology that emanated from the aristocracy as it rationalized its position and interests against the French Revolution of 1789 — *aristocratic conservatism;* (2) an ideology that contains substantive prescription about the organization of social and political life — *autonomous conservatism;* (3) and lastly, an ideology arising from a given situation in which the status quo is threatened by the prophets and the activists of change — *a situational ideology.* Conservatism is ". . . the articulate, systematic, theoretical resistance to change. It is primarily an ideology that defends the status quo." (In *American Political Science Review,* v. LI, June 1957, no. 2, pp. 454–473)

5. Religion, with the feeling for reverence to authority with which it is associated, is dear to the conservatives.
6. They distrust "reason" and the propriety of using it for the solution of social problems.
7. Almost all conservative ideologies are elitist. Some people are better equipped than others; some are superior, while some (generally the many) are inferior.

These principles were invoked throughout the nineteenth century as certain groups fought to maintain their position against the egalitarian and reformist principles of democracy, liberalism, and, later on, socialism and Marxism.

A final note: the terms "conservative" and "reactionary" should not be confused as they so often are. A conservative doesn't want change — but will acquiesce to it — at least to gradual change. A "reactionary," on the other hand, is often one who wants to change things radically in order to reestablish the past. A conservative is against rapid change; a reactionary is one who doesn't accept the change that has already taken place! Nor should conservatism be confused with authoritarianism. The latter favors a concentration of political power in the hands of a leader or a group, is against individual and political freedoms, rejects popular participation in almost any form, and accepts repression and the use of force.

Classic Conservatism: The British Model

The best formulation of conservative ideology was given by Edmund Burke, in the latter part of the eighteenth century. The best implementation of it has been, through the nineteenth century and until today, that of the British Conservative party.[2] Variants of the British model could be found in Germany under Bismarck, in France during the so-called Orleanist period (1830–1848) and in some of its offshoots during the period of the Third French Republic (1871–1940), and in Gaullism. But almost nowhere on the Continent did an alliance of the aristocracy and the upper classes, the Church, the monarchy, and the army lead to the posture of conservatism tied to constitutional democracy that prevailed in England.

European conservatives chose in many instances to reject constitutional democracy and representative government. In the United States there have been many variants of a conservative ideology, but the absence of a nobility and the success of the egalitarian ethic and liberalism account for the virtual absence of any genuine conservative movement or ideology that has had any impact.

2. An excellent discussion of the evolution of conservative ideology can be found in the relevant parts of Samuel H. Beer. *British Politics in the Collectivist Age.* New York: Vintage, 1949.

Classic conservatism is characterized by certain basic propositions that relate to political authority, to a conception of society and the nature of the individual, and to the relationship between national economy and the State.

The Political Society

Society, according to early British conservative thought, is organic and hierarchical. Classes and social groups fit together in the same way as do the various organs of our bodies. One is indispensable to the others; it cannot function without them. Relations between them must be harmonious and balanced, and each group and each class performs the functions that are necessary to the others for the good health of the whole. Society is not like a machine, say a clock, in which the motions are eternally identical and where each part has no idea of what the other parts are doing. It is, rather, a combination of many parts, each one of which understands its role and perceives society as a whole. Unlike the machine, society knows it has a purpose; unlike a clock it grows and changes. "The whole," wrote Edmund Burke, ". . . is never old, middle-aged, or young." It "moves on through . . . perpetual decay, fall, renovation, and progression."[3]

Society thus consists of interdependent parts — and all the parts are equally conscious of the interdependence. Each one does its own work, but what it does makes sense only when the whole is understood and valued. Farmers grow crops; soldiers keep order and give protection; priests improve our minds and souls; the leaders govern and balance the various parts. The parts working together almost lose the sense of their separateness. Society is not a "mixture" of various roles, groups, qualities, and activities. It is, as Aristotle said, much more of a "compound" in which the parts blend with each other to become something different from what they are individually. They become a society.

Different functions and roles inevitably suggest a hierarchical organization and social inequality. Some of society's roles are more important than others, and some people do more important things than others. This means that there must be a subordination of some individuals to others. Persons endowed by nature with certain qualities that others do not have should play the most important roles. Equality and freedom, as abstract propositions, are not acceptable to the conservative ideology. Rather, it emphasizes *rights* and *liberties*. These derive not from rational principles or from natural law but from specific institutional and legal arrangements, and from history and tradition. They give to individuals and to groups specific benefits, protections, and claims that are commensurate with their functions and roles. Nor is the idea of material equality for all seriously entertained. Material benefits should correspond to the talent shown and the work done.

The "whole" — this society that consists of the harmonious interdependence of many parts — is formalized in the Constitution. This is not a

---

3. Burke. *Reflections on the French Revolution.* p. 162.

written document, and in fact there is no way, according to conservative thinkers, a constitution can be set down. The Constitution is a set of customs, understandings, rules, and especially traditions, that define political power and set limits upon its exercise. Power thus enshrined by habit, custom, and tradition becomes authority; that is, it is accepted and respected. In this way, it is the Constitution that binds the whole of the citizenry to its rulers and the rulers to the citizenry within the nation. Conservatives, however, are not necessarily nationalists. To them the nation-state is a social and historical reality, the product of many centuries of common life and togetherness. But it is not a supreme moral value unless it has managed to embody justice and order. "To make us love our country, our country must be lovely" was the pithy comment of Burke.

Political Authority

In contrast to those who establish the foundations of political authority on contract and consent, conservatives find it in tradition, custom, and in what they call inheritance and prescription. Society as a living whole is the result of natural evolution. The Constitution of England and its various parts — the monarchy, the House of Lords and the nobility, the House of Commons, individual rights, the judiciary — are an "entailed inheritance." One accepts it, to live on it, but cannot waste it. In a famous passage, Burke sees in the State something like a mystery: its parts and its majesty cannot be dissected, analyzed, and put back together in the same or in a different way. *The State cannot be made.* He wrote:

> The state ought . . . to be looked upon with . . . reverence.
> . . . It is a partnership in all science; a partnership in all art; a
> partnership in all perfection . . . between those who are living,
> those who are dead and those who are to be born. . . . Each
> contract is but a clause in the great primeval contract of eternal
> society, linking the lower with the higher natures, connecting the
> visible with the invisible world, according to a fixed compact
> sanctioned by the inviolable oath which holds all physical and all
> moral natures, each in their appointed place.[4]

Conservatives, therefore, have no use for the "contract" theory of the State propounded by the early liberals. The idea runs counter to the organic theory of society and to the role history and tradition play in the formation of a state. Burke insisted that even if there were a contract it was shaped by history and tradition, and once made "it attaches upon every individual of that society, without any formal act of his own." We are born into political society like our fathers and forefathers; we do not make it.

---

4. Ibid., pp. 139–40.

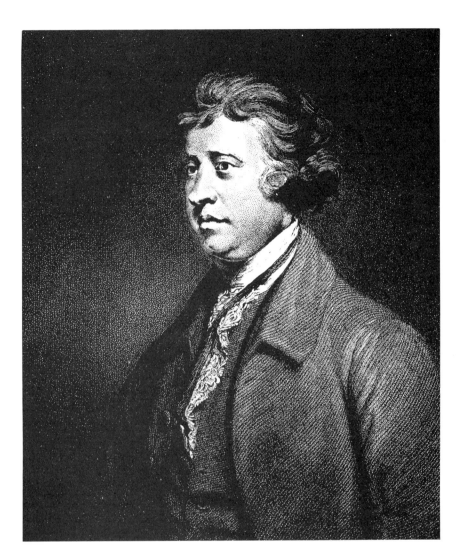

Edmund Burke (1729–1797)

Edmund Burke was the most eloquent expounder of British conservative ideology. Originally, Burke appeared to be a liberal arguing not only against the prerogatives of the crown and in favor of parliament, but also for the autonomy of the colonies in North America. These views were expressed in *Thoughts on the Causes of the Present Discontents* (1770). It was the French Revolution and its excesses that accounted for his masterpiece *Reflections on the French Revolution* (1790), in which he presented arguments favoring tradition and prescription, and the sanctity of law and authority, while cautioning against anything but the most gradual expansion of popular participation in affairs of the State.

Change

Given the emphasis on tradition, conservative thought is generally opposed to change unless it is gradual. Our "partnership with the dead" should not be broken, for fear that this would undermine the living and those still to be born. Modifications become necessary, but on balance the past carries more weight than the present. As for the future, there are many would-be reformers and social engineers, and conservatives distrust them. Innovation is suspect, and Burke claimed it was prompted by "selfish temper and confined views." As a result, the conservatives fall back upon the existing and widely shared values that have kept the society together. Religion is one of the most important; so is common law and even prejudices. As Edmund Burke put it, "wise prejudice," consecrated by long usage, is "better than thoughts untried and untested."

Religion, tradition, the common law, and prejudice — all give the individual shelter and solace; they provide stability that in the last analysis is a higher value than change. All these things, together with the State and its organs, must be strengthened with the proper pomp and ritual that appeal to the common people. The crown itself is a symbol that, through ritual, secures support and obedience. More than fifty years after Burke, another British conservative, Walter Bagehot, (1826–1877) spoke of the "symbolic" or "ceremonial" part of the Constitution (that is, the monarch) providing for the attachment of the common people and unifying political society. The cabinet, the prime minister, and parliament were the "efficient part," though this was understood only by the elite and hardly appreciated by the common people.[5]

If change is to come, however, it must be natural and slow — one and the same thing for conservatives. Conservatives may even favor change in order to preserve. Change must reflect new needs and be the result of cautious adjustment with past practices. The British conservatives *allowed* for changes in the Constitution, which they venerated; thus came about the gradual extension of the franchise, the ascendancy of the popularly elected House of Commons over the hereditary House of Lords, and the development of a civil service based on merit, as well as economic and social reforms. But they did so often under pressure, and with the aim of preserving what they valued most. In their efforts to slow down reform, however, British conservatives remained firmly attached to the basic democratic principles of representative government, elections, and the rule of law.

Leadership

The purpose of the State and its leaders is to balance the whole and to create unity and commonality of purpose out of diversity. Government leadership and decision making should be entrusted to "natural leaders" — men or women of talent, high birth, and property, who have a stake in the interests of the country and in its fortunes. As late as the middle of the nineteenth

5. Bagehot. *The English Constitution.* New York: Oxford U.P., 1936.

century many argued in England that noblemen could own, outfit, and command whole regiments in the army and the explanation given was simple — they cared more about England's welfare than did the common people. They had a greater stake in the defense of the country.

As a conservative put it recently, "Government is instituted to secure justice and order . . . and . . . the first principle of good government allows the more energetic natures among a people to fulfill their promise while ensuring that these persons shall not tyrannize over the mass of men."[6] Quality and not election should therefore be the source of leadership. Conservatives fought against the rapid extension of the franchise, acquiescing to it reluctantly, and did not accept the full logic of majority rule until very recently. The principle of one man-one vote was unacceptable, and the notion that decisions could be made by simple arithmetic majority was considered "a violent fiction." The idea of decision making by a majority could be entertained only when that majority, by long habits of obedience, had become self-disciplined. That would be when the majority had accepted the restraints that law and tradition had inculcated so as to act in accordance with the fundamental rules of the past.

The natural leaders hold the interests of the country in trust. They act on behalf of the people and the society. The trust, however, is almost a complete and blanket grant of power — it is not a delegation.

Another way of explaining the same conservative notion of trusteeship is to refer to it as the theory of *virtual representation*. Today we agree that representatives represent their constituency, those who elect them, and the country in general, but their capacity to make decisions for us stems directly from elections and from the *mandate* they receive from their constituency or the electorate at large. Virtual representation, on the other hand, is the capacity to represent and make decisions by virtue of qualities other than mere election. Conservative thinking returns to the idea of birth and wealth. Persons who have one or both can represent the people and the nation by virtue of their position better than elected representatives. They are what in medieval times were called the *valentior pars* (the better part) of the community. This again shows the reluctance by conservatives to extend the franchise and accept majoritarianism.

Thus, the natural leaders should govern and the many should follow. This reflects the typical British conservative attitude, which still is evident today. Many of the members and leaders of the Conservative party still think that they are endowed with capabilities with which they can govern better than any other party and its leadership. They still believe that they can hold the interest of the country in trust better than all others. They also think that the government has autonomous and independent powers to govern and that, once elected, it is free to exercise them. It is a government that once elected cannot be given instructions or be delegated to do some things and not others. So, there is an element of authoritarianism and elitism still lurking in the

6. Russell Kirk. "Prescription, Authority and Ordered Freedom" in F. S. Meyer (ed.). *What is Conservatism?*, p. 33.

hearts of all good conservatives, together with a certain distrust for the "common people" or the "mass."

Paternalism

While conservatives believe that the propertied classes and the landed aristocracy have special privileges, they also agree that such privileges and their exercise have corresponding social obligations. Here there is a strong element of paternalism, whereby the natural leaders have to cater to the well-being of the common people by providing them with relief when out of work and at other times improving their living conditions. Because of their organic theory of the society, conservatives tended to subordinate economic interests to the overall interest of the collectivity. Social solidarity and social cooperation are given precedence over particular interests. Finally, the purpose of "the whole" goes beyond simple material considerations. The State is an all-encompassing agency for providing justice and order. It has a moral purpose to which particularisms and economic interests must yield.

For all these reasons conservatives reject the utilitarian philosophy of economic liberalism. Self-interest, unrestrained competition, individualism, and the very notion that the society is held together by competing claims and antagonisms is repugnant to them. They reject laissez-faire economics, or at best tolerate it on condition that individual effort and competition not be allowed to tear apart the fabric of the society. They accept economic individualism if it allows everybody to show his or her worth and capabilities; they reject it if it were to lead to sharp inequalities and social strife that would upset the balance of the whole. British conservatives have favored State intervention and welfare measures, unlike other conservative parties on the Continent and elsewhere.

Constitutional Government and Democracy

The British conservatives and their Conservative party became strong advocates of constitutional and representative government. In contrast to the European conservatives they did not waver in their support of democracy and parliamentary institutions. Authoritarian and totalitarian solutions appealed to only a negligible number of their leaders and followers. In this way conservatism, while representing the status quo groups, recognized the realities of social change and the necessity of guiding it and reducing its speed rather than arresting it altogether. Classic conservatives appear something like a well-controlled dam in this way and not a bulwark against the forces of all change.

After the nineteenth century, conservatives not only accepted major economic changes, such as the establishment of Britain's Welfare State and the nationalization of its industries, but they themselves also *introduced* social and economic reforms. In 1951, when the Conservatives replaced the Labour government, they assumed the direction and the management of the nationalized industries and the welfare system Labour had built. The Conservative party did not reject Labour's social economic and welfare legislation; it tried to slow their pace of reform until it judged society as a whole had time to adjust to it. Thus, conservatives reconciled themselves to a new social and economic order.

The Conservative party remains staunchly committed to democratic principles. While the authority of the leader of the party is given greater scope than in the case of other parties, notably Labour, the Conservative party developed into a mass party with three to four million members. It holds annual conferences, allows its various organs considerable autonomy, holds free debates in which policy resolutions come from the floor, and can be endorsed despite the opposition of the leadership. It now recruits its candidates for the House of Commons without consideration of their personal wealth and ability to contribute to their own campaign or to the party. In general, despite its affinities with the upper status groups and wealthier segments of the population, it has managed to appeal to and get support from many of the voters who belong to the working or lower middle classes. The marriage between the cottage and the throne that the great Tory leader of the Victorian period, Disraeli, had suggested, developed into strong ties between the people and the Conservative party leadership. As a result the party has survived as one of the two major political groups in England. Since 1945 it has held the reins of government for almost twenty years.

To sum up some of the basic characteristics of classic conservative thought: there is a belief that society is like an organism; that its parts are hierarchically arranged; that authority should be entrusted to natural leaders. There is a rejection of individualism and egalitarianism; a strong belief in custom and tradition and an aversion to change; emphasis upon religious and ritualistic symbolisms to solidify the union of the whole. Yet, at the same time, there is a strong commitment to a government under law guaranteeing individual rights, an acceptance of representative government, and with it an acknowledgment of the increased participation of all the people, an implementation of the Welfare State, and above all, a rejection of authoritarian solutions. Conservatism has thus legitimized itself as an ideology consistent with democracy.

People who like change and innovation, and find themselves at odds with the conservative ideology, should not be particularly hasty in rejecting it. Classic conservatism, as portrayed here, was and remains a brake to rapid change. But it channelled the well-to-do and, what is more, millions of voters, into accepting gradual and peaceful change. Conservatives have been distrustful of human reason and majoritarianism. But they never attempted to control the first or to outlaw the second. They (like the British socialists) presented their position and policies in the context of democracy. The conservative ideology — in a sense the creature of the British ruling groups — tamed the class that formulated it, disciplined its followers to act within the logic of individual and associational freedoms, and accepted free political competition without which democracy cannot exist. By creating an ideology that taught the British ruling classes how to bend in order not to break, they legitimized not only gradual change but all change, if and when the electorate demanded it, and they prepared their followers to accept change, if not always with grace, at least without resorting to force.

Conservatives and Neo-Conservatives in the U.S.A.

Until World War II the term "conservative" was virtually unknown in American political life. When used it was considered a slur. Yet in 1978, an opinion poll revealed that 8 percent of a representative population sample considered themselves "very conservative," 31 percent declared themselves to be "conservative," and 31 percent called themselves "moderates." Only 19 percent called themselves "liberals" and only a small fraction, 4 percent, proclaimed themselves to be "very liberal." Either the terms have changed meaning, or the American people have undergone a dramatic change in the configuration of their political beliefs and attitudes. A change, that is, in political ideology. This was reflected in the overwhelming victory of President Ronald Reagan in 1980. He had been favored by the "conservatives" within the Republican party and had spoken out in favor of many of the positions they advocated.

As we saw in our discussion of British conservative ideology, conservatives admire and try to preserve the past; they are elitist in that they believe in natural leaders; they accept only gradual and incremental change; they admire a well-balanced and hierarchically structured society, and they emphasize the need for authority. "Civilized man lives by authority," according to a (British-born) American conservative.[7] Conservatives believe that societies develop norms — that is, enduring standards of behavior — and that we obey them because of habit and tradition. "The sanction to norms," writes the same author, "must come from a source other than private advantage or rationality" — the two basic propositions used by liberals to explain our obedience to the State. The real source of authority and obedience "is tradition." For conservatives, "the good citizen is a law-abiding traditionalist."[8]

To most Americans these propositions are alien. "Man is created equal"; all of us are "endowed" with liberty. The American dream has been that change, through the manipulation of the environment in order to get more out of it, is equated with progress toward a better future, and a person's worth lies in achievement, not birth, inheritance, or status. As for society, it has no meaning and reality outside of the individuals who make it and can remake it. There is no hierarchy and no organic quality about it; there is no fixed subordination of some to others, and no structure of deference. The self-made person is still the symbol of Americanism, and of the constant restlessness, mobility, and change of Americans and American society. Law is but a convenient external standard that we set up to accommodate our

7. Ibid., p. 23.
8. Ibid., p. 31.

domestic conflicts — hardly a norm maturing and gaining strength and respect with time until obedience to it becomes a tradition.

American history and practice have both shaped and strengthened these attitudes. The vast land to be conquered by individual effort in the days when the frontier was open to the west; the immensity of the resources available; the freedom of all (except, until recently, the blacks) to move at will since they were not bound to a lord or master; the relative weakness of the central government to impose law and order, allowing individual groups and vigilante organizations to do it — all these strengthened egalitarian and individualistic values and determined the spirit of liberalism. To quote the famous phrase of the Greek philosopher Protagoras, the individual remained "the measure of all things" in America.

Liberalism became the dominant American political creed, and virtually all social thinkers called themselves liberal. Few dared call themselves conservatives until very recently. There was little to conserve and a lot to change and to conquer: more wealth to amass and greater material benefits to realize for all. Outside of individual effort and achievement neither norms nor "tradition" nor "wise prejudice," as Burke had put it, restrained the myth of material success and self-improvement that was the heart of the beliefs of Americans. When the labor leader Samuel Gompers was asked in the latter part of the nineteenth century what it was that American labor wanted, he gave the answer that all Americans understood: "More!" In a society holding such an ideal, genuine conservatives were likely to find themselves out of place or, what amounts to the same thing, there was no place for them.

American Conservatives and the British Model

The American political tradition has few conservative authors or leaders in any way comparable to the British ones: Henry Adams, John Calhoun, Herman Melville, Brooks Adams, Irving Babbitt, Santayana, and Walter Lippmann. Calhoun, without any doubt, had a profound influence in the years until the Civil War. But his impact has not been a more lasting one than that of the others. The real classic conservatives — the "humanistic value preservers" — who venerate tradition, order, and natural law, have been very few indeed. The reason is that the American system and the American society were made in the name of human reason and individual rights, not tradition. Real conservatives in the United States must either go directly to the British sources for inspiration, which they often do, or try to find the particular institutions and ideas that best correspond to the conservative ideology in the American experience, which they have tried to do. The only conservative ideology they claim to find is in the Constitution and in the thinking of the framers that produced it and, of course, in the political philosophy of some of them as it was expounded in the Federalist Papers.

American conservatives have tried to draw their inspiration from the Constitution because of the limitations upon direct democracy that it embodies and because of its emphasis upon law. The American republic is "a government of law and not men." It is a republic and not a democracy — a state in which separation and the balance of powers make it impossible for any single branch of government to concentrate, in its hands, enough power to endanger the rights of the people. It is a system carefully engineered to make it impossible for a numerical majority to control all branches of government, at one and the same time, and to establish its "tyranny" — one that is considered just as bad as the tyranny of a minority or a group of men or of one man. Restraints are built into the system not only against the governmental organs, federal and state, but against the people as well. It is in this that American conservatives find the "wisdom of the framers."

Similarly, in the Federalist Papers that provide for a defense of the Constitution and embody the philosophy of the "framers," notably Madison and Hamilton, references are made and institutions are defended in terms that are close to British conservative ideas and vocabulary. Thus, the "electoral college", that was supposed to be free, once chosen, to elect the president, is viewed and defended as a body of wise men who are considered more reliable to make the proper choice than the people directly. The early mode of election for the Senate, by the state legislatures, again provides for an indirect mode of election whose purpose was to filter the popular choice. It is significant, however, that the electoral college has ceased to play the independent role it was supposed to play, and that the Senate is now elected directly by the peoples of the various states.

Emphasis upon law — a government of law and not men — remains an important ingredient of a conservative ideology, yet only a careful examination of the jurisprudence of the Supreme Court, the ultimate custodian of the Constitution, can answer to what extent. Furthermore, it should be remembered that nowhere did the Constitution grant power to the Supreme Court to declare acts of Congress unconstitutional and to set them aside.

This interpretation of the Constitution and of the intentions of its framers, as being essentially conservative and a reflection of a conservative ideology, must be considered seriously. The framers were afraid of "the people," the majority, and they looked for "natural leaders." Many had a profound respect for tradition, but this hardly makes them and the Constitution, as it developed, conservative. Conservatives in England believed in the wise exercise of power and extolled established authority; they put politics and political wisdom above everything else except religion and divine or natural law; they thought, as we have seen, that a political society was a living organism to which material and functional interests were subordinated. Wise leadership kept this organism together.

The framers of the United States Constitution, on the other hand, feared political power. It could be abused and might be abused by anybody and everybody — even by "wise rulers." They were skeptical about the possibility of legitimizing power and of creating a strong political authority. Their solution was to weaken authority as much as possible by fragmenting it and dividing it. The solution was a mechanical one — it reflected no belief in tradition, custom, or in natural leaders. Like the Newtonian physics which influenced its framers, the policy was one in which, at best, an equilibrium of forces and of governmental organs would result.

This philosophy was fully consistent with the climate of opinion of the times. By downgrading the powers of the government and by providing for checks and balances for each and all of its organs, the framers hoped to liberate society (i.e., the individual, the economy, voluntary associations, the churches, and so on) from the State and from political domination. The best government was the one that governed the least and left individuals free to pursue their material interest in the best utilitarian manner, and to maximize their pleasure and avoid pain as they saw fit. The "do-it-yourself man" of Benjamin Franklin was to emerge not only unfettered by political power, free of tradition and prescription, but also free from the wisdom of political elites and their natural leaders! This was, and remains, the very opposite of classic conservatism.

The American Neo-Conservatives: Who Are They?

Despite the foregoing, in the last twenty years the term conservative has gained respectability, and the conservative ideology has gained many followers. There are many who proudly claim to be conservative. What is the meaning of the term? And who are these new conservatives? To begin with, conservatives today in the United States are very different from British conservatives. They are, in fact, liberals who subscribe by and large to the tenets of nineteenth-century liberalism. They accept the institutions and policies of nineteenth-century liberalism and want to preserve what, in their opinion, worked so well for this country. They believe in economic individualism, competition, the free enterprise system, and are against State intervention. Until 1932 *they* were the liberals. Herbert Hoover called himself a liberal!

It was the economic depression of 1929 and the New Deal under Franklin D. Roosevelt that accounted for a change of terms. Roosevelt, who also called himself a liberal, introduced sweeping social reforms, most of which involved the direct intervention of the federal government in economic and social matters. These included public works, social security, insurance schemes, a minimum wage, legislation that favored the growth of trade-union membership and gave them a new role in collective bargaining with employers, direct and indirect controls over agriculture and farm prices, unemployment compensation, production of electricity by a federal public corporation, federal loans to business and prospective house-buyers, stringent controls on banks and federal guarantees to protect people's savings, and so on. Without ever rejecting the free market economy the New Deal fashioned a system of controls and regulations unprecedented in American history. As a result, the federal budget swelled and taxes rose. The New Deal asserted the role of the State and the nation over the economy. Political power was used directly to compensate for the weaknesses of the market economy that was presumed to have brought about the depression — a depression that halved the national income, arrested economic growth, and accounted for the most severe unemployment that the country had experienced. About ten million people were unemployed between 1929 and 1938.

With the "statism" and State intervention of the Roosevelt era in economic affairs, the meaning of liberalism changed. Those who supported Roosevelt and favored the intervention of State controls in the economy and who endorsed the welfare measures became the liberals or the "neoliberals." From 1932 until World War II and until very recently, political leaders, whether Republican or Democrat, accepted this general philosophy, and the federal government continued to expand and to spend more. Defense has been one reason for high spending, but welfare legislation is just as responsible. Education subsidies, loans and grants, antipoverty programs, expansion of welfare benefits and of the number of beneficiaries, Medicare, more comprehensive old age and related benefits, hospital subsidies and health care, and an ever-growing expansion of the social security system to provide more to larger numbers accounted for this vast amount. Taxes increase accordingly.

The neo-liberals also sought to expand the basis of political power, and with it *their* power. Since the New Deal there has been a growing involvement of groups of people who previously had been excluded from the political process. Labor was the first to assume a greater degree of power thanks to the New Deal legislation favoring the growth of trade unions and their role in collective bargaining. Ethnic and religious minorities came next — Catholics, Jews, Poles, Italians, Irish, Greeks, and so on. Al Smith, running for president in 1928, faced strong and overt hostility in many parts of the country because he was a Catholic. But by 1960 the religious issue did not play a critical role when another Catholic, John F. Kennedy, was elected.

The assimilation of the blacks came in the late 1950s and 1960s, and by 1970 the federal government was actively intervening through a variety of programs to ensure that ethnic minorities were not discriminated against in employment or education. The 1970s saw, finally, the same protection extended to women in employment and education. The neo-liberals have been responsible both for the widening of political and social opportunities to all and for comprehensive economic controls and welfare measures. Equality has become, gradually, synonymous with social justice; it is no longer solely a matter of equality of opportunities, but of real equality in substantive benefits and achievements.

It is through this process that the meaning of liberalism has changed. Those who accepted the New Deal and its philosophy and policies are called the *neo-liberals,* or *welfare liberals,* or *collectivist liberals.* However, the liberals who rejected it became known as *conservatives,* or, the term we use here, *neo-conservatives. Paleo-liberals* (old-time liberals), or *"autonomist liberals"* (believers in the independence and freedom of the economy and the market) are other terms used to describe them.

What do the neo-conservatives stand for? First and foremost, for individual initiative and freedoms. But they narrowly interpret both to mean in particular *economic freedom* — freedom of enterprise, freedom to work irrespective of whether or not one belongs to a union, freedom of contract, a free market economy. One of the most sophisticated of the neo-conservatives, William F. Buckley, points this out:

Conservatives have failed to alert the community to the interconnection between economic freedom and — freedom. . . . It is a part of the conservative intuition that economic freedom is the most precious temporal freedom, for the reason that it alone gives to each one of us, in our comings and goings in our complex society, sovereignty — and over that part of existence in which by far the most choices have in fact to be made, and in which it is possible to make choices, involving oneself, without damage to other people. And for the further reason that without economic freedom, political and other freedoms are likely to be taken from us.[9]

Thus, neo-conservatives ask that the federal government (and often the state government) move out of the economy; that if and when welfare measures are needed they should be undertaken at the state and local levels and not the federal one; that the federal budget and federal expenditures be sharply reduced; that income taxes and also many other federal and state taxes be sharply curtailed. In effect, neo-conservatives ask for the dismantling of much of the New Deal legislation and of the Welfare State.

Many arguments favor the position of the neo-conservatives, and we are already familiar with some of them: bureaucracy leads to inefficiency; state controls and regulations stifle competition and are wasteful because they increase the cost of production. State controls lead to increasing deprivation of moral freedoms, and, most important, of the freedom to make our own choices and to assume our own responsibilities. We become dependent upon bureaucratic, impersonal services for which nobody is responsible. In 1946 Friedrich von Hayek, a professor of economics at the University of Chicago, wrote *The Road to Serfdom*, in which he sounded the alarm and set the tone for the neo-conservatives. State intervention and economic planning, he argued, and the end of individual economic freedoms, would result in moral degradation for all of us and the ultimate loss of our political freedoms as well. The bureaucratic state would make choices for us — what to produce and what to consume, where to work and where to live, what income to make, and so on. The same theme is repeated by Buckley:

What all conservatives in this country fear, and have plenty of reason to fear, is the loss of freedom by attrition. It is therefore for the most realistic reasons, as well as those of principle, that we must resist every single accretion of power by the State. . . .[10]

What do neo-conservatives propose? Buckley provides a list of particulars:

. . . to maintain and wherever possible enhance the freedom of the individual to acquire property and dispose of that property in ways that he decides on. To deal with unemployment by eliminat-

9. William F. Buckley, Jr. *Up From Liberalism*. New York: McDonnell, Oblensky, 1959, p. 166.
10. Ibid., p. 179.

ing monopoly unionism, featherbedding, and inflexibilities in the labor market, and be prepared, where residual unemployment persists, to cope with it locally, placing the political and humanitarian responsibility on the lowest feasible political unit. . . .[11]

We can identify the neo-conservatives, then, in terms of a cluster of issues. Less taxation, reduction of the federal budget, withdrawal of the State from economic regulation and control, reduction of public expenditures (federal and state), sharp reduction in welfare services and in the size of the bureaucracies, and more initiative and freedom to local government bodies are some of the issues. Yet neo-conservatives, irrespective of the positions they take regarding social and economic matters, have remained within the framework of constitutional democracy. At no time do they envisage the use of force or repressive tactics, in or out of government. They believe in political competition and political freedoms, and use the political process to gain support.

Neo-conservatives have been gaining strength. Increased taxation in the 1970s, coupled with inflation and unemployment, have turned the public away from the neo-liberals, whether Democrat or Republican. The middle classes feel threatened. Reduction in taxes is the slogan of many neo-conservative leaders, and the passage of Proposition 13 in California, mandating an across-the-board reduction of state taxes and consequent reduction in state expenditures, has set a precedent that other states may follow, and that may affect Congress and the federal government as well. The disillusionment with the neo-liberalism that the New Deal spawned seems to be strong, and as we noted, this may well have accounted for Ronald Reagan's victory in the presidential election of 1980. He favored lower taxes; reduction in welfare spending; reduction in the scope of the federal government — with a "new federalism" that would return many welfare services to the states, and a promise to give more freedom to the private sector of the economy and the market.

Neo-conservatives in the United States today echo the liberal voices of the nineteenth century. They stress the economic core of liberalism and remain attached to the moral and political core. Their growing strength derives from the disenchantment of many — in particular the middle classes — with what now seem to be the deficiencies of State controls, public spending, high taxes, and centralized decision making through an ever-growing bureaucracy. But there is also the argument that public spending and public controls undermine the moral initiative of individuals and dull their incentives and inventiveness so that, in the last analysis, productivity and economic growth are undermined. The myth of "rugged individualism," so central to nineteenth century American liberalism, remains remarkably strong. So, too, is the notion that the character and moral fiber of a person can be tested only through competition and individual effort — a struggle in which only the best survive.

11. Ibid., p. 202.

In the last few years, nobody has better expressed the position of the "neo-conservatives" than Nobel Prize winner economist Milton I. Friedman. His book[12] (written with his wife Rose) popularized the basic arguments against State intervention in the economy and the notion that such intervention will inevitably lead to controls that will undermine the moral autonomy of the individuals and erode their political freedoms. Very much in the spirit of von Hayek (1946) and John Stuart Mill (1856), Friedman distinguishes between the areas where political or social constraints exist and the areas where voluntary activity and choice should prevail. Both are necessary. But the constraints should be limited to what is absolutely indispensable; freedoms and choices should be protected and, whenever possible, broadened.

Socialism, State intervention, welfare politics, restrictions upon consumer freedom and choice — all constitute an invasion upon our freedoms and destroy the voluntarism that provides both for challenge and innovation in our society. In short, economic individualism goes hand in hand with political liberties and democracy. The liberal perspective continues to have its knights and faithful followers. Their armor is free enterprise and their shrine is individual freedom. They move from the one to the other with what often appears to be superficial ease, but they do offer compelling arguments.

Bibliography

Banfield, Edward C. *The Unheavenly City*. Boston: Little, Brown, 1970.

Burke, Edmund. *Reflections on the Revolution in France*. New York: Bobbs-Merrill, Library of Liberal Arts, 1955.

Cecil, Lord Hugh Richard. *Conservatism*. London: Williams and Nurgate, 1912.

Friedman, Milton and Rose. *Free to Choose*. New York: Harcourt Brace Jovanovich, 1980.

Hayek, Friedrich von. *The Road to Serfdom*. Chicago: University of Chicago Press, 1946.

Hearnshaw, F. J. C. *Conservatism in England*. London, Macmillan 1933.

Kirk, Russell. *The Conservative Mind*. Rev. ed. Chicago: Henry Regnery, 1960.

Meyer, Frank S. (ed). *What Is Conservatism?* New York: Holt, Rinehart & Winston, 1964.

Nash, George H. *The Conservative Intellectual Movement in America*. New York: Basic Books, 1976.

Nisbet, Robert A. *The Quest for Community*. New York: Oxford U.P., 1953.

Rossiter, Clinton. *Conservatism in America*. 2nd rev. ed. New York: Knopf, 1966.

Viereck, Peter. *Conservatism: From John Adams to Churchill*. Princeton, N.J.: Van Nostrand, 1956.

von Mises, Ludwig. *Planned Chaos*. New York: The Foundation For Economic Education, 1947.

12. Friedman, Milton I. and Rose. *Free To Choose*, New York: Harcourt Brace Jovanovich, 1980.

Part Two

Communism: from One to Many

In place of the old bourgeois society . . . we shall have an association in which the free development of each is the condition for the free development of all.

KARL MARX AND FRIEDRICH ENGELS
The Communist Manifesto

The socialist and conservative political ideologies, as outlined in Chapters 3 and 4, remain solidly within the democratic tradition. They fully accept individual freedoms, political liberties, political competition, representative assemblies, and constitutionalism. This is not the case with totalitarian or authoritarian ideologies and regimes like communism or fascism. They are antidemocratic; they reject individual and associational freedoms; they use force as an instrument of governance; they rely upon a single party, excluding all political competition among parties and groups. Representative assemblies in these regimes are but a rubber stamp unanimously accepting the policies formulated by the leadership. Elections are controlled by the State apparatus and by party officials.

Totalitarianism and Communism

Totalitarian movements and totalitarian regimes show the following characteristics:

1. The ideology is total and comprehensive and everything becomes subordinate to it. Society is to be restructured in terms of the posited ideological goals.
2. The single party becomes a party to control, intimidate, and govern. It becomes the major vehicle of political mobilization and recruitment. No political competition is tolerated.

3. All associations, all groups, and all individuals become subordinate to the party, the State, and the leader. There is no cultural pluralism. Education, literature, art, music, architecture — all must yield and conform to the overriding objectives and goals of the political ideology. Groups and individuals, family life, social and recreational activities, the schools, and the economy must all be synchronized with the political regime. All must "march in step" with it.
4. The use of violence is institutionalized through the police and other specialized instruments of coercion and intimidation.
5. The party directly, or through the State, has a monopolistic control of mass communications and overall economic activities.

Needless to say, these characteristics represent extreme or "ideal" types, helpful for the purposes of analysis. None of them are likely to be found in their pure form. Even in portrayals of the most extreme of totalitarian systems, like Huxley's *Brave New World* or Orwell's *1984*, the total conformity of the society and the individual to the ideology and leader are shown to be impossible. Dissent and nonconformity can never be eliminated entirely.

For some time the view of totalitarianism as an exclusively right-wing phenomenon was widely held. Marxists argued that it represented, in fact, the last stage of capitalism, in which the economic oligarchy was forced to jettison democracy in order to preserve its position, economic power, property, and profits. For instance, Palmiro Togliatti, the Italian Communist leader, defined fascism as a revolutionary movement "for counterrevolutionary purposes." It was aimed at stopping the proletarian revolution and socialism. Totalitarianism, however, as we have outlined it, is a political regime that subordinates individuals and their freedom to the political objectives of the party and the State. In this sense communism and fascism are *both* totalitarian ideologies.

Both left- and right-wing totalitarian ideologies and regimes reject economic and political liberalism, democracy, and representative assemblies that have genuine power to deliberate and decide, economic and political freedoms, and civil rights. In their tactics for the seizure of power, both advocate force and both prepare for it through a well-disciplined political party. Similarly, when totalitarian parties of either left or right gain power, both eliminate freedoms and political competition, both establish one-party rule, both promise to develop a planned economy and to replace the free market, and both stress social and communitarian goals as opposed to individualistic ones. Both subordinate the individual, in fact, to the State or the party, and to the new ideology they establish and whose orthodoxy they try to impose.

Some Differences

With regard to ultimate goals, there are fundamental differences between communism and fascism. In communist regimes totalitarian controls are supposed to be temporary — they represent a historical phase after which individual freedoms will return. The "dictatorship of the proletariat" paves the way to the disappearance of the State; the socialization of the means of production destroys the class structure of the society and makes the use of force unnecessary; production is not geared to profit but to need. A true communist system not only will become increasingly egalitarian but also will become more open and free. Finally, nations and national wars will give place to a fraternal and egalitarian international community.

Right-wing totalitarian movements, on the other hand, project an entirely different set of goals. Domination of the few over the many is to be permanent; the elite will continue to govern. Property is respected, even if under State control, and so are profits. The role of the State as a coercive agency is strengthened. Inequalities on the basis of a number of factors that include race are considered natural and are legitimized. Finally, nationalism is consolidated, thanks to the exaltation of the superiority of one nation over others.

These differences appear to be impressive. However, there is no assurance that the professed goals of communism will ever be realized. There is no clear evidence that they are being implemented in any communist regime, and especially in the Soviet Union. Stalinism represented, as we shall see, a political movement that remained very remote from the professed doctrinal goals of communism. There is also no indication that communist regimes are immune either to war or nationalism. The appeal to past or newly fabricated nationalist myths, in an effort to integrate the people, characterizes communist movements and regimes, just as it does right-wing totalitarian ones. Conflict seems to be very much in evidence today, pitting some communist regimes against each other while the prospect of expansion or domination of others is ever-present. The Chinese Communists, for instance, are accusing the Soviet Union of a "hegemonic" foreign policy.

Thus, until there is a clear indication that the professed ideological goals of left-wing totalitarian regimes are beginning to be implemented, we seem to be dealing with a similar *political* phenomenon — totalitarianism — irrespective of whether it is associated with the left or the right. In this part we shall deal with communist ideology and communist regimes.

5 | *Communism and Marxism*

Marx was a genius; we others were at best talented.
Without him the theory would not be by far what it is
today. It, therefore, rightly bears his name.
FRIEDRICH ENGELS   Selected Works (vol. 2)

Communism is, literally, the economic and social system whereby all the means of production are concentrated in the hands of the community or the State, and in which the production and allocation of goods and services is decided upon by the community and the State. Generally, however, communism has meant much more. It has been "an ideal, a political movement, a method of analysis and a way of life."[1] As an ideal it promises an egalitarian society with production geared to need — a society in which the dream of abundance will be realized. As a political movement it represents the organization of men and women striving to attain freedom; as a method of analysis it sets forth propositions that explain the past and point to the future development of our societies; finally, as a way of life it portrays a new type of citizen for whom the communitarian and social attributes of human nature will gain ascendancy over egotism and private interest.

Whether taken singly, or all together as they usually are, the trends represent what communism has been — one of the most powerful myths and ideologies in history. It takes the form of a moral imperative — how to create a collective and social ethic that will override self-interest and do away with the demons of profit and private property, which are seen as the cause of subjugation of the many to the few.

Ever since antiquity, the theme of the *moral* superiority of communal ownership, in contrast to private property, interest, and individualistic aspirations, has been kept alive. It is defended in Plato's *Republic*, where no private property is allowed the rulers, the Guardians, in order that they can give their full attention to communitarian values and govern in the interest of the whole. The myth of communism appears and reappears in many religious

1. Alfred Meyer. *Marxism*, p. 1.

writings in which property is viewed as the result of "man's fall." It is part of secular law and does not exist through "divine" or "natural" law. The theme reemerges with particular force in the writings of many utopian socialists in the decades after the French Revolution and well into the nineteenth century. After the Industrial Revolution, the dream of favoring collective ownership and eliminating all income inequalities and poverty has been particularly potent.

Not until the middle of the nineteenth century, however, did the ideal become transformed into a political movement, and not until the end of the century did the ideology take on flesh and blood with the formation of political parties. In 1920, communism gained ascendancy in one country, the Soviet Union, and spread thereafter with renewed vigor all over Europe. By World War II the ideology had crystallized firmly into the Soviet political system, and after the war it had established itself in other countries — in Eastern Europe and China, with noticeable spillovers elsewhere. But at about the same time, under the impact of a number of forces, communism began to splinter into various sects (national or ideological) to such an extent that today a discussion of the movement has to specify *what kind* of communism we are talking about. Even more, the early fraternal cooperation among communist states has given place to rivalries.

Today communism plays two quite separate roles. In a number of countries it sustains a political system, which is the official, or, as we called it, the *status quo* ideology. This is clearly the case in the Soviet Union, Eastern Europe, and some of the Balkan countries. In Asia, such countries as Republican China, North Korea, Laos, Vietnam, and Cambodia have communist regimes. In parts of Africa and Arabia, such as Angola, Ethiopia, Mozambique, and South Yemen, communism has gained a foothold. Even in the North American sphere of influence, there is, despite the vigilance of the United States, one fully established communist regime, Cuba. Today, at least 30 percent of all peoples of the world live under communist regimes and the communist ideology.

In virtually all other countries communist ideologies and movements play *a revolutionary role*, seeking political power and domination through various means. There are powerful communist parties in France and Italy, and moderately strong ones in Portugal, Spain, Greece, throughout the rest of Europe, and in countries of the Third World.

Almost a century and a half ago, in 1848, Marx wrote *The Communist Manifesto;* it transformed communism from only a theory into a strong political movement. In his opening sentence he spoke of "a specter" that haunted Europe — "the specter of communism." Today it is a reality. Communism, either in the form of established political regimes or as a powerful political revolutionary movement, inspires, mobilizes, and organizes for political action a greater number of people than any other political ideology. But what kind of communism is it?

As with other ideologies, communism can be viewed in two different ways. Firstly, as a body of theory and philosophy it requires us to examine and analyze it with one question in mind: how valid is its theory and underly-

HISTORICAL PICTURES SERVICE, INC., CHICAGO

Karl Marx (1818–1883)

Born in Germany, where he studied law, philosophy, and history, Karl Marx and his family settled in London when he was thirty years old. There he began a lifelong cooperation with Engels to develop a communist ideology and to translate it into political action. In 1848 they produced *The Communist Manifesto,* urging the workers to rise and take over the means of production from the exploiting capitalist class. In 1864 he founded the First International whose purpose was to unite the workers everywhere in a revolutionary struggle. A prodigious worker, a committed man, and also one of the most learned and creative minds of the nineteenth century, Marx, like Freud half a century later, suggested a new way of looking at social life and history. Accordingly, material and economic conditions are responsible for the shaping of our values, morality, attitudes, and political institutions. Marx singled out property relations to be the key element and the exploitation of "have-nots" by the "haves" to be at the heart of liberal capitalism. It was, at the same time, the reason for a working-class revolution, and the vindication of communism. He wrote voluminously, but his major work is the analysis of the capitalist economy in *Capital,* the first volume of which was published in 1867 and the second and third posthumously, by Engels, in 1885 and 1894.

ing philosophic assumptions? Secondly, as a political ideology and movement it requires us to examine the way in which its basic philosophic and theoretical propositions have been translated into an action-oriented movement (i.e., an ideology). While the first level of analysis is important, we shall emphasize communism here as a political ideology and a movement for political action, and stress some of its contemporary characteristics.

The Legacy of Marx

It was Karl Marx and his associate Friedrich Engels who provided us, through their writings and their political activities, with the foundations of contemporary communism. Of the two, Marx was the dominant intellectual figure. He published major theoretical works on economics and philosophy and produced a series of pamphlets on various aspects of political tactics. After his death in 1883, Engels synthesized, some might say simplified, some of his ideas. When we speak of Marxism, however, we are referring to the combined work of Marx and Engels.

Marx and Engels provide us with a comprehensive philosophy of economic, social, and political life, that includes the rejection of capitalist society, the dynamics of a communist revolution, and the promise of a new society.

The Sources That Inspired Marx

Four sources combined to produce the overall synthesis that constitutes Marxism. They are:

1. Hegel's philosophy, especially his philosophy of history.
2. The works of the British economists; notably, Ricardo, Adam Smith, Malthus, and others.
3. The French utopian socialists, even though they were criticized sharply by Marx and Engels.
4. The social and economic reality of the mid-nineteenth century, particularly in England.

The first of these gave Marx a dynamic and evolutionary theory of history based on conflict; the second provided him with a new objective analysis of economic phenomena in which all economic factors were viewed in abstract terms as commodities, or variables, relating to each other on the basis of demonstrable and quantifiable laws; the third provided hints on the construction of the future society.

As for the reality of British industrial society in the middle of the nineteenth century, it had a profound impact on both Marx and Engels. Working conditions were dismal, hours of work long, children and women were employed at starvation wages for twelve, fourteen, and sometimes sixteen hours a day, living conditions were abominable, and life expectancy low. The miseries of the workers contrasted sharply with the well-being of those

HISTORICAL PICTURES SERVICE, INC., CHICAGO

Friedrich Engels (1820–1895)

Friedrich Engels was Karl Marx's companion, associate, and collaborator. Born in Germany, he lived most of his life in England. He collaborated with Marx on many publications including *The Communist Manifesto,* and edited the second and third volumes of *Capital* after Marx's death. While he played an important role in the formulation of the communist doctrine, Engels himself admitted that the real theoretical inspiration came from Marx. Engels himself wrote *The Origins of the Family; The Condition of the Working Class in England in 1844; Socialism: Utopian and Scientific* (1892); *Anti-Dühring* (1877–78) and a number of other less important essays. He took part in the founding of the First International in 1864 and the Second International in 1889.

who had land, property, and money (i.e., capital), and could employ others. Conditions like these provoked not only moral indignation but also widespread protest. Workers rebelled and wrecked the new machines for fear they would deprive them of work; regimentation in the factory under the new industrial order was deeply resented, and workers attempted to use their numbers against the employers who, in turn, made use of the instruments of coercion available to them.

But this movement of protest against the early conditions of industrialization and capitalism was unorganized and diffuse. Marx and Engels provided a theory that gave an order and a direction to it.

The Rejection of Capitalism

For Marx, the rejection of capitalism is *not* based on moral or humanitarian considerations. It derives from what he considered to be the empirical reality of the capitalist economy. It obeys certain laws. Understanding them and studying them leads to the unavoidable conclusion that capitalism is doomed. Marx's anatomy of capitalism is also its autopsy!

The key to the understanding of capitalism and of its inevitable demise is the notion of value, surplus value, and profit. The student can easily follow the Marxist critique of the capitalist economy by following Marx's own steps:

1. Only labor creates value.
2. Machines, land, and all other factors of production create no new value. They pass on to the product a value equivalent to the portion of their value used as they depreciate during the process of production.
3. The capitalist (the entrepreneur) pays the worker only a subsistence wage.
4. The worker produces a value that is twice as much (generally speaking) as what he or she gets in wages.
5. The difference between what the capitalist pays the worker and what the worker produces is the *surplus value* pocketed by the capitalist.
6. All profits derive from the surplus value, though the actual profit does not correspond to the amount of surplus value extracted by a given capitalist.
7. In the market there is a fierce competition among capitalists. Each tries to sell more; a large volume of goods sold, even at lower prices, will bring added income.
8. This incites the capitalist to modernize and mass-produce, to introduce better machines, and to increase the productivity of labor.
9. A modern firm manages with fewer workers to produce and, hence, sell more. As a result more and more workers are laid off.
10. Thus the modern firm can reduce prices by lowering its profit *per unit*.
11. Many firms that fail to modernize are gradually driven out of business. They employ more workers and they pay out more in wages, and thus cannot compete with the lower prices the modernized firms set.

12. As a result, many firms have to close down. Capital becomes increasingly concentrated into fewer and fewer hands and in larger and more modern firms, in which more machinery and modern technology is introduced.

13. Capitalism reaches a point where a small number of highly modernized large firms can produce goods efficiently and cheaply. However, with a great number of people out of work there are not enough buyers for the products, so firms can no longer make a profit. Production becomes restricted.

14. Profit and private property, the great incentives of the Industrial Revolution, now become obstacles to the plentiful production of goods.

15. The legal forms of capitalism (private profit and private property) come into conflict with the means of production (efficiency, high productivity, and potential abundance).

This is the Marxist scheme in a nutshell. Some explanations must be added.

The heart of capitalism and capitalist production is to be found in private property and profit. Capitalism emerged when landed property began to give place to capital and to the manufacturing of goods in the factory. The purpose of production is profit — that is, how the capitalist can get from the market a value for the product that is higher than all he spent to produce it, including the use of land, the cost of machines as they are amortized over the years, and, of course, wages paid. The difference between what the entrepreneurs spend to produce and what they receive for the product is *the profit* — one of the most dynamic incentives for capitalist production and growth.

Marx develops an ingenious theory to explain profit. It is *the theory of surplus value*. The worker is paid wages that are determined by the market through the law of supply and demand. The daily wage corresponds to the price of goods the worker and his family need and consume in one day. During the same day, however, the worker has produced goods that have a much higher value. The difference between value produced (owned and sold by the entrepreneur) and what is paid out in wages is *the surplus value*. Marx contends that generally wages tend to correspond to not more than half of the value the worker produces. So, the other half goes to the entrepreneur — to the capitalist. This is Marx's argument.

There are, of course, qualifications. For instance, the increased growth of mechanization in the plant (what we call today technological advances) gives to some capitalists and firms the possibility of producing more with very few workers. Consider automation, for instance, and computers. The firms that make technological advances and invest in machines make the highest profit. Where does it come from? Marx answers by making a distinction between what he calls *constant capital* (technology, machines, and so on) and *variable capital* (workers employed). Since only workers produce value, the greater their number, the greater their surplus value, and hence the profit.

Yet the truth seems to be precisely the other way around. The more modern the firm, the more advanced its machines and technology, the fewer the workers, the higher the profit. The reason for this apparent contradiction is quite simple: competition among industrialists in the market is ferocious. The one who manages to improve the productivity of the worker through the use of machines, increasing the units the worker can produce every hour, manages to produce in the same given period of time twice as many goods as his competitors and is therefore able to sell the same product at a lower price. By selling twice as much, he will thus take in more than his competitors, even if his profit *per unit* is smaller. Industrialists are thus able to derive a profit from the surplus value their competitors make, compete with them successfully, and, by selling cheaper, drive them out of the market. The margin of profit begins to fall on each item but as productivity goes up, the fall is compensated by the volume of sales.

The Law of Capitalist Accumulation

The distinction between *constant capital* and *variable capital,* and the fact that the technologically advanced firms with the newest machines make profit at the expense of the backward ones, who rely upon a higher percentage of variable capital (workers), accounts for the trend towards technology and modernization. Many firms go bankrupt but the survivors accumulate in their hands an ever greater part of the capital. Fewer and fewer capitalists own the means of production, while more and more small firms disappear. The whole social structure becomes lopsided with a tiny minority controlling production for the purpose of making profit, while the vast majority of the people have nothing but their labor to sell, exactly when it becomes less needed!

However, the capitalists who survive become the victims of their success. Having established firm control over the means of production, the capitalist class now finds it difficult to find enough buyers for their products. This is implicit in the law of capitalist accumulation, or rather, it is the other side of the coin of the same law — the law of pauperization.

The Law of Pauperization

More and more people are dispossessed of the means to produce. More and more fall into the category of proletariat. Thus, as the firms develop more sophisticated machinery, a greater number of people find themselves living in a state of misery. Many cannot find work. Many become "marginals" moving from one place to another without a role, without skills, and in a state of constant deprivation and humiliation. They are the *lumpenproletariat* — the army of the unemployed and also unemployable, people from the countryside or those recently demoted from the middle or low middle classes. They become a permanent fixture of capitalist societies.

Unemployment, however, affects also the qualified, skilled and semi-skilled workers. It becomes permanent. Capitalism, therefore, inevitably reaches a point at which it cannot utilize all resources and satisfy all needs, even basic ones. In fact, a point comes when a given percentage of the population may not be part of the economic system — they do not work in it and they cannot buy and enjoy what it produces. Millions of human beings become "surplus labor," unwanted and useless.

To conclude: the profit motive — a driving and dynamic motive in the early stages of capitalism — becomes a drag and an impediment in its most advanced stage. It has pushed the capitalists to modernize and to accumulate capital and industrial equipment; it has indeed made production easier and much more efficient; *objectively speaking* it has made it possible for human beings in a society to supply all their wants and more. Capitalism thus achieves a most remarkable breakthrough by creating all the material conditions for the good life. Marx is full of praise for the bourgeoisie and for capitalism when he views its historical role:

> The bourgeoisie . . . has been the first to show what man's activity can bring about. It has accomplished wonders far surpassing the Egyptian pyramids, Roman aqueducts, the Gothic cathedrals; it has conducted expeditions that put in the shade all former Exoduses and crusades. . . .

> The bourgeoisie has through its exploitation of the world market given a cosmopolitan character to production and consumption in every country. In place of the old wants, satisfied by the production of the country, we find new wants, requiring for their satisfaction the products of distant lands and climes. In place of the old local and national seclusion and self-sufficiency, we have intercourse in every direction, universal interdependence of nations. And as in material, so also in intellectual production. The intellectual creations of individual nations become common property. National onesidedness and narrow-mindedness become more and more impossible, and from the numerous national and local literatures there arises a world literature.

> The bourgeoisie, by the rapid improvement of all instruments of production, by the immensely facilitated means of communication, draws all, even the most barbarian, nations into civilization. . . .

> The bourgeoisie has created enormous cities, has greatly increased the urban population as compared with the rural, and has thus rescued a considerable part of the population from the idiocy of rural life. . . .[2]

Yet it is precisely at this point that the capitalistic economy can no longer provide for profits. By pressing heavily upon the middle class, and by creating a chronic state of unemployment among the independent artisans and the small farmers, which reduces them gradually to the ranks of the poor and the dispossessed, many have been deprived of the means to buy things and meet their needs. Demand goes down and with it comes lower profit. To

---

2. In *The Communist Manifesto.* See Tucker (ed.) *The Marx-Engels Reader*, pp. 469–500.

keep the rate of profit the capitalist now is forced to produce less, to control prices, to develop monopolies in order to avoid competition, and to form cartels to keep prices up. Whereas profit was a positive incentive to industrial growth and production, now it becomes a shackle. This is the point when capitalism has outlived its purpose — it can produce plenty but there is no incentive to do so. It is at this point that Marx pronounces its death sentence!

The student will note that thus far there has not been a single note of moral approbation or disapprobation. Marx gives us a "scientific" account, i.e., a description of what he sees happening, a description which fits his basic laws of the capitalist economy. As capitalist production and the capitalist economy develop they begin to show contradictions that *inevitably*, that is to say, for reasons inherent in the system itself, will be self-destructive. The major contradiction which ultimately unfolds itself is the discrepancy between the productive capacities that the system has developed and the forms of production (i.e., private property and profit). Capitalism will collapse because private property and profit become *dysfunctional* — they are no longer adequate incentives for production.

The analysis of the laws accounting for the demise of capitalism, however, do not amount to a "rejection" of capitalism. People must become aware of something, become dissatisfied with something, and move actively against something in order for there to be a rejection. Rejection is a subjective phenomenon associated with a collective desire and consciousness and with concerted action. *This is the revolutionary side of Marxism.*

The Dynamics
of the Communist Revolution

In contrast to his economic analysis, in which Marx set up theories and hypotheses and sought their confirmation in the empirical world of the capitalist economy, his whole notion of a revolution is the culminating point of philosophic speculation and is not amenable to the same rules of scientific inquiry. It includes: (a) a philosophy of history, (b) a theory of class struggles, (c) a theory of the State, (d) the historical act of "revolution" and (e) the utopian world to follow. We shall discuss each of them.

A Philosophy of History

History has been defined as a set of tricks that the living play upon the dead. For Marx, there are no such tricks! For him, the living constantly interact with the dead. Men and women are both the product of history, bound by the conditions it creates, and also the makers of history in reacting to those conditions and changing them. But this is only within the limits that history itself allows.

We can look at history in evolutionary terms — gradual changes occur not only in our material world but also in human knowledge and the way we think. The individual gets better and better control of his or her environment. In this sense there is progress. Another method is to look at history without any notion of direction at all — just as all a matter of chance. We can conquer war and misery but they can defeat us too! The third view is that we move in circles with periods of great achievement, material well-being and knowledge, alternating with periods of decay and ignorance. Our task in this case is like that of Sisyphus (cursed by the gods to carry a rock to the top of the mountain and to tumble down with it the moment he reached the peak) but with the destiny of humankind, so to speak, on our backs. We rise and then crash down into the ravine, only to start again and again and again. This is the cyclical theory.

All these theories are interesting but none of them answers the question of why there is "history" at all, why there is change and movement. Why do we change our ways? Why do we find out about germs? Why did we move from the Stone Age? Why did we invent a new language called mathematics and find out about regularities in the universe which surrounds us? Is it out of "love"? Is it because human beings are "rational"? Is it the divine will that pushes us? Marx answers this crucial question by using the works of the German philosopher G. W. F. Hegel (1770–1831) to develop a theory of history and change.

According to Hegel,[3] history moves through conflict — a conflict of ideas. He believes that there is something like a divine will, an Absolute, destined to finally unfold itself fully in the universe, but the process of unfolding is not evolutionary. It takes place through struggle between opposing ideas. The idea of beauty has opposing it the idea of ugliness, the idea of truth that of falsehood, the idea of liberty that of slavery, and so on. Throughout history and its various stages there is a constant and Homeric battle between opposing ideas, called by Hegel *dialectic idealism*. It goes something like this: each phase in history corresponds to the manifestation of certain ideas or an idea. It is called the *thesis*. It includes, however, its opposite, its *antithesis*. Thesis and antithesis struggle with each other until the antithesis manages to absorb the thesis or to combine with it in one form or another. This combination is called a *synthesis*, representing a new stage in history. Every synthesis in turn becomes a thesis that suggests automatically its antithesis which comes into conflict with it to lead to a new synthesis and so forth. . . . A point comes *when history will have exhausted itself — the best possible synthesis will have occurred*. God or the Spirit will have fully unfolded itself in the universe!

This sounds abstruse and it is. But the important thing to retain is that Hegel makes conflict the mother, the father, and the midwife of history. He is not an evolutionary, he does not believe in cyclical movements, he traces all change to conflict between ideas.

Marx maintains the dialectic (the notion of conflicting opposites); he maintains the whole scheme of historical movement in terms of thesis-antithesis-synthesis. However, he is clearly not an idealist. Writing in his

---

3. Hegel. *The Philosophy of History*, New York: The Colonial Press, 1900.

preface to *Capital*, Marx tells us himself how he changed the very foundations of Hegel's philosophy of history while maintaining the basic structure.

105

*Communism
and Marxism*

> My dialectic method is not only different from the Hegelian, but its direct opposite. To Hegel, the life-process of the brain, i.e. the process of thinking, which under the name of "the Idea," he even transforms into an independent subject, is the demiurgos (creator) of the real world, and the real world is only the external, phenomenal form of "the idea." With me on the contrary the idea is nothing else than the material world reflected by the human mind, and translated into forms of thought . . . With Hegel (the dialectic) . . . is standing on its head. It must be turned rightside up again. . . .[4]

In other words, Marx found, in the material world of our senses and our working conditions, the source of ideas and the source of conflict and change and not the other way around, as Hegel had done.

Dialectic Materialism   This is what, in contrast to "dialectic idealism," has become known as *dialectic materialism.* The stages of historical development, the specific contents of a thesis, an antithesis, and a synthesis are not to be found in the not-so-easily observable world of ideas but in the empirical world — in our society. It is a momentous shift. It makes Marx a social scientist, an empiricist, and one concerned with observable phenomena. The Hegelian abstraction now becomes a theory leading to hypotheses about human and social life that can be observed and tested.

Types of Conflict   What is the conflict that generates movement and change and accounts for history? There are two types of conflict according to Marx, the first between the human being as a social being (society) and the environment (the outside world). The second is between social groups.

Man Against Nature   Every social group, from the primitive tribe on, attempts to carve, out of its environment and out of nature, as much as it can in order to live and meet its needs. It is a basic struggle and human beings are affected deeply by it; their thoughts, their social institutions, their law and values are influenced by this interaction between themselves and the world in which they live. They depend on it in part; they are its creatures and even its slaves. Yet they try to overcome it and survive in it; they try to change it and emancipate themselves from its mastery. Real freedom will come when they have fully conquered it. Marx believes that one day they will succeed. The whole of humanity will be free. It will conquer nature and use it to its own ends.

4. Marx. Preface to *Capital.*

Class Conflict

The second conflict is that among individuals and groups in one and the same society. It is not an indiscriminate conflict haphazardly pitting individual against individual; it is highly structured. The conflict is between classes; it is a *class struggle.*

But what is a class? The word has been used to define nobility, riches, education, intellect, and other characteristics of certain groups. Marx, however, gives a very precise definition to the term. *A class is defined in terms of the relationship individuals have to the means of production.* Very simply, there are two classes, consisting of those who own property and those who do not. This has been the reality of social life and the basic source of conflict and change. Class struggle is the motor force of dialectic materialism.

Property, however, has taken many forms. To each form corresponds a different "class." For each class there has been an "antithesis" corresponding to the emerging new class. The antithesis "devours" the thesis, borrowing from it what was most useful and discarding what was useless. In every case it is conflict — a revolution — that brings the antithesis — the emerging class — to power.

Each historical phase corresponded to new and different forms of private property. Landed property was the characteristic of the feudal period and the landed aristocracy; but within it money, gold, and commerce made their appearance. Artisans, small manufacturers, and merchants emerged, with them commercial capital, and finally manufacturing and industry. They were destined to become a new class, an antithesis, the *bourgeoisie.* The French Revolution of 1789 epitomized, in a way, the end of the landed aristocracy and the coming of the middle class to power, emphasizing new types of property and new productive forces. But the moment the capitalists and the various groups allied to them emerged, the antithesis was already present. It was *the working class* — a small cloud on the blue horizon of bourgeois capitalism. With no property of its own, with nothing to sell but its labor, and subject to the laws of capitalistic economy, the cloud of working-class grew bigger and bigger. The class struggle was on, presaging the storm and the inevitable revolutionary conflict between the workers and the bourgeoisie.

Infrastructure and Superstructure   In the constant interaction between society and environment, and in the constant class struggle that corresponds to various historical stages, human beings not only develop particular forms of property they also change them. For each phase there is a particular set of ideas and norms, and these correspond to and are fashioned by the interests of the property-owning class. They rationalize and legitimize (i.e., make acceptable to all) the dominance of the ruling and property-owning class. This theory, which traces and attributes moral ideas and norms directly or indirectly to economic factors, is called *economic determinism:* it states that how and where we live and work fashion our ideas about the world. Capitalists have a set of ideas about society and the world that correspond to their interests and to their dominance. The workers begin to develop theirs to express their needs and interests.

In the Marxist vocabulary the totality of factors that determine a person's relations to private property and work constitute the *infrastructure:* they are the material and objective social conditions. On the other hand, the way we look upon society — the ideas we have about it, in a word our ideology — is the *superstructure.* This superstructure includes religion, law, education, literature, even the State. It is an ideology fashioned by the dominant class, the one that owns property, and its view of society is forced upon all (including the workers) until a moment comes when other groups begin to question it.

Objective and Subjective Conditions Each phase of the class struggle and each form of property relations differs in content from the preceding one. Bourgeois capitalism revolutionized the *objective economic conditions* of production. Division of labor, capital accumulation, technological progress—all these profit-inspired activities changed the world in the late eighteenth century and throughout the nineteenth. Marx conceded this, as we have seen. But by also creating a vast proletarian army, by divesting the lower classes of property, and by concentrating capital in a small number of firms, individuals, and banks, society found it easier to replace the capitalist class. A mass of people began to demand the end of capitalist rule and were ready to replace it. These were the *subjective conditions.* Thus capitalism, at one and the same time, creates the conditions for greater productive effort and lays the groundwork for expropriation of it by the community at large. A point comes when objective conditions (technology, concentration of capital, the capability of the economy to provide abundance) coincide with the subjective conditions (i.e., the will and the consciousness of the workers to take over the industrial apparatus created by the capitalist and use it for the whole community). When subjective and objective conditions converge, it is the moment of revolution.

Note this carefully: The revolution is not, according to Marx, a matter of will, indignation, or even leadership. Conditions, both objective and subjective, must be ripe. The workers must gain full consciousness that they are a class and that they must demand the change in the existing property relations. Only then can revolution under the appropriate leadership be envisaged.

The Theory of the State

The State is viewed by Marx as part of the "superstructure." It is used to keep the majority of the people, who do not own the means of production, under the control of the small minority who do. While many (including Hegel) see in the State the embodiment of noble purposes — rationality, an agency for social justice and protection, the equitable distribution of goods, an impartial umpire keeping and administering the rules and laws equitably — Marx sees in it the instrument of the capitalist class. It is a repressive agency — a policeman!

It is not alone in this, for the whole superstructure, as we have noted, is fashioned by the ruling class. Religion inculcates observance of bourgeois values and respect for property; the family and the laws of inheritance perpetuate the rule of property; the educational system socializes everybody to respect the capitalist ethic and, most important, private property; art and literature extol the same virtues. No matter where they turn, the workers and their children will confront the same values and principles and many of them will be brainwashed into accepting them. The peculiar characteristic of the State, however, is that it is the only part of the superstructure that can use force. Hence, it is necessary to use force against it.

The Revolution

Revolution, therefore, is necessary and unavoidable. "But what about democracy?" the student asks. "What about free and equal voting, freedom of association and of trade unions, of political parties and even of socialist parties?"

The answer is complex. Firstly, when Marx wrote, trade unions were only beginning to develop; secondly, there were no socialist parties, although some were just making their appearance; thirdly, political parties almost everywhere were just about to become national parties with national organizations and members; fourthly, outside the United States, universal suffrage did not exist or could not be freely exercised. Most important of all, however, Marx did not really believe that a capitalist system and the capitalist State would ever allow socialist parties to gain ascendancy, nor did he believe that such parties would ever be allowed to directly challenge private property nor to control production and the allocation of goods and services. If they did, the State would use force against them.

It is true that at times Marx wavered, and Engels did even more so. On occasions they both conceded that it was possible for well-established democracies, in which the parliamentary system and universal franchise had gained deep roots — *where in other words the superstructure was genuinely democratic* — to radically transform property relations and socialize the means of production. This might happen, but it was very unlikely: the use of force against socialists would be virtually inevitable everywhere. The workers had to gain freedom from their oppressors, therefore, by force. They had to make a revolution when conditions were ripe, when and where there was a convergence of subjective and objective factors in the industrialized countries.

The Utopian Goal: The Communist Society

Marx gives us only a sketchy account of the communist society to come. In fact, he provides us with what amounts to a two-stage scheme. The first corresponds to the transitional stage towards socialism, and the second is the ultimate one, the utopian level of communism.

In the first, the revolution is followed by the "dictatorship of the proletariat." The workers take over the State and all the instruments of coercion that it disposed and use them against the capitalist class. "The development towards communism," he writes, "proceeds through the dictatorship of the proletariat; it cannot do otherwise, for the resistance of the capitalist exploiters cannot be broken by anyone else or in any other way."[5] In contrast to all other dictatorships, however, this is one by the majority against the minority. It is necessary, he claims, in order to avert a counter-revolution. This is a dictatorship, therefore, that corresponds to, and gradually becomes, a democracy of the people and the workers. The few — the capitalists — are excluded and suppressed by force.

What are the measures to be taken during this stage? Marx advocates abolition of the ownership of land, heavy progressive income tax, abolition of all rights of inheritance, centralization of credit and all means of transport, extensive socialization of factories and all means of production, equal obligation of all to work, public education, and so on. They are to pave the way for the complete abolition of property and to the full and comprehensive socialization of the means of production.

As the State is now being used by the workers against the capitalists, its substance changes. It becomes the instrument of the many against the few. As the means of production become socialized, classes disappear, since there can be no classes without property. Without classes there is no need for coercion. *The dictatorship paves the way towards its own disappearance and to the establishment of a classless and stateless society.* The State simply "withers away."

The second phase corresponds to communism. The economy, both production and distribution, is now in the hands of the community. Nobody can exploit anybody; "bourgeois rights" (individual rights) give their place to "common rights." The final and ultimate phase is reached with the collectivization of all the means of production, with the harnessing of production to common purposes, with the transformation of the State from a coercive power to a purely administrative one. The objective conditions of production bequeathed to the new society from capitalism can now be used to make the slogan *"From each according to his ability to each according to his needs"* possible.

This is the apocalyptic or utopian element. And although Marx did not go to the lengths some earlier utopian socialists did, he shared their general optimism and was influenced by it. Crime would disappear, the span of life would increase, brotherhood and cooperation would inculcate a new morality, scientific progress would grow by leaps and bounds. Above all, with socialism spreading around the world, war, the greatest blight of humankind, and its twin, nationalism, would have no place. International brotherhood would follow. Engels waxes enthusiastic over the prospects and goes so far as to declare that, with the socialist revolution, humanity will complete its "prehistoric" stage and enter for the first time into what might be called

5. In *The Communist Manifesto.*

its own history. Until the revolution, he claims, society submits to outside forces while the majority of humans within a society submit to a ruling class. After the revolution a united classless society will be able, for the first time, to decide which way to go and what to do with its resources and capabilities. For the first time we shall make our own history! It is a "leap from slavery into freedom; from darkness into light," he announced.

For the first time the skeptics were now confronted with the anatomy of capitalism, a theory of history, a theory of revolution, a theory of the State — all of them pointing in the same direction, to the communist society. With it, of course, the laws developed by Marx would come to an end, for individuals and society would be free to make their own laws and shape their own future.

The Diffusion of Marxism: Success and Failure

Marxism represented the synthesis of many socialist writers and of movements that were active before the body of Marx's thought became known and disseminated. The first volume of *Capital*, incorporating Marx's analysis of capitalism, was completed in 1867; it was translated from German into French and English by 1886. Most of his other works, especially the many political pamphlets, including, of course, *The Communist Manifesto* of 1848, were translated, at least in French and English, almost as soon as they came out. They all were read by socialists, anarchists, utopians, and the many other radical groups of the time. The work of Marx helped shape ideas, create a firm ideological orientation, and ultimately brought together various sects and factions into well-organized large socialist movements and parties. It became an ideology.

In 1864, the International Working Men's Association (the First International) was founded by representatives of English, French, Italian, and German labor organizations. Marx wrote the basic guidelines for the International, including among others the need for a federation of all workers of various nations, the destruction of class domination, and the emancipation of the working class. With its headquarters in London, the First International never attained a large membership, and most of its efforts were devoted not so much to the organization of the workers but to fighting a strong anarchist faction. It held a few congresses and gradually disappeared.

The spread of Marxism took place after his death in 1883, with the development and consolidation of socialist parties not only throughout most of Europe, but also in the United States. These were dedicated to the expropriation of the capitalist class, to class struggle, and to internationalism. The German Social Democratic party became the dominant socialist party of Europe, receiving 4,250,000 votes in the 1912 elections — almost 35 percent of the total. In France, after many internal struggles, a Socialist party was founded in 1904 and in the election of 1914, on the eve of World War I, received over one million votes. By 1904 the British Labour party had been established — perhaps the only socialist party of the world, however, that did not owe much directly to Marx. It made appreciable electoral gains. In Russia, a clandestine Social Democratic party was founded in 1898. The Socialist Party of America was founded in 1901. It gained a million votes in the presidential election of 1920 — while its leader, Eugene Debs, was in the penitentiary for speaking against the war.

Many of these socialist parties, and others from Italy, Belgium, and Holland, were represented at the founding of the Second International in Paris in 1889, called to organize all workers against anarchism, to prepare them to combat the dangers of war that threatened Europe at the time, to commit them to class struggle and, of course, to commit them to socialism and internationalism. "If war threatens to break out," the leadership of the Second International declared, ". . . the working class pledge themselves . . . to use their utmost exertions to prevent the outbreak of war by using the means which seem most effective to them. . . ." If war should break out however, they pledged themselves "to work for its speedy termination and to exploit with all their strength the economic and political crisis induced by the war to arouse the people and thereby hasten the abolition of the class domination of capitalism."[6]

While socialist movements and parties were spreading all over the world, so was trade unionism. After the end of the nineteenth century, the freedom of workers to establish trade unions, to bargain collectively, and, in some instances, to strike, had become assured in most of the western democracies. Millions of workers in the advanced capitalistic countries, notably Germany, France, and England, became union members and engaged, legally or illegally, in strikes. Some theorists saw in the strike the special weapon of the working class — the ability to undermine the capitalist order. Others used it simply to extract local benefits from the employers and still others saw in the trade-union movement a prerequisite for the development of working class consciousness. One Marxist leader (Lenin), however, was fearful that trade unionism might divert the workers from revolution and limit them only to the search for immediate benefits within the capitalistic order.

Revisionism and Nationalism

The year of crisis for Marxism was 1914, as it was for socialism and for the Second International. There were at least two separate crises: revisionism and nationalism.

We have already discussed revisionism in regards to evolutionary socialism. It had abandoned revolutionary tactics to become increasingly

6. Quoted in Max Beer. *The General History of Socialism and Socialist Struggles,* Vol. 2. New York, Russell and Russell, 1957, pp. 157–58.

gradualistic and reformist, and it accepted the principles of democracy and representative government. By 1914 virtually all socialist parties had become revisionist and paid only lip-service to Marxist formulas and slogans.

Nationalism was a different and perhaps even more serious problem. Its tenacity, both before, during, and also after World War I, indicated that the *class* consciousness of the workers was not as strong as their *national* consciousness. Although according to Marx the workers of all the countries shared the same predicament, and should have united against their common masters everywhere, the German, French, British, Austrian, and all other workers and socialists in all countries supported their government (with very few exceptions) and fought against each other in the war. Workers' international solidarity remained a dream, and the Second International was broken.

Revisionism and nationalism, the former dealing directly with the validity of the Marxist theory and blueprint, the latter denying explicitly its internationalist aspirations, were, of course, only two forces that undermined and weakened Marxism. Criticism came from many other sources—from the left as well as the right. Anarchists already objected to the Marxist scientific scheme that subordinated revolution to specific conditions. They preferred to stress individual and revolutionary political will, but they also rejected the blueprint of the "dictatorship of the proletariat" and the imposition of socialism through State controls. Anarchists felt that the society envisioned by Marx provided little prospects for individual freedom and initiative, and that the communist regime would substitute one form of tyranny for another. Similarly, many socialists, as we have seen, shied away from the advocacy of force. They believed that change through persuasion and education would in the long run prove to be far more lasting and creative than one undertaken by force.

Many other philosophic assumptions and conclusions of Marx were criticized. Economic determinism came under attack by philosophers and also by the Church and the many strong religious organizations. Religious leaders argued that it reduced men and women to passive instruments whose fate and actions, and ideas and beliefs were fashioned by the material conditions of life. The individual was deprived of his or her vaunted "freedom of will." A strong reaction among intellectual and educational leaders against dialectic materialism developed, often leading them to the other extreme of proclaiming the complete and unfettered freedom of individuals to choose and shape their own lives.

By 1914, therefore, Marxism as a philosophy and a revolutionary political ideology had become increasingly isolated. Socialist parties had accepted parliamentary democracy, negotiations, and compromises with their capitalist "masters" as well as the reality of the nation-states within which they lived. The hard core of the Marxist doctrine had been abandoned. It seemed like a monumental defeat.

But one man had recognized the reasons for the failure, had reflected on them, and was determined to revive Marxism. This man was Lenin; to his efforts, and the establishment of communism in Russia, we now turn.

Bibliography

Avineri, Shlomo. *The Social and Political Thought of Karl Marx*. New York: Cambridge U.P., 1968.

Bernstein, Eduard. *Evolutionary Socialism*. Trans. E. C. Harvey. New York: Schocken, 1961.

Bober, M. M. *Karl Marx's Interpretation of History*. New York: Norton, 1965.

Burns, Emile. *An Introduction to Marxism*. New York: International, 1966.

Drackhovitch, Milorad M. (ed.). *Marxism in the Modern World*. Stanford, Calif.: Stanford U.P., 1965.

Gregor, James. *A Survey of Marxism*. New York: Random House, 1965.

Lichtheim, George. *Marxism: An Historical and Critical Study*. 2nd ed. New York: Praeger, 1965.

Marx, Karl and Engels, Friedrich. *Selected Works*. New York: International Publishers, 1968.

McLellan, David. *Karl Marx*. Baltimore: Penguin, 1976.

———. (ed.) *The Karl Marx Reader*. New York: Oxford, U.P., 1977.

Meyer, Alfred G. *Marxism: The Unity of Theory and Practice*. Ann Arbor: University of Michigan Press, 1963.

Miliband, Ralph. *Marxism and Politics*. New York: Oxford U.P., 1977.

Plamenatz, John. *German Marxism and Russian Communism*. New York: Longmans-Green, 1954.

Tucker, Robert C. (ed.) *Philosophy and Myth in Karl Marx*. 2nd ed. New York: Cambridge U.P., 1972.

———. *The Marx-Engels Reader*. 2nd ed. New York: Norton, 1978.

Wolfe, Bertram D. *Marxism: One Hundred Years in the Life of a Doctrine*. New York: Dial Press, 1965.

6 | *Soviet Communism*

> *The organization of the Party takes the place of the Party itself; the Central Committee takes the place of the organization; and, finally, the dictator takes the place of the Central Committee.*
>
> LEON TROTSKY   Our Political Tasks

With Lenin, Marxist ideology and revolutionary tactics were given a new sharpness and urgency. Lenin was able to take the theoretical Marxist blueprint and adapt it not only to the revolutionary movement of Russia in the early part of the twentieth century, but also to the independence movements of the colonial world. The first successful revolution in the name of Marxism, the Bolshevik Revolution, was made under his leadership in Russia on November 7, 1917.

Stalin succeeded Lenin in 1924 and became in a true sense the architect of Soviet communism. He remained in power for almost thirty years until his death in 1953. Collectivization, economic planning, rapid industrialization, the expansion of Soviet power and also one-man authoritarian government are associated with his rule. Since Stalin's death the same blueprint has been retained by the Soviet leaders, while at the same time a number of communist movements have emerged that differ sharply from the Soviet model.

Leninism

Lenin faithfully accepted the body of Marxist thought and devoted a good part of his life to defending it against its many critics. He accepted the idea of dialectic materialism, endorsed and developed Marx's theory of the State, and sharpened and refined Marx's theory of revolution — especially revolutionary tactics. His two most important contributions to communist thought can be found in two pamphlets — *What is to be Done?* (1903), and *Imperialism, the Highest Stage of Capitalism* (1917). In the first, Lenin developed a new theory for the organization of the proletariat through the Communist party; in the second, he attempted to show that the highest stage (and last

114

Lenin (1870–1924)

Vladimir Ilyich Ulyanov ("Lenin" was originally a pseudonym, but became the better-known name) spent his childhood — a happy one according to all accounts — in the province of Kazan. After receiving his law degree he was arrested for revolutionary activity and exiled to Siberia. In 1900 he was allowed to go abroad where, as a professed Marxist, he pursued his revolutionary activity with remarkable energy. He formulated, and imposed on his followers, a program for a highly centralized party consisting of trained revolutionaries.

The collapse of the Tsarist armies and the democratic revolution of February 1917 found Lenin in Switzerland. He managed to negotiate with the German government for a passage across the front line between the German and Russian armies; on the night of November 6–7, 1917, the Bolsheviks seized power and Lenin was made chairman of the new government. By 1918, Lenin had established what amounted to a dictatorship. He dissolved the Constituent Assembly after the Bolsheviks failed to get a majority in the elections, but his main attention was given to the war against the Tsarist loyalists. Not until 1920 did the Russian Civil War come to an end with the victory of the communist forces.

stage) of capitalism was inextricably associated with colonial wars among capitalist nations. In a third long essay, *The State and Revolution* (1918), he elaborated on such key concepts as the revolutionary takeover of power, the period of the dictatorship of the proletariat, and the final stage of communism where the State was to disappear and material abundance become a reality. But his most important contribution, as the head of the Russian Bolshevik party, was to make a revolution and to preside over its consolidation.

Because of Lenin's theoretical contributions to the works of the founding fathers Marx and Engels, and also because of the political tactics he developed as a revolutionary, Lenin's name has been permanently attached to theirs. The new term of orthodox ideology became *Marxism-Leninism*.

Lenin's Revolutionary Doctrine

The greater part of Lenin's life was devoted to the development of a revolutionary doctrine. In *The State and Revolution* he summarized the Marxist theses: the State is the product of the irreconcilability of class antagonisms and the agency of the capitalist class; liberal democracy is another name for capitalism, ensuring domination of the workers; law and the State are instruments for the domination of the ruling class against the working classes; and, of course, revolution and the triumph of the working class is both desirable and inevitable.

The revolutionary stages Lenin envisages are the following:

1. The armed uprising of the proletariat, under proper leadership.
2. The seizure of political control by the workers, in the form of a temporary "dictatorship of the proletariat," against the remnants of the capitalist classes.

    Lenin's concept of dictatorship was as succinct as it was brutal. "The scientific concept of dictatorship (of the proletariat) means neither more nor less than unlimited power, resting directly on force, not limited by anything, not restricted by any law or any absolute rules. Nothing else but that."[1]
3. The socialization of the means of production and the abolition of private property.
4. Finally, the slow "withering away of the State" as an instrument of coercion and class oppression, and the emergence of a classless, stateless society.

The Communist Party

What does Lenin mean by a revolution of the working class *under proper leadership?* Marx's position was that objective economic factors and the class consciousness of the masses would move in parallel. The maturing of

---

1. Quoted in Bertram Wolfe, "Leninism" in Milorad Drackhovitch (ed.). *Marxism in the Modern World*. Stanford, Calif.: Stanford U.P., p. 69.

capitalism would mean the maturing of the social (i.e., revolutionary) consciousness of the workers.

Lenin posits from the very beginning, however, the need for leadership and organization, and stresses the inability of the masses by themselves to develop a proper social consciousness. The working class — and particularly the Russian working class — could never develop revolutionary consciousness by itself. An elite, organized into a Communist party, would have to educate the masses, infuse them with revolutionary spirit, and inculcate in them class consciousness. This would lead them toward the revolution and, ultimately, communism. *Dialectic materialism is brushed aside here to be replaced by a theory of voluntarism.* The Communist party is based on the will and dedication of Marxists. They are the revolutionaries. They can make the revolution irrespective of the prevailing social conditions.

A number of consequences, both at the theoretical and tactical levels, follow these assumptions.

Elitism The party is to be composed of gifted individuals who understand Marxism and therefore understand the direction of history better than the rest of the people. The leaders of the party are particularly endowed with scientific knowledge and foresight that the common people lack. Leadership is likely to come not from the ranks of the working class but from "outside" — from middle-class intellectuals who are able to comprehend the totality of the society's interests and hence promote socialism. They are trained in Marxist dialectics and can discern the historical pattern leading to socialism. This party is the *vanguard* of the proletariat. It speaks and acts on behalf of the proletariat.

Organization of the Party The rank and file of the party is united with its leaders by bonds of allegiance and common action, and also obedience and discipline. They must be prepared for any kind of action, legal or illegal, at any time. "The one serious organizational principle for workers in our movement," Lenin wrote, "must be the strictest secrecy, strictest choice of members, training of professional revolutionaries. . . ."[2]

The party, Lenin asserts, has to be organized on the basis of *democratic centralism,* according to which:

1. All decisions are to be made in an open and free debate by the representative organ of the party, the congress.
2. Once a decision is thus made, it is binding upon all. No factions are to be allowed within the party and no minority within the party is permitted either to secede or to air its grievances in public.
3. All officers of the party — secretaries, the central committee, and other executive organs — are elected indirectly from lowest membership upwards.
4. All decisions and instructions of the party executive officials are binding upon all inferior organs and officers.

2. Ibid., p. 78.

Thus, the party can be democratic if the principles of open debate and elections are followed, but it can also become authoritarian, and even autocratic, if emphasis is put on the right of the superior officers to command and the obligation of inferior officers to obey.

The organization of the Soviet Communist party became, in fact, hierarchical. Orders for action flowed from top to bottom. Throughout his whole life Lenin was able, despite opposition, to hold the supreme decision-making power in his hands, and to control the nomination of local party leaders.

The party did not tolerate dissent and, under Lenin's leadership, indulged in purges in the years after the revolution. He invented the notion "enemies of the people." It was during this same period that thousands of so-called wreckers, saboteurs, petit-bourgeois, and many others were jailed, and "thieves" and "speculators" sentenced to death.

From Lenin's model of the party, it is obvious that he had no respect for democracy. In his view, representation, universal and secret franchise, political parties, and periodic elections had no value in themselves. If suitable to the revolutionary struggle they ought to be defended, but if they proved to be obstacles to the proletarian revolutionary movement at one moment or another, they should be brushed aside without a moment's thought.

The second congress of the Russian Social-Democratic Workers' party was held in Brussels in 1903. Writing of it, Sir Isaiah Berlin says: "There occurred an event which marked the culmination of a process which has altered the history of the world . . . Lenin and his friends [insisted] upon the need of absolute authority by the revolutionary nucleus of the party." When this concept was questioned one of the founders of Russian Marxism took Lenin's side with the statement that the "revolution is the supreme law." "If the revolution demanded it . . . everything — democracy, liberty, the rights of the individual — must be sacrificed to it."[3] Accordingly, Lenin had no scruples at all in dissolving democratically elected bodies whenever the Bolsheviks were in a minority in them.

Trade Unionism   One might have thought that Lenin would see in the growth of the trade-union movement a proper medium for the development of class and revolutionary consciousness. This was not so. From the very beginning Lenin looked upon trade unions with apprehension. He feared that workers bargaining with capitalists through their trade unions would increasingly tend to pay attention to their conditions of work, to ways to improve conditions, and to their wages and benefits. If so, they would gradually adjust themselves to the capitalistic economy and learn to act within it. Instead of gaining revolutionary consciousness, they would, on the contrary, shed it in favor of opportunistic compromises and bargains.

---

3. Isaiah Berlin. "Political Ideas in the Twentieth Century" in *Foreign Affairs*, April 1950. Reprinted in Roy Macridis (ed.). *Political Parties: Contemporary Trends and Ideas*. New York: Harper and Row, 1967, pp. 205–37.

There was also a second danger. If trade unions represented only a part of the working class — usually the most favored one and the better organized — the working class would split and lose its solidarity. A situation would develop in which some workers would have a great deal to gain by staying within the capitalistic system while others would want to destroy it. One part of the working class would be pitted against another. Trade-union activity was therefore detrimental to revolutionary Marxism. According to Lenin, unionism is an infantile disease of the working classes and the faster they are cured of it the sooner they will reach adolescence and revolutionary maturity.

Colonies and World Revolution

In *Imperialism: the Highest Stage of Capitalism,* published in 1917, Lenin attempted to show that the highest last stage of capitalism ("monopoly capitalism") corresponds to a period of control by the big banks and trusts that have investment in overseas colonies, and the division of the world into colonial areas of domination and exploitation, and wars. The most important thesis of the book, however, was that capitalist countries had divided the world and that, as a result, capitalism had become a world phenomenon despite the uneven economic development of the various countries and the backwardness of the colonies. From this he drew the conclusion that revolutions were advisable and tactically desirable irrespective of whether they take place in an advanced or backward country. Any revolution, anywhere, was legitimized because it was directed against capitalism as a world-wide phenomenon.

This account of *imperialism* appeared at a most opportune moment, shoring up the waverings of many Marxists. It explained why Marx appeared to be "wrong" in predicting the pauperization of the masses in industrially advanced nations. Now it was claimed that it was because of these nations' foreign colonies that this had not come to pass. Surplus values derived by the capitalists in the colonies was also shared in part by the workers of the imperialist powers. This in turn accounted for the delay in the development of working-class revolutionary consciousness and the successes of revisionism. It also explained nationalism and wars. Above all it vindicated revolutions in underdeveloped areas (including, of course, Russia). With this brilliant (no matter how inaccurate) pamphlet, Lenin revived Marxism and, indirectly, justified the revolutionary takeover of power in Russia in the name of Marx.

Telescoping the Revolution   If capitalism had indeed become a world-wide phenomenon, if the imperialist nations had divided the world among themselves, and if they had managed to blunt the revolutionary class consciousness of the workers by providing them with benefits and advantages that were being extracted from the colonial peoples, where would the revolution come from? For Lenin, as we have seen, it would have to come from trained revolutionaries, well-organized and sharing a common will. But where would the revolution take place?

One of the answers given by Lenin, with the support of Leon Trotsky, was that one should not wait for the stages of capitalistic development to unfold themselves. History could somehow be telescoped so that even if capitalism had not matured, and even if there were no strong working class, a combination of the peasantry and the workers could support a revolutionary seizure of power in the name of communism. The capitalistic stage could be combined with the socialist stage at an accelerated rhythm. It was possible, therefore, and indeed desirable, to push for revolutionary seizures of power anywhere in the world rather than wait until each and every country had reached the level of maturity required by Marx and Engels.

This analysis provided a theoretical justification and also a powerful tactical weapon for colonial revolutions. Capitalism was not as strong on its colonial periphery as it was at its center. The capitalistic chain which bound the world had some weak links, particularly its colonies, where it was vulnerable when colonial peoples demanded what many liberal bourgeois leaders had advocated for themselves — national independence, political rights, equality, and so on. One part of the fight against the capitalists, therefore, was to try to snap their chain at its various weak links. Communists were asked, in the name of Marx, to promote revolutions in countries where the peasantry and not the workers represented the most numerous social group; they were to do this in the name of nationalism, rather than internationalism. From a tactical point of view, every colonial independence movement that succeeded was a break of the capitalistic chain and hence a victory for Communist Russia.

It was a masterly tactical twist designed both to defend communism in Russia against potential enemies (and in so doing defend Russia as well), and also to expand and export the Communist revolution made in Russia. At this point we enter the stage of ideology where communism as a political ideology becomes very closely linked with the interests of Russia as a nation-state. This was a phenomenon that became particularly pronounced under Stalin.

Conclusion

Emphasis upon political and revolutionary tactics, no matter what the objective conditions, are the hallmarks of Leninism: reliance upon the human factors of will, leadership, and organization irrespective of their social contents; and the subordination of everything else to political organization and political will and leadership to make the revolution. Very often this is referred to as the theory of *substitutism*. With Marx, the working class develops the consciousness to make the revolution and establish communism, thus substituting itself for the whole of the society. With Lenin the Communist party substitutes itself for the working class and speaks for the interest of the working class. Then, thanks to the principle of democratic centralism, it becomes the executive and higher organs of the party, the central committee, who speaks for the interests of the working class, which speaks for the interests of the whole. But since the same central committee controlled the

Third International it also spoke for the interests of all the Communist parties, which spoke for their respective working classes!

It takes only one more step for the single leader to substitute for all the others in order to arrive at the logical outcome of such an organization — the subordination of *everything* to the leadership of *one* man. Such was the essence of Stalinism.

Stalinism

The name of Stalin is becoming as remote as that of Napoleon. But for many contemporary Communists, Stalin and Stalinism remain important and highly controversial. A member of the Russian Communist party and an associate of Lenin, Stalin succeeded him after his death in 1924. After five years, during which he managed to eliminate all opposition within the Communist party, he became its absolute ruler. While Lenin was backed by his enormous prestige and was respected for his intelligence and writings, Stalin relied upon the organization he had built with the party and upon outright force. Stalin institutionalized in his own person the dictatorship of the proletariat: not bound by any law, indeed being above any law.

In 1929, Stalin undertook what became known as the Second Revolution, collectivizing agriculture, socializing all means of production, establishing a rigorous planned economy, and attempting to industrialize the country as fast as possible through massive capital investment. He controlled not only all the instruments of coercion at home, but through the Third International he managed to impose his will upon foreign communist parties. His personal rule emulated that of the tsars. Intellectuals, poets, novelists, and scientists were forced to pay constant homage to him. During his lifetime the term Marxism-Leninism became transformed to Marxism-Leninism-Stalinism — an indication that he was considered one of the "founders."

With Stalin an important transformation in communist ideology occurs. From a revolutionary ideology it becomes the official *status quo ideology*. Even after the 1917 Revolution with Lenin trying to consolidate it, Marxism was still a revolutionary movement. He hoped that what he had started in Russia would be only a spark to ignite a world-wide revolutionary conflagration.

Stalin succeeded Lenin at a moment when the revolutionary spirit in Russia, and everywhere else, was at an ebb. Long years of strife, civil war, and economic hardships had disillusioned a number of revolutionary leaders and undermined the morale of the rank and file of the party. The inability, or unwillingness, of the European working classes to follow the Bolshevik Revolution left the Soviet Union in a precarious economic and international position. Times called no longer for the revolutionary, but for the administrator and the organizer. The period needed stability and reconstruction.

Stalin's rise to power reflected this basic desire. A party organizer above all, with all the qualities and limitations of an administrator, Stalin was able to succeed Lenin because of his administrative functions and position within

Joseph Stalin (1879–1953)

Born in Georgia, Stalin became the head of the Communist party of the Soviet Union after Lenin's death in 1924. Though originally a lesser figure among the Communist leaders who made the revolution, and lacking the literary, oratory, or intellectual talents of many of them, Stalin, nevertheless, assumed a controlling position within the organization of the party, becoming its Secretary General, and his system prevailed. He launched what is generally called the Second Revolution, collectivizing agriculture and socializing all the means of production. His rule, which lasted until his death, saw the rapid increase of Soviet power, economically, internationally, and militarily. But it was in substance a personal dictatorship based upon the most ruthless application of force and terror, and is characterized by many to be a great betrayal of the original principles upon which the revolution was predicated. His regime brought about the most rapid industrialization any country has managed to achieve within such a short period of time.

the party. Patiently he wove within the central committee of the party and within the regional and district committees at large a web of personal and organizational contacts. He controlled the appointments of Communist party members to local and district administrative jobs; he was in charge of party admissions; he was asked to reorganize and purge the administrative apparatus of the State. He used these powers to the best of his ability in order to consolidate and promote his own personal position.

Almost a year before his death, Lenin dictated the following in his political testament:

> Comrade Stalin, having become secretary-general, has boundless power concentrated in his hands, and I am not sure whether he will always be capable of using that power with sufficient caution.[4]

A man of rather limited philosophic and speculative capacities, Stalin did not share the broader outlook of other communists. He set for himself the task of reconstructing the economic and political institutions of Russia, without concern for world-wide socialism. Neither did he share the faith of the other party leaders in the possibility of a proletarian revolution in Western Europe. In fact, he had a deep distrust, even enmity, for the western world about which, in contrast to the other Russian Communist leaders, he knew and understood little.

Gradually the terms Soviet Union and Russia came to be identified with communism, and the survival of communism became identifiable with the well-being of the Soviet Union. Loyalty to the one also meant loyalty to the other. With Stalin, what was a revolutionary ideology and a revolutionary movement became State and party orthodoxy. Speculation, argument, and debate gave place to imposition and dogma. Arguments, or even mere disagreements, were magnified to mean treason. Persuasion gave place to force, and the State and the party became the agencies to administer it. Marxism (so rich in speculative thought, and claiming to be a rational and scientific doctrine) was now presented in simple didactic terms to settle every dispute — especially when the presentation of the ideas involved was made by Stalin himself. It became a catechism repeated through all the socializing mechanisms available to the party — the party agitators, the press, the schools, the radio, the universities, the trade unions, and so on.

Socialism in One Country

The first element of Stalinism is a nationalism closely associated with the traditional patterns of Russian history. Stalin decided to forge ahead with socialism in Russia without much concern for the fate of communist revolutions in Western Europe, though he continued to exert influence over all communist parties in Europe, China, and Southeast Asia. He set before him the task of building "socialism in one country" (a phase first used by Lenin) in Russia. His decision, though made in the name of socialism, evoked a

4. Richard Tucker (ed.). *The Lenin Anthology.* New York: Norton, 1975, p. 727.

genuine patriotic response among the members of his party and at least part of the Russian people. Russia was backward when compared to the West. The assertion that Russia alone could perform the miracle of building socialism was in itself an expression of faith in the strength of Russian society, a defiance of the West, and a proclamation of Russian independence and self-sufficiency.

The Organization of the Communist Party The organization and functions of the Communist party under Stalin represent the ultimate development of what Lenin had started. The party remained an *elite* composed of loyal and energetic members. Its mission was to maintain and further the cause of Soviet socialism and to educate the masses into socialism. Its membership continued to be relatively small. Sometimes it was described as the "chief of staff of the proletariat" and sometimes as "the teacher" of the Russian masses and the "vanguard of the working class and the masses." It grew into an exclusive organization which controlled every aspect of governmental and social life of the Soviet society.

The Leninist conception of the hierarchical relationship between leadership and rank and file hardened into an institution. The role of the leader began to be expounded upon in a semireligious, semi-Byzantine manner: he was omniscient and omnipresent, he was the father of the people, his word was law. There was in Stalinism a marked similarity to the despotic paternalism of the tsarist regime.

The development of this concept of leadership is also related to the internal development of the party organization. Decision-making powers became concentrated exclusively in the hands of the executive organs of the party, and any semblance of democratic centralism was abandoned in favor of rigid centralization and control from the top. Nominations to party posts were made from above and not by the rank and file. Criticism was allowed only when leaders would permit it, and only on subjects selected in advance by them; periodic purges accounted for a constant turnover of the rank and file and middle-echelon officers and organizers.

No Internal Democracy Another indication of the demotion of the status of the party was the lack of any genuine free deliberation and criticism among its assembled delegates. Congresses, whenever they were convened, spent their time in giving their approbation without any debate to the resolutions of the leadership. After 1927 not a single protest was raised; not a single dissenting voice or vote expressed. The slate of candidates for the various executive organs was prepared in advance by Stalin and his immediate associates and was always approved unanimously.

The Police The new organ, that in effect replaced the party, was the police, which operated directly under Stalin. It was the duty of the police to maintain communist legality. Lenin had used it to first operate against "deviationists" and "dissenters," but it was always understood that it was to be an adjunct of the party acting on its behalf. But by 1935 the secret police became, in the hands of Stalin, the instrument of control and intimidation not only of society as a whole but also vis-à-vis the party. Party members were totally at its mercy as were high-placed party officials. The secret police gradually became the most feared coercive and punitive force. It had its own private army (including tanks), a huge network of spies and informers, and was in command of the forced labor camps where the inmates — variously estimated to range from three to four million to as many as ten million over the whole Stalinist period — were interned. Terror thus became an instrument of government.

Stalinism and the Social Order When the revolution took place in Russia in 1917, the attention of all intellectuals, socialist leaders, and that of the people of Western Europe was directed to the first genuine revolutionary experiment to be made in the name of Marx. Expectations and hopes ran high for many and the leaders of the revolution shared them. Trotsky, for instance, on becoming Minister of Foreign Affairs, claimed that all he had to do was to publish the various secret (and imperialist) treaties signed by the victorious powers in World War I, issue some revolutionary proclamations, and then "close shop" — national boundaries would then melt away and internationalism would come about! The early policy of war communism — a blanket socialization of all property and the direct control by the socialist state of the economy — would pave the way to the transitional stage leading to communism. Throughout these first years, these social developments were carefully watched. Lack of democracy was consistent with the idea of the dictatorship of the proletariat, but it was fully compensated by the prospect of economic equality, many argued. The argument was repeatedly made that the West protected political (formal) rights while the Soviet socialist system was ushering in economic (substantive) rights.

Industrialization Reality, however, differed sharply from expectations based on ideology. Communism failed to initiate any economic recovery, just as national boundaries had failed to melt away. Lenin, a masterful tactician, was the first to retreat. His New Economic Policy of 1921 reestablished freedom of commerce, agriculture, and manufacturing, but the State kept in its hands what he called the "commanding heights" of the economy — banks, steel, iron, coal, transportation, energy. The rest went back to private hands: private employers who could hire labor and presumably get surplus value and make profit, private tradesmen, and individual farmers who owned farms could buy land and employ farmhands.

This was the situation that Stalin had inherited and decided to resolve in 1929. All means of production and all private property were socialized and agriculture was collectivized. Marxism-Leninism became the convenient political instrument for controlling society and bending it to the task of rapid industrialization. This entailed a rigorous centralization and bureaucratic control of the national economy. Economic targets were formulated over five-year periods (the Five-Year Plans) with priorities and specific quantitative quotas. Capital investment — the building of factories and industrial equipment — and the training of the labor force took precedence over consumption. Education became an indispensable part of industrialization, for technicians, scientists, skilled workers, engineers, and service personnel such as doctors, administrators, accountants, and so on, were vital to economic growth. A crucial problem was to find the human resources to train, and Stalin's answer was a massive transfer of the population from the farm and the country into the new industrial urban centers.

Force and Incentives The overall effort amounted to a radical overhaul of Russian society. In the name of socialism the task was to create what socialism should have inherited, an industrialized society. Three basic incentives could be used. The first was propaganda and persuasion: to extol the myth of socialism and incite people to communal efforts and sacrifices. But ideological exhortation has limits. Stalin had therefore to fall back upon the two classic means of encouraging compliance: the carrot and the stick. The carrot was monetary incentive; the stick, force.

He who did not work would not eat. Income was to be proportionate to the quality and quantity of work done; inequality of income was declared to be unavoidable. Trade unions who had favored equality of pay were put in their place — their leaders arrested and eliminated — the right to bargain was abolished, and the right to participate in the decisions of the plant manager were withdrawn.

The differences in pay created a salary structure that began to resemble that of the capitalistic societies, with the right of certain individuals to save and get interest, to pass on some of their gains to their heirs, to provide their children with better education, and to enjoy special advantages for vacation, leisure, and travel. There was even status — the recognition that they belonged to an elite class consisting of the top group of the *intelligentsia* (the Russian word denotes a very large class of people, comprising all groups other than workers and farmers). In recognition of their services and as an added incentive, they were allowed membership within the party — thus bestowing upon them political status as well. The percentage of workers and farmers within the party decreased correspondingly.

Force took a number of forms and served many purposes. It was used against those who did not work, or did not work regularly, and failed to live up to the quotas assigned to them. These found their way to labor camps, and their disappearance was only a reminder to others of what they might have to face. Force was also used directly to create regiments of workers in labor camps who were responsible for tasks that nobody else would take (except for very high pay) such as mining of gold, lumber cutting, and road construction. In a more comprehensive sense, force was also a constant reminder, even to those who received a good pay for their work, that any relaxation or negligence would be followed by swift punishment.

The Impact of Stalinism

Stalin and Stalinism can be viewed from three different points of view. Stalin can be considered, in line with Marx and Lenin, to be one of the chief exponents of communist philosophy and practice. One may also attribute to him the consolidation of the revolution in Russia. As Communist dictator in charge of the party, he expropriated the farms, socialized the means of production, and established economic planning. Finally, he may be viewed as a modernizer. He started Russia on the road to economic modernization. As Isaac Deutscher puts it, he found Russia with the wooden plough and left it with atomic weapons.[5]

Stalin, in fact, may go down in history as another Peter the Great, as one of the grat modernizers. Under his rule and in a short period of time the Russian economy and society underwent a great change with an emphasis on education, technology, mass production, urbanization, the movement from the farm to the city, the development of science and above all, a rapid economic growth.

It was inevitable that rapid economic and industrial development would be linked to socialism, and that in the process the political aspects of Stalinist rule would be glossed over. It was also unavoidable that the modernizing aspects of socialism would be emphasized and presented as the most attractive side of the Stalinist regime.

But the great loyalty to Stalin during his lifetime and to the Soviet system in general, by other communist parties and so many intellectuals in Western Europe and elsewhere, is due to the profound impact of Marxism. As an ideology, it provided simple answers to the three most fundamental questions we ask about our society and our lives. Where are we going? How do we get there? What will it be like?

By answering them, Marxism, like all great ideologies, gave a particular meaning and therefore direction of history: it is not haphazard; it is not indefinite; it is not aimless. We are moving in the direction of freedom, equality, and abundance to fulfill the ultimate goal of our nature as individuals and social beings. We can get there when conditions are ready but only by an act of our own will or by revolution.

History and its purpose may be realized through the most unexpected or repugnant agencies, but it moves inexorably to its predetermined goal of communism — and humanity's salvation! Stalin is thought of as a dictator, as a perpetrator of inhuman acts, as the murderer of friends and relatives. He is considered to have deprived millions of their freedom and their lives, and all of this is true, but to some he incarnated history. Jean-Paul Sartre spoke of the "monster dripping with blood," but still remained very sympathetic to the Soviet ideology and with it, of course, to Stalin. To attack *him* would have been to endanger the citadel of communism and with it the future of humankind. There *was* no alternative. Belief, a powerful ingredient of all ideologies, came to stifle critical inquiry.

As we pointed out, an ideology is a lens through which some people share a view of reality. Reality cannot be used to disprove them as for them reality is what they see in terms of the ideology. It is only in the last years that intellectuals from the left — even communist ones, in Spain, France, and Italy — are beginning to raise embarrassing questions about Soviet communism and Stalinism.

5. Isaac Deutscher. *Russia, What Next?* New York: Oxford U.P., 1953.

Milovan Djilas: A Critique

The most scathing critique of the Stalinist system, and also more generally a critique addressed against virtually all communist systems, has come from a Yugoslav Communist, Milovan Djilas, in a book entitled *The New Class*. It was written only three years after Stalin's death and published in the United States in 1957. "Everything," writes Djilas, "happened differently in the Soviet Russia and other communist countries from what the leaders — even such prominent ones as Lenin, Trotsky, Stalin, and Bukharin — anticipated."[6] They expected, he points out wistfully, that the State would wither away, democracy would be strengthened, the standard of living would go up, and internationalism would supplant nationalisms. Exactly the reverse has happened; neither industrialization nor collectivization has accounted for economic improvement, let alone plenty. And the dream of a classless society remains a dream. In fact a new class has developed: it is the Communist party and "the Communist party State" with a huge bureaucracy. In the process of industrializing, and even after industrialization had been in part achieved, "the new class . . . can do nothing more than to strengthen its brute force and pillage the people. It ceases to create. Its spiritual heritage is overtaken by darkness."[7]

The new class legitimizes itself the way all classes have done in the past. It uses indoctrination and force, relies upon handouts to secure loyal supporters, and develops a nationalist ideology to appeal to the same forces on which the bourgeoisie had relied in the past. The party oligarchy and its bureaucratic apparatus maintains not only a monopoly of political control but allocates to itself a disproportionate part of the national wealth and income. Despite their rhetoric, the communist regimes thus far, and Soviet communism in particular, have continued to perpetuate class rule.

Leon Trotsky: A New Revolution?

Leon Trotsky (1879–1940) was one of the architects of the Bolshevik Revolution and a theoretician and tactician just as brilliant as Lenin. Much of his work — after he was expelled from the Communist party and forced out of the country by Stalin in 1925 — is remembered, however, for his criticism of the Stalinist system. It embodied all the shortcomings of "socialism in one country." Russia did not provide an adequate base for the building of socialism; economic growth and development would remain slow, and the bureaucracy would become the privileged class. Under Stalin it had, in fact, grown into an independent state — not responsive and responsible to the people. It had become a dictatorship that began to move against and to exploit the workers. The bureaucracy must be overthrown, and, to do so, in 1938 Trotsky urged the formation of an illegal revolutionary party in the Soviet Union and a world-wide revolution by the workers everywhere.

6. Djilas. *The New Class: An Analysis of the Communist System*, p. 37.
7. Ibid., p. 69.

It was the last world-wide appeal for a Communist revolution; Trotsky was assassinated in 1940. "National communisms" inspired by the Soviet leadership developed, but they began to pit themselves against the Soviet control and domination, as well as against each other. Without genuine internationalism, two alternatives to Communism remained: "national communisms" or Soviet-controlled and dominated communism.

Soviet Domination: The Comintern 1919–1943

How would the communist parties and the movements that sprang up almost everywhere after the Bolshevik Revolution be organized? The answer was the Third International — the Comintern — founded in 1919. Communist parties, formed in many countries, agreed to coordinate revolutionary strategy and tactics. There were thirty-five national parties in the Comintern when it was founded. By 1939 — on the eve of World War II — the number had grown to about sixty.

The 21 Conditions

What bound all these new Communist parties and movements together in the Third International were the famous twenty-one conditions suggested by Lenin, that were accepted. The same (or almost the same) characteristics of discipline, organization, and loyalty which Lenin imposed upon his Bolshevik party were required of all other national communist parties. Some of the conditions for Communist parties everywhere were as follows:

—They must accept absolute ideological commitment to communism.
—They were to assume direct control over their communist press and publications.
—They accepted the principle and practice of democratic centralism. (i.e., the compliance of the rank and file to the instructions of the higher authorities and the obligation not to allow any factions to exist within their party. Reformists, revisionists, trade unionists, were to be ruthlessly eliminated from their ranks.)
—Underground and illegal organizations and activities were to be established and party members should be ready for illegal work.
—A pledge was taken to make special efforts to undermine and disorganize the national armies.
—Pacifists and pacifism were not to be tolerated.
—All Communists undertook the obligation to give aid and support to revolutionary movements of the colonial peoples.
—They were ordered to break with all trade unions affiliated with the Second International.
—Communist members in national parliaments were mere delegates of the party.

—All Communist parties in the world undertook to support the Soviet Union and "every Soviet republic."

—The Communist party program for every country had to be accepted by the executive committee of the Third International.

In this manner Lenin transformed the communist movement into a world-wide organization to counter the world-wide grip that he claimed the capitalists had established. Any threats on the part of the capitalists against socialist Russia would meet with the resistance of this well-organized force everywhere outside of Russia.

With the offices of the Comintern in Moscow, the Soviet leadership was able to establish its control over all other parties. Aside from ideology, many organizational and financial ties linked the individual Communist parties of various countries with the Soviet Union. Seven Congresses of the Third International were held and, in the beginning, there was freedom on the part of delegates from abroad to express their points of view and engage in dialogue. Soon the choice of these delegates became controlled by the Soviets, and the Congresses simply confirmed the "line" suggested by the Soviet leaders.

The Third International became the Vatican of the Communist movement; in its various pronouncements it analyzed the world-wide forces at work, and set forth the strategy and the tactics to be followed by the individual national Communist parties and their leaders. The Soviet Union, through the International, maintained surveillance and control over all national Communist parties. The most direct method of control was through the exchange of delegates. Every Communist party was expected to have a delegate-in-residence at the headquarters of the Third International in Moscow; the Third International in turn dispatched its own delegates to the headquarters of the national Communist parties. They sat at their deliberations and often shaped their decisions. Many of the national Communist party leaders had served time as delegates. After World War II, almost all of the leaders of all Communist parties throughout the world had been trained, if not "made," in the Soviet Union. Most behaved as Moscow expected; only a handful did not.

Major ideological pronouncements defining the party line to follow, with regard to both domestic and international politics, came from the Third International. The two most significant ones were the pronouncements made in 1928 (Sixth Congress) and in 1935 (Seventh and last Congress). In the Sixth Congress, the socialist parties were declared to be the principle enemies of communism and no cooperation with them was permitted. The socialists became known as "social-fascists."

In the Seventh Congress of 1935 and the Communist party line changed by 180 degrees. It now favored cooperation with all democratic parties — not only the socialists, but also middle class liberal parties and often conservative parties — that were opposed to Nazi Germany. This became known as the policy of the "popular front." It lasted until August 1939 when the Executive Committee of the Third International, under the control of the Soviet leaders, again reversed its position. The Soviets signed a "nonaggression" pact with the Nazis.

In 1943, the Third International was formally dissolved. The reasons given were that the various Communist parties in the world were "mature" enough to take care of their own programs and tactics and move about in their own way. The dissolution, however, was meant to placate the Western Allies (especially the United States) by showing that the Soviet Union was no longer bent on world revolution. But the Third International had played its role — it had coordinated tightly the Communist movements throughout the world according to the Soviet designs and had solidly infused the belief that the defense and protection of the Soviet Union was the ultimate duty of all workers.

The Communist Information Bureau: Cominform (1947–1956)

After World War II, another effort by the Soviet leadership was made to control the communist movements and parties and to marshall their forces in support of Soviet foreign policy and strategic objectives. The Communist Information Bureau (Cominform) was established for this purpose in 1947. It was comprised of nine European Communist parties — the Soviet Union, Yugoslavia, Bulgaria, Rumania, Hungary, Poland, Czechoslavakia, France, and Italy. (Albania was absent and so was Germany — East and West). Parties were required "to give an account" of their activities. The headquarters of the Cominform were in Belgrade, but within a year they were moved to Prague. A bimonthly publication, *For a Lasting Peace for a People's Democracy*, setting forth guidelines for action and analyzing world trends was published.

The formation of the Cominform was based on the assumptions that (a) war with "imperialism" — notably the United States — was inevitable; (b) the Soviet Union — the fatherland of revolution — was being encircled by the "imperialists"; and (c) all Communist parties should continue by all possible means to defend the Soviet Union. It was also assumed — but not accepted by some Communist parties — that the Soviet Communist parties that had made its revolution first had the historical right to "guide" the other parties in the building of socialism and that the Soviet "model" was to be followed elsewhere. In this way the claims of the Soviet Union went far beyond the claims made by the Third International at the time when it was founded.

By 1947 nationalism in the form of national resistance movements and national liberation movements made it increasingly difficult for the Soviets to impose their control. "Socialism in one country" had been Stalin's slogan and his "great patriotic war" against Germany involved a direct appeal to nationalism as a mobilizing force. The non-Soviet Communists had learned this and could now use it against Russian domination.

The Cominform was not capable of coordinating the activities of the various parties and putting them under Soviet leadership. First, there was the defection of Albania; then there was the Soviet-Yugoslav schism; subsequently conflicts emerged between the Soviet and the Italian Communist parties — all of them long before the Sino-Soviet conflict. The changing international conditions and the death of Stalin put an end to the Cominform, and it was formally dissolved in 1956.

After the dissolution of the Cominform, other instruments of cooperation and coordination were tried with varying success as other Communist parties and regimes — China, Spain, Italy, and occasionally France, began to balk at even the intimation of Soviet ideological or political domination. There were world congresses of Communist parties in Bucharest, East Berlin, Budapest, and Moscow — bringing together many of the Communist parties of the world. They numbered from sixty to as many as eighty-one. None of them managed to decide on common and comprehensive policy guidelines.

Soviet Communism After Stalin

In 1956, Nikita Krushchev, having replaced Stalin after a short power struggle as General Secretary of the party and Chairman of the Council of Ministers of the Soviet Union, gave a "secret report" to the delegates of the Soviet Communist party at its twentieth Congress. He criticized Stalin sharply for the many crimes committed during his long stay in office.

> Comrades! . . .
>
> After Stalin's death the Central Committee of the party began to implement a policy of explaining concisely and consistently that it is impermissible and foreign to the spirit of Marxism-Leninism to elevate one person, to transform him into a superman possessing supernatural characteristics akin to those of a god. Such a man supposedly knows everything, sees everything, thinks for everyone, can do anything, is infallible in his behavior.
>
> Such a belief about a man, and specifically about Stalin, was cultivated among us for many years . . . Stalin acted not through persuasion, explanation, and patient cooperation with people, but by imposing his concepts and demanding absolute submission to his opinion. Whoever opposed this concept or tried to prove his viewpoint and the correctness of his position was doomed to removal from the leading collective and to subsequent moral and physical annihilation. . . .
>
> Arbitrary behavior by one person encouraged and permitted arbitrariness in others. Mass arrests and deportations of many thousands of people, execution without trial and without normal

investigation created conditions of insecurity, fear, and even despair.[8]

The Nobel Prize novelist, Aleksander Solzhenitsyn, in his *Gulag Archipelago* describes the utter capriciousness behind the terror that Stalin used. One of the inmates is asked for how many years he was sentenced in the labor camp. "For ten," he answers. "What did you do?" "Nothing." His companion seems surprised. "Nothing!" he exclaims. "People usually get five years for doing nothing."

Since the time of the Khrushchev report, but particularly since 1961, Stalin's name has been virtually removed from every corner of Soviet life. Streets and villages and towns no longer bear his name. He is no longer part of the Marxist-Leninist-Stalinist trinity, and no longer regarded as a founder of the communist ideology. Occasional efforts to "rehabilitate" him have failed but similar efforts to rehabilitate some of the Communist leaders who were put to death or "disappeared" during his reign have also failed. The regime has attempted to liberalize itself but few, if any, significant changes in the overall ideology of the communist leadership and its practices are noticeable.

International Communism

The control that the Soviet leadership once exercised over the other communist parties in the world has declined. First it was Tito in Yugoslavia, then Mao in China, and then Eurocommunism, together with various "deviant" forms of communism that emerged in a number of countries, all of which we discuss in our next chapter. They all differed or claimed to be different from Soviet communism. The Third International was abolished in 1943 and the Cominform (the Communist Information Bureau), which was to maintain links with all communist parties, was disbanded shortly after it was founded in 1947. References were now made to polycentrism, with multiple and independent centers of communist rule and to "national communism" where communist parties would follow a path dictated by specific national conditions and not by the Soviet leadership according to the Soviet model. The ability of the Soviets to impose their course of action declined.

Peaceful Coexistence

Communist leaders had posited the inevitability of a conflict between communist and capitalist blocs. After Stalin's death it was abandoned in favor of "peaceful coexistence," which assumed conflict between the two blocs but denied that it would inevitably lead to war. Such an admission in itself weakened Soviet control over other communist parties since war was no longer considered inevitable. Peaceful coexistence allayed the fears of many

8. Krushchev's "Secret Report" to the Twentieth Congress of the Communist party of the Soviet Union, in Bertram Wolfe. *Krushchev and Stalin's Ghost.* London: Atlantis Press, pp. 88–100.

communists and gave them time to develop their own individual strategies and domestic politics. It is only within the Eastern bloc — the Warsaw Pact countries — that Soviet control has been maintained, by virtue of the presence of Soviet military forces.

Domestic Developments

Stalin's rule has come under increasing criticism both with regard to the political practices he used and with reference to the overall kind of socialism that developed. The State had not withered away; on the contrary, many pointed out that it had blossomed forth in the form of excessive centralization and bureaucratization. Freedoms virtually disappeared, and the development of a consumer-oriented economy was still far off. Inequalities increased and coercive practices were still prominent even when more incentives were introduced.

Why was this so, many asked. Was Stalinism a phenomenon peculiar to Russia? Did it obey characteristics embedded in the Russian political culture and history? Was the continuing backwardness of the Soviet economy the inevitable result of its manifest backwardness at the time the revolution was made? As we pointed out, many communists and socialists considered that Stalinism was a temporary phase — inevitable, but destined to pass. Many hoped that democratization would be possible after Stalin's death. The disappearance of the cult of personality; the downgrading of the role of the police; the growth of intraparty democracy; the development of some degree of pluralism, and a more tolerant attitude to dissent — all of them would indicate that liberalization was at long last on the way.

The Cult of Personality   Stalin, as the leader — omniscient and omnipotent — was replaced by "collective leadership." The General Secretary of the party, however, continues to have ascendancy. Yet the servile adulation and deference is gone. Through the party, Stalin's successors continue to exercise control, but it is no longer the direct and personal iron grip that Stalin held through the police and through outright intimidation.

Succession   The problem of succession seems to have been resolved in a manner that allows for the peaceful removal of a leader and the designation of another. The organs of the party — the Central Committee and the Politburo — are consulted. The ousting of top leaders does not lead to their physical extinction. There will be jobs for them in Uzbek or in Georgia . . . or in other remote parts of the Soviet Union.

The Police   The police and their arbitrary practices have come under party control thanks to the development of some general rules and procedures. To be sure, Soviet legality may be a very flexible concept, but some search for legality has been going on and efforts to curb the police and to subordinate them to procedural and legal requirements have been made. People no longer disappear overnight; they are not sent to labor camps without proper investigation and "trial." Intimidation is not as pervasive as it used to be.

Dissent There has been a great interest in dissent and dissenters abroad, with the obvious conclusion that it is still not open to Soviet citizens, Jewish or non-Jewish. Yet despite harassment and persecution, dissenters remain active; they give interviews to foreign reporters, and they seem to be protected by the interest that world opinion has focused on them. Some are allowed to leave; others are not. The Nobel Prize winner Andrei Sakharov is active — something impossible to imagine under the Stalin regime. Others, however, have been less fortunate and sentenced to long years in jail or to death. The regime continues to show its reluctance to allow for freedom of criticism — even the kind of freedom that does not question the foundations of the socialist system, but rather attempts to reconcile it with political freedoms and civil rights.

Bureaucratization and Centralization Nor is the regime sensitive to demands for decentralization in the economy. Economic centralized planning remains the general rule, despite some efforts to give more autonomy to firms. It applies to industry, trade, and agriculture. No efforts have been made to provide for genuine autonomy or to allow for the participation of trade unions in the decision-making process. The system, therefore, remains inflexible to consumer demand and needs.

All in all, little seems to have been modified in the official ideological orthodoxy of the party. The "dictatorship of the proletariat" continues to be proclaimed necessary and as long as there is a capitalist sector in the world it is to be maintained. The period of genuine communism as envisaged by Marx and Engels is still far off. Society is still going through a process of adjustment, allegedly to prepare the conditions for a truly classless society. The State in the hands of the Communist party maintains its coercive traits and is likely to continue to do so.

Modernization It is in the social composition of the Communist party, and the bureaucracy, that many begin to detect changes which may affect the official ideology. With industrialization and socioeconomic modernization there has been a proliferation of new social groups — engineers, scientists, intellectuals, teachers, and various types of experts such as the military, the managerial, and so on. These groups begin to develop their own particular interests and to become conscious of the special roles they play within the society. They, as a result, tend to express these interests in order to promote them or to safeguard them. They begin to act like all interests do by trying to influence policy decisions. The result is a certain degree of pluralism that affects the decision making and the deliberative processes of the system. Interests begin to influence and even to colonize the party, the huge bureaucracy, and other organs of the State. There is a constant pull and tug among them which breaks the monolithic structure of the State and of the party apparatus. Concessions have to be made; compromises are negotiated. Ideological requirements often yield to pragmatic considerations, and the totalitarian structure beings to soften up.

Connected with this development is the effort on the part of many groups and their spokesmen to defend their positions. A defensive posture

The most powerful and prominent leaders of the Soviet Union in 1982 —
Leonid Breshnev, 75; Nikolai Tikhonov, 78; Andrei Kirilenko, 76;
Andrei Gromyko, 74 — follow their comrade Mikhail Suslov, 79, to his
grave. The aging of the top leadership in the Soviet Communist Party
and government is but an illustration of the bureaucratization of Soviet
politics. (*Photo: Wide World Photos*)

grows that, in effect, does not allow the State and the party to intervene
consistently in dictating policies or shaping and reshaping the values of those
who operate within their assigned roles and expertise. Limitations upon the
totalitarian State begin to develop. This should, *logically,* lead to the granting
of freedoms and privileges and autonomies that were denied in the past. The
groups and interests must be given representation, and their views should be
voiced.

It is in such a development, consistent with the industrialization and the
modernization of the Soviet society, that some authors find the seeds of its
liberalization. But the seeds have not quite broken through the soil yet, and it
will be some time before they bring forth the promised flowers — if ever.
The Communist party will be the first to feel them, for inevitably interest and
other groups will have to begin to operate within the party in order to gain
representation in it and to change its internal organization from democratic
centralism to one of relative freedom to criticize and deliberate on different
policies.

For the present, the Soviet system continues to remain highly centralized and bureaucratic. The party and the police maintain their rule. A class
consisting of party members, government officials, members of the
intelligentsia — experts, scientists, defense personnel and officers, loyal au-

thors and writers, top managers — are well off as compared to the average citizen. Among *them* the Russian minority is in a privileged position compared to the other nationalities, and Russian nationalism remains strong. The critique of Milovan Djilas, published more than twenty years ago, remains substantially very pertinent. A powerful ruling class is maintaining its priveleges.

Bibliography

Blaler, Seweryn. *Stalin's Successors.* New York: Cambridge U.P., 1980.

Borkenau, F. *The Communist International.* London: Faber, 1938.

Brauntahl, Julius. *History of the International 1914–1943,* (2 vols.). New York: Praeger, 1967.

Conquest, Robert. *The Soviet Political Sytem.* New York: Praeger, 1968.

Deutscher, Isaac. *Stalin.* New York: Oxford U.P., 1949.

Djilas, Milovan. *The New Class: An Analysis of the Communist System.* New York: Praeger, 1957.

Lenin, V. I. *What Is To Be Done?* New York: International Publishers, 1969.

———. "Imperialism: The Highest Stage of Capitalism" and "The State and Revolution" in *Lenin: Selected Works in One Volume.* New York: International Publishers, 1971.

McNeal, Robert H. *The Bolshevik Tradition.* Englewood Cliffs, N.J.: Prentice-Hall, 1975.

Medvedev, Roy. *On Socialist Democracy.* New York: Knopf, 1975.

Meyer, Alfred G. *Leninism.* New York: Praeger, 1957.

———. *The Soviet Political System: An Interpretation.* New York: Random House, 1965.

Schammell, Michael. *Russia's Other Writers: Selections From Samizdat Literature.* New York: Praeger, 1971.

Schapiro, Leonard. *The Communist Party of the Soviet Union.* Rev. ed. New York: Vintage, 1978.

———. *The Government and Politics of the Soviet Union.* New York: Vintage Books, 1978.

Shub, David. *Lenin: A Biography.* New York: Penguin, 1976.

Simon, Gerhard. *Church, State, and Opposition in the USSR.* London: C. Hurst, 1974.

Solzhenitsyn, Aleksander. *The Gulag Archipelago.* Three volumes. New York: Harper & Row, 1974–1979.

Stalin, Joseph. *The Essential Stalin.* Edited by Bruce Franklin. New York: Anchor/Doubleday, 1972.

Tucker, Robert C. (ed.). *Stalinism: Essays in Historical Interpretation.* New York: Norton, 1977.

Ulam, Adam B. *The Bolsheviks.* New York: Macmillan, 1968.

———. *Stalin: The Man and His Era.* New York: Viking, 1973.

Wolfe, Bertram D. *Three Who Made A Revolution.* New York: Delta/Dell, 1964.

7 | *Communist Variations*

*The most successful, and the most fanatically
revolutionary and communist, group of followers . . .
found itself compelled to defy the claims of the
Kremlin to dominate unconditionally every
Communist Party of the world.*
ADAM ULAM   Titoism and the Cominform

The aftermath of World War II accounted for the consolidation of the Soviet Union as a world power. In the name of socialism, and because of the presence of Soviet forces, most of Eastern Europe established Communist regimes and came under the control of the Soviets: Eastern Germany (the German Democratic Republic), Hungary, Czechoslovakia, Rumania, Bulgaria, Poland, together with the small border states of Latvia, Estonia, and Lithuania. Yugoslavia had already made its own socialist revolution while the war was going on thanks to the organization of a strong partisan army which fought the Germans under communist leadership.

In Asia it took only a few years after the end of the war for nationalist forces and the Chinese warlords to give way to the communist forces led by Mao. Though they had received some Soviet help, these forces were homemade and homegrown and, as in Yugoslavia, there was no direct Soviet military involvement.

Would the Communist bloc act as one? Would ideological ties overcome national rivalries? Would the Soviets manage to maintain their hegemony over the Communist bloc — over its "satellites," as they came to be known, in the name of ideological unity, and power? Would they be able to extend their influence over other parts of the world, and especially among the new nations?

A brief glance at two dissident movements, Titoism and Maoism, indicates the emergence of ideological conflicts and national rivalries *within* what we called the Communist bloc. Eurocommunism, too, may be viewed as the beginning of a new ideological movement among Western European communist parties claiming independence from the tight bureaucratic, organizational, ideological, and financial control that the Soviets had managed to impose in the years of Stalin and until the 1960s.

138

The result has been a break in Soviet control and in the monolithic kind of communism that many, especially American political leaders, had taken for granted.

Titoism

Titoism is the label given to the prevailing communist movement and the ideology of Yugoslavia. It began to develop after the German occupation of the country in 1941. Throughout the war, the Yugoslav Communist party under Tito assumed the leadership of the resistance and organized and fought a sustained guerrilla war against the Nazis. In 1945, the party assumed political control of Yugoslavia, but in 1948–1949, Communist Yugoslavia and the Soviet Union disagreed on a number of issues. Ever since, Titoism has been synonymous with a national communist regime that has declared itself independent of the Soviet Union, and that differs on a number of domestic and international questions.

Adam Ulam writes that Titoism is " . . . a proper name for the historical moment of the break between Tito and Stalin, but not for an ideology. . . . "[1] Yet he points out also that "Titoism . . . has a broad meaning [that] might be translated as resistance on the part of a communist party to the domination of the Russian communists." We shall not be concerned here with the specifics of the historical moment — that is, of how Tito defied Soviet leadership and control — nor of the circumstances surrounding it. We shall discuss, rather, the development of an ideology in terms of which the Yugoslav political, social, and economic experiment seeks an identity separate from that of Soviet communism.

The Nationalist Urge

As we have seen, it was Lenin's genius that knit together the various Marxist groups and parties into an international organization, the Third International. This was accomplished at a time when communism was still a movement whose chances of survival, even in Russia, were dim. How would the international proletariat react when communism had triumphed in a number of countries? Would they disregard their national borders in favor of cooperation? Or would they follow the way of the socialist parties on the eve of World War I and put their country above proletarian brotherhood and solidarity?

Stalin's answer was simply to subordinate the communist ideology and the communist movements to the national interests and needs of Russia. One might argue this was only a tactical move, and that if and when communist regimes spread in other countries, then, indeed, cooperation among them would be spontaneous and would be carried out on a footing of equality.

1. "Titoism" in Drachkovitch (ed.). *Marxism in the Modern World,* p. 137.

YUGOSLAV PRESS AND CULTURAL CENTER

Josip Broz Tito (1892–1980)

Josip Broz was born on May 25, 1892 in Croatia. Wounded in World War I and captured by the Russians in 1915, he eventually joined the Red Army and married a Russian woman (whom he later divorced). In 1920, Broz returned to Yugoslavia and joined the Communist party. After serving a five-year prison sentence received in 1928 for subversive activities, he went to Moscow to work for the Communist International. In 1937, he became Secretary-General of the Yugoslav Communist party. In June 1941, after the invasion of the Soviet Union by the Germans, Broz returned again to Yugoslavia under the name Tito to organize resistance against the occupation forces there. It was one of the most successful partisan operations of the war. In 1945, Tito became prime minister of Yugoslavia. His independent, nationalistic brand of communism eventually brought verbal attacks, along with threat of military invasion, from Stalin in 1948.

Again Stalin gave the answer: the communist regimes that emerged in Eastern Europe in the wake of World War II were imposed and controlled by the Soviet leadership. They were consolidated in the period of the Cold War to answer the needs of the Soviet Union. Their leaders were handpicked; their economies were controlled; their relations with each other and with the Soviet Union were fully dominated by the latter. There was no semblance of international communism on a footing of equality, only the control of the Soviet Communists.

Tito and his Yugoslav Communist party, as they emerged from the war, felt they merited special attention and looked forward to genuine cooperation with their Soviet comrades. There was in Yugoslavia, more than in any other country in Europe, a strong Stalinist faction in the Communist party. It had waged war against the Germans, tying down a number of their divisions and keeping them away from the Russian front. It was able to lead the resistance successfully enough to force the Germans out without the intervention of the Soviet Army. Tito's Communist Yugoslavia was a homemade product with proper communist credentials, its own cadres, its strong popular support, its own roots and, therefore, freedom to claim its "own road" to the building of socialism.

The historical moment for breaking with the Soviets came after the end of the war when the Yugoslav leadership showed remarkable unity in resisting attempts by the Soviet Union to dictate their policies. The leaders took exception to Soviet spying and machinations; to the lack of open and fraternal discussions; and to Soviet "arrogance" and "interference." They asked the Soviet technicians and advisers to leave. The conflict which had been muted for some time came out into the open in the spring of 1948 and the Yugoslavs stood alone. It was like a mouse taunting the big bear . . . and the mouse survived.

The ability of the Yugoslav Communists to resist was due to the strong national base that the Communist party had developed as a *national* party. Some time after the split, the Yugoslav Communist leaders began to search for their own ideology and to take a foreign policy that differed from that of the Soviet Union. It was only then that Titoism became transformed into the *Titoist ideology*. This took at least two new directions: the establishment of, or at least the effort to establish, political and economic institutions that differentiate Yugoslavia from the Soviet Union, and the search for a foreign policy that differed from and was independent of that of the Soviets.

New Institutions

The Yugoslav Communist party numbered only some 15,000 members in the years before World War II. It was a Stalinist party like all other European communist parties: tightly organized and disciplined, committed to revolution, but always ready to follow the tactical shifts and changes that Moscow ordered. By the end of the war — within a matter of six years — it numbered 120,000 members and had made a revolution at home by destroying the industrial and financial elites, expropriating the land of the landowners, reducing the middle classes, and gaining the support of the peasantry and the overwhelming backing of the workers. It also gained the support of the ethnic minorities. It was a remarkably youthful party, primarily recruiting from among those who had entered the partisan forces and who were waging war against the Germans. Thus, the party developed a solid base that gave it the independence to defy the Soviets and the strength to maintain its separate course and ideological orientation.

Tito's partisans took the lead in fighting the occupying German forces in Yugoslavia. The struggle was hard but the successes often spectacular: here, partisans lead large numbers of enemy prisoners down from their mountain hideouts. (*Photo: Yugoslav Press and Cultural Center*)

Communism and Patriotism Nowhere in Europe was communism so deeply associated with national resistance against the Germans, and with patriotism, as in Yugoslavia. The communist leaders were the leaders of this resistance. They organized the partisans, provided for political and military direction, and gradually gained the support of many of the social strata of the population. The more brutal the German repression, the greater the support for the partisans, and the greater the influence and control of the communists over the countryside. Young men and women fled to the mountains to join the partisans. As the predominance of the communist leaders asserted itself, and as they gained greater popular support, the elimination of opposition became easier. Rival partisan formations, and groups that collaborated, were destroyed in what amounted to a civil war fought alongside the guerrilla war against the Germans.

In this manner a social revolution took place in the context of a vast patriotic uprising against the Germans and the collaborators. The Communist party emerged after the war with few enemies at home and with the backbone of the conservative forces broken. It had gained wide popular support.

Freedoms, Linkages, and Participation The Yugoslav Communist party grew during the period of the occupation of the country.[2] It built its support by encouraging and directing the mobilization of the population. Given the nature of the guerrilla warfare against the Germans, however, it was not always easy to establish a centralized direction. It had to rely upon local initiative and effort. Thus, at the local and village levels, and often at the regional level, the partisan forces had to be given initiative to act. A certain and quite considerable degree of freedom was left, in other words, to the regional cadres and to lower echelons. It would not be an exaggeration to say that the party was built from bottom upwards. Inevitably a certain degree of democracy within the party developed, which was based upon common effort and mutuality of trust. The camaraderie of the partisans and their relative degree of isolation from the leaders strengthened this.

The partisan war necessitated also the building of solid links with the population and its various strata — peasants, workers, students, intellectuals, even some of the units of the army, as well as various religious and ethnic groups. The communists created a National Liberation Front as an umbrella organization designed to be as inclusive as possible. In so doing they had to build links with as many groups as possible, and to exclude virtually none. The need for repressive tactics was secondary, and slogan appeals to class hatred were superfluous. These linkages not only provided and strengthened support but created a more open and conciliatory attitude on the part of the communist leaders to all population groups, excluding only those who collaborated with the Germans.

Communist and socialist slogans were used of course, and the program of the Communist party was to establish socialism and to deprive the established groups of political and economic power. But again, this was done (at least in part) by the Germans. The Yugoslav Army had been discredited after its defeat, and the financial, industrial, and commercial elites that collaborated with the Germans were also discredited: those among them who refused to collaborate were destroyed by the Germans. The "class enemy" had been vanquished. The churches — Orthodox, Catholic, and Moslem — lost their influence. They simply lost their base in the peasant and village populations, and, especially, they felt the loss of the young people who left the countryside to join the partisans.

Almost a whole generation of people between the ages of eighteen and thirty-five came under the guidance of the Yugoslav Communist party. They were the people most willing to embrace new ideas and turn their backs on old values and attitudes. The more they participated in the war the more committed they became to the liberation of their country *and* to communism. Communism assumed the character of a "generational revolution" bringing together the most enthusiastic and dynamic age groups of the population.

All the prospects, therefore, for the emergence of a national communism, open and populist in character, based on broad cooperation among

---

2. This is fully developed in B. Denitch, *The Legitimization of a Revolution.* As mentioned in my preface, I am indebted to the author for many of my observations in this section.

the various social, regional, and ethnic groups and with strong links between the party and the people, were present. The Communist party relied less upon repressive and police measures than anywhere else. It had disposed of its actual or potential enemies or, more accurately, saw them disposed of by their own enemies, the German occupying forces. No better conditions could be found for the establishment and the consolidation of a communist regime.

After the Split: A New Communism?   This brief account of the role and of the conditions under which the Yugoslav Communist party grew explains not only why the party managed to survive the split with the Soviet Union, but also it may explain the split itself. The party emerged with grass roots support, with faith in its own ability to lead, and with few enemies at home. The split with Soviet Russia forced it to consider alternative models of Communist rule, and in fact, it triggered a search for a new model of communism which began to emerge some ten years later, by 1958.

The model is by no means complete. Yugoslav communists have been moving, and are still moving, into uncharted waters in the attempt to launch a new and different kind of socialism. The political regime and the ideology to sustain it have also been going through numerous modifications as they adjust to national and international pressures, demands and counterpressures. How the regime will evolve is uncertain since the very symbol of legitimacy, Marshall Tito, who played the role of unifier and ultimate arbiter for almost forty years, is now dead.

A Communist Society. Yugoslavia is a socialist society. Property belongs to the State, and to various State agencies, and to the people. Except for the farmers who own their farms (nobody is allowed to have more than sixty acres of land) and small artisans and shopkeepers, the rest of the economy is owned by the collectivity. Industry, manufacturing, mining — over 90 percent of the total nonagricultural economic activity — is in the hands of public bodies. Even in agriculture, publicly owned farms account for a significant percentage of the total production of some crops.

A Modernizing System? Yugoslav Communist leadership emphasized from the very beginning economic modernization. One of Tito's associates wrote:

> It was necessary after the war to undertake a number of measures that had been requested by the people . . . It was necessary to raise the country from its semicolonial position, to develop its vast natural resources . . . Plans were made for the industrialization of the country, so that it should no longer be a country of muddy roads and general backwardness . . . Foreign capital in Yugoslavia held the key positions . . . It was in a position to pursue its own economic policy . . . [It] increased the inequality of development in our country. It was necessary to eliminate the glaring inconsistencies between different sections of the population: abundance on one side and wretchedness on the other . . . The

land was redistributed . . . These tasks . . . were accomplished with relative ease, because during the war the majority of the people had declared themselves for their enactment. That was why our People's Front readily accepted nationalization after the war: if the Communists had been alone in seeking to carry out this task, they would have been in a minority and civil war would have been inevitable.[3]

To modernize, one needs capital, ample supplies of labor, technical cadres (which means education), and of course the elimination of the traditionalist forces and values that impede change. In all these, the situation of Yugoslavia was a propitious one for modernization. For if capital was difficult to find, the other required conditions were present: the will to modernize, shared by the Communist leadership and the Communist-led elites; a great supply of labor, consisting of young men and women who had already left their villages; an adequate supply of technicians and cadres, at least for the initial phase of industrialization and modernization. The traditional elites had been virtually eliminated, so no resistance was possible. The broadening of educational opportunities, one of the first tasks of the regime, gradually provided the required expertise and skilled workers. Finally, when after the split with the Soviets the hope of getting economic aid from them disappeared, Yugoslavia profited from its independent status and received economic aid directly from Western Europe and the United States.

The indicators of economic growth have been impressive. Gradually, the number of people employed in agriculture has diminished from about 65 percent before the war to just about 38 percent. The number of workers and semiskilled and skilled workers, and also white-collar workers and technicians and managers, has increased rapidly. Economic growth was one of the highest in the world, averaging over 7 percent a year in the 1960s. There has also been a remarkable increase among university students — from eleven out of every thousand young people aged eighteen to twenty-five before the war to seventy-six out of every thousand in 1960, a percentage that has remained about the same since. What is more, the social composition of the student body showed a remarkable influx of students from poor or previously disenfranchised groups — 21 percent came from working-class families and 39 percent from white-collar.[4] Despite the slump that has affected all economies in the last few years and present-day signs of stagnation and unemployment, the record of the economy has been impressive.

Economic Democracy? By 1958, Yugoslavia had definitely abandoned the Stalinist model of modernization involving State control and subordination of economic activities to a highly centralized bureaucracy. Instead, it put the premium on *decentralization* through the development of quasi-independent units of production with grass-roots controls. This is in essence the principle of self-government in industry and the economy. The bureaucratic model has

3. Dedijer, Vladimir. *Tito Speaks*. London: Weidenfield and Nicolson, 1953 pp. 257–58.
4. Figures from Denitch, op. cit.

been turned upside down and economic activity has been returned, so to speak, to the producers. State socialism of the Stalinist model fixes production in advance, in the form of quotas, and it controls prices, wages, and consumption. The "socialist model" of Yugoslavia allows for competition among firms and decentralizes decision making on what and how much to produce. It allows, therefore, for self-regulatory mechanisms, (i.e., for a market economy that generally determines prices, production, and consumption). The system allows for a great degree of freedom for each and every individual firm. It encourages competition among enterprises and allows some to earn more while the others strive to do the same. Though property is "socialized," it is managed by thousands of separate firms and public enterprises. Efficient management brings higher profits from which everybody within the firm benefits.

Institutions of Self-management: Workers' Councils. Decentralization simply means that decisions are not made by one single central authority but are left in the hands of individual units and firms. Self-management, on the other hand, refers to the institutions and procedures under which decisions in a firm or in any other economic unit are made by all those who work in it.

The most important institution, which allows for such an internal democracy, is the workers' council in industry and in all other branches of the economy. The representatives elect the managers and have the right to dismiss them, and they review and deliberate on all aspects of the firm's decisions — what to produce, how much, how to distribute income, how much to allot for capital formation. They have a strong, and at times, the definitive voice on policies of hiring and firing, promotions, and standards for promotion.

No doubt tensions between managers and the workers' councils exist; firms everywhere may be run with an eye to profit, like capitalistic ones, at the expense of other social considerations. But Yugoslavia provides the only case of such a widespread participation of workers, and perhaps the unique case of workers' control. It is the only society that claims to have managed to embark upon industrial democracy.

What are the advantages of this system? They are social, economic, and political. Politically, the workers are increasingly allowed to participate. Even if it is for economic matters only, they are drawn into the system and, therefore, the more they benefit from it the more they are likely to support it and to support the political regime as well. From a social point of view, workers' councils and workers' control may overcome the sentiment of alienation and powerlessness that afflicts workers in industrial societies, including the Soviet one. They have a voice and a stake in what is being decided and what is being produced, and they benefit or suffer directly because of the decisions they make. Furthermore, in making decisions of an economic nature, they have to balance their own direct and immediate self-interest against the interest of the collectivity where they live and work, and those of society as a whole. The system, in contrast to bureaucratic ones, presumes that the workers may be able to learn how to balance these various interests and to shed gradually the selfish motivation that "economic man" displays.

But one of the advantages of the system is that it does not do away with private interests. On the contrary, it allows for the expression of self-interest and, within limits, legitimizes it. It gives to the workers a sense of direct economic responsibility for their own well-being, since bad decisions may well mean less income. From a more general point of view the system allows competing self-managed firms to seek the highest possible efficiency in order to show a profit.

Toward a Political Democracy? The present regime appears to be relatively open and free to a far greater extent than the Soviet Union and any of the Eastern European regimes. The country is open to millions of tourists every year and, in turn, Yugoslavs are free to travel abroad. There is no *prior* censorship in the publication of books, and much of the press that is not directly controlled by the party is relatively free. But controls vary from one republic to another. Authors have been sentenced for their publications and some have found themselves in jail.

Within the various representative assemblies, debate is free and many policies are not agreed upon until an elaborate process of compromise has yielded agreement. The constitution provides for federal organs: a government and a parliament where national policies are hammered out; six individual republics and two autonomous provinces, each representing different ethnic and religious populations. The federal bodies represent the country and the "nation" as a whole. Every effort has been made to avoid the domination of one nationality (i.e., Serbian) over others.

The overall purpose is to create a multinational political society in which all ethnic groups have equal representation and participation as well as freedom to use their own language and to enjoy their own ways, including the expression of their religious beliefs. The same is the case with another national institution, the army. Whereas in the past, 100 percent of the officer corps was Serbian, we find today not more than 60 percent. Only 46 percent of the generals and only 33 percent of the members of the high command are Serbian.

The League of Communists. Yugoslavia has a one-party system. The League of Communists of Yugoslavia (the new name for the Communist party) is a national organization with a membership of over a million and a quarter. It is both a horizontal organization cutting across republics and a vertical one reaching down into every republic, region, locality, firm, and social institution. Elective office is generally limited to the members of the league, for at election time candidates for office must be approved by it. Thus, the league remains a monopolistic organization and competition for elective office is controlled by it.

There are three important considerations regarding the composition of the league that should be kept in mind. Over 60 percent of its members have joined it since about 1960. They are still relatively young, and all came into the party *after* the Yugoslav-Soviet split. Their entry coincides roughly with the shift away from the centralized model of Stalinism in the direction of self-management. To them, the institutions of the workers' councils and direct participation and control *is* socialism. Secondly, every effort has been made, despite the inevitable growth of white-collar and managerial groups, to keep the league a working-class party. Workers, white-collar workers, technicians, managers, and students comprise a majority and are considerably over-represented in comparison to their population strength. These are the more dynamic groups of the population that are interested in continuing modernization and anxious to maintain and enlarge their opportunities and advantages in the regime. Thirdly, every effort has been made to make the league as faithfully representative as possible of the ethnic composition of the country as a whole.

What is the major function of the league today? "The league," writes Bogdan Denitch, ". . . even though it renounces the role of direct shaper of day-to-day policy and defines itself primarily as the leading ideological guardian of an essentially self-managing society and economy, is a key factor in the social changes taking place in Yugoslavia. . . . " "It is hard," he points out, "to imagine an active citizen . . . who is not a member of the league." The league "is the active vehicle for active political participation in the system as a whole." Finally, "The league functions as the representative of the new values of industrialization and modernization."[5]

One might add that the league is also the major instrument for the organization and integrity of a multinational political society both against internal disruptive forces and external enemies. It is the custodian, in other words, of the nation, the State, and of the official ideology.

The elite that constitutes the league is drawn from the population on the basis of their ability and achievement. It is an elite that believes in rapid modernization and progress, and takes it for granted that the communism they practice is the best way of bringing it about. The leadership is quite conscious that it needs widespread support, and that force may be both costly and ineffective. Support is inculcated not only through education, socialization, and propaganda but through participatory mechanisms and rewards. Self-management and the workers' council promote participation, and the modernizing sectors and strata of the population, whether in industry, among engineers, white-collar workers, or managers, are rewarded with prospects of social mobility and higher material benefits. The league acts as a catalyst in providing and encouraging participatory politics and seeing to it that rewards will be channeled, in the name of modernization and socialism, to the more active and productive segments of the population — something that *both* motivates them and secures their support.

It is conceivable, however, that self-management and participatory politics may lead the citizenry to a point at which the basic values of the regime may be questioned; in other words, when persuasive politics will give place to confrontation politics. The league stands as a guardian against such an eventuality. If dissent spills over the limits set by the ideology on which the regime is based, then it is inevitable that there will be a sharp confrontation between the league and the participatory and self-managing institutions it has created. The league, in other words, remains the only watchdog of the existing values, and together with the army, may have to protect them even

5. Ibid.

by force. In the meantime, it acts as the nervous system of a highly complicated organism, promoting the acceptance of common values, facilitating compromise and decision making, reconciling ethnic or group antagonisms, supervising, from a distance, the effective application of self-government in industry and in all other social local institutions, while making sure that no rival force develops.

It is precisely this openness, within the limits that a socialist regime can allow, that has been for the Yugoslavs both a source of pride and a lever of criticism against the Soviet Union. The words of Tito show why Yugoslavs are led both to glorify their own regime and to criticize the Soviet system. To explain the Soviet-Yugoslav split Tito wrote: "Progress toward socialism has been arrested and the Soviet Union has become an enormous terror state. . . . The fundamental question on which Stalin failed is the problem of freedom of the individual in socialism, for there can be no socialism without freedom. These two concepts are identical."[6] But freedom and openness are tolerated only within a socialist context, where most property has been socialized and the Communist party enjoys a political monopoly.

Foreign Policy

An ideological profile is beginning to emerge; one of relatively open and participatory socialism, of decentralization and industrial democracy, of socialism with a market economy. It is a system, however, whose democratic credentials depend, in the last analysis, upon what the League of Communists (i.e., the Communist party) will or will not allow.

It was far more difficult for Yugoslavia to develop a new image in the international world. Tito split from the Soviets and managed to survive in the name of national communism. He planted seeds then that have continued to grow, and are now thorns that plague the Soviet Union. The most important one is the concept of "national communism." It means that nations, despite their acceptance of communism, are fundamentally and irrevocably committed to their full independence and reject any intervention in any form. "Titoism" as national communism spread all over Eastern Europe.

A second effort by Tito to find an image was his sponsorship of "nonalignment" — that is, the effort to organize nations, mostly in the Third World, which refused to become dependent politically, diplomatically or militarily upon either the western world led by the United States or the Communist world led by the Soviet Union. While these nations constitute a large bloc numerically, they are generally poor and torn with internal disputes and conflicts. They have been unable to organize thus far and have failed to agree on any basic foreign policy objectives.

Faced by the Soviet power, Tito and the present Yugoslav leaders fell back discreetly on the only possible course of action left to a small state — support from the United States. There was no alternative. It will have to be so until Titoism develops elsewhere in Eastern Europe, and until fellow-

6. Dedijer, op. cit.

Communist China, whose concerns and ideological posture parallel those of Communist Yugoslavia, takes a more active part in European affairs. For the time being, the assertion of an independent stance by a Communist state in the name of national communism, and its consolidation, remain Tito's most enduring legacy in international affairs.

Titoism Without Tito

On May 4, 1980, Tito died, after a long illness, and as with the death of Stalin in 1953, the question was raised: After Tito What? The intensely personal element of the leadership he had provided, the deep respect and attachment of the Yugoslavs for their leader — irrespective of ethnic origin, religion, or language — made the question even more relevant for the people of Yugoslavia. Tito was "the founder." When the institutions did not provide the accommodation of conflicting points of view, especially among the nationalities comprising Yugoslavia, Tito could be counted upon to provide an authoritative solution or, if need be, to apply force. Without him the mosaic that had been written into the Yugoslav federal Constitution giving autonomy and in substance a veto to various governmental units might not work, and the League itself might reflect the fragments of the many political forces at work rather than provide the glue to keep them together.

It is still too early, however, to answer the question. The remarkable thing is that more than three years after Tito's death, and in the midst of a renewed cold war, Yugoslavia remains united and its institutions have functioned fairly smoothly. Conflicts among nationalities about the allocation of resources have found resolution, and there has been no change in the independent stance Tito imparted to Yugoslavia's foreign policy. Titoism remains very much alive. While the Party Congress held in June 1982, two years after Tito's death, was an indication of the durability of the regime, it was also an occasion to note the many strains and conflicts that have been aggravated by the world economic crisis. Disparities between the autonomous republics remain great. For instance, the per capita income in Croatia or Slovenia is about seven times as high as that of Kossovo, which is inhabited by Albanians. The rate of inflation is possibly the highest of all the countries in Europe (it was about 40 percent in 1981), and unemployment went up to 12 percent in the same year. The Yugoslavs owe over fifteen billion dollars to western banks and to the United States, and their trade balance showed a deficit of one billion dollars in 1981. Efforts to distribute the economic activity evenly among the countries' autonomous republics, and thus attempt to equalize the national wealth, have not been successful thus far. The economic problems aggravate existing ethnic and religious conflicts so much that the individual republics have developed separatist tendencies that divide and fragment the regime. The unifying force remains the Communist league and a long-term functioning of the regime will depend, as Tito's legacy begins to fade, upon its ability to generate and sustain the kind of ideology that will transcend individual particularisms and contain separatist movements.

Maoism

Like Titoism in Yugoslavia, Maoism is the label for the Communist movement and its ideology that developed in China under the leadership of Mao Tse-tung. "Chairman Mao" was, for more than forty years, the undisputed leader of the Chinese Communist party and the head of the Communist government in China after the civil war (1946–1949) and until his death in 1977.

Maoism represents the first, apparently successful, communist revolution in an underdeveloped non-European society and the first viable non-European communist regime. Like Yugoslavia, China broke off from the direct political and economic oversight of the Soviet Union to follow its own path to communism, but the reasons for the break can be traced to the very beginnings of the Chinese Communist movement, as expounded by Mao Tse-tung.

Background

Two powerful forces dominated pre-Communist Chinese society: the landlords and the warlords. The first owned and controlled the land and squeezed out of the peasantry whatever they could, keeping them at a bare level of subsistence, if not starvation. The second controlled the means of coercion. Military commanders in various regions and provinces, however, asserted their independent authority and engaged frequently in war with each other.

There were at least three other important forces: the rich merchants, acting on behalf of foreign firms and exporters, British, American, French, Japanese; the foreign governments, who controlled, with their own military forces, many of China's eastern seaports, including a great part of Shanghai (these were the "concessions" that had been granted to foreign powers); and, finally, there were the Japanese, who after taking Taiwan in 1898 began to eye Manchuria and the eastern part of China. After World War I they, too, were given special concessions in Shanghai.

Foreign presence fanned the flame of a growing nationalism precisely when the internal quarrels of the warlords, the speculation, and manipulations of the landlords and the merchants, the overall corruption of the elites, and the weakness of the political regime deprived the country of unity and direction. The circumstances, therefore, seemed propitious for the development of a new party, such as a Communist one with unified direction and clear ideological goals. It could at one and the same time harness the widespread discontent, and give direction to the spirit of nationalism and the demands for national independence.

The Chinese Communist party, founded in 1921, at first accepted fully the 21 conditions imposed by the Third International. It accepted the "dictatorship of the proletariat" and subscribed to the concept of revolutionary class struggle. Yet at the express insistence of the Soviet leadership, the Chinese Communist leaders abandoned their party's revolutionary position

WIDE WORLD PHOTOS

Mao Tse-Tung (1893–1977)

Mao Tse-tung was from Hunan. In 1918 he became a librarian at Peking University where his socialist leanings were strengthened as a result of contact with the works of Marx and those of Li Ta-chao and Ch'en Tuhsiu, two professors who with Mao were to help found the Chinese Communist party (CCP) in 1921. Although attaining leadership positions in the CCP, Mao's devotion to the peasantry as a revolutionary force, and his theory of guerrilla warfare rather than urban insurrection, alienated him from much of the party leadership. After the persecution and elimination of the communists in 1927, Mao proclaimed a "soviet republic" in southwestern Kiangsi Province. In 1934 he led his forces on the two-year "Long March" to regroup in northwestern China. The Chinese Communist forces finally triumphed over their nationalist opponents in 1949 and established the People's Republic of China, which Mao served as President in addition to his post as Party Chairman. Among Mao's major works are *On Contradictions, On Practice* and *Quotations From Chairman Mao,* an anthology that served as the textbook for the young Red Guard cadres of the Cultural Revolution.

and gave their support to the leader of what appeared to be a middle-of-the-road coalition of political forces in China — the Kuomintang, led by Chiang Kai-shek. Almost immediately Chiang turned against the Communists, arrested and imprisoned thousands of leaders, cadres, and members, and shot many of them. The Communist party was destroyed in virtually all urban centers where it was supported by workers and intellectuals. Its proletarian base was wiped out. Perhaps it was from this moment on that the peasant base of the Chinese Communist party became indispensable in the eyes of Mao. He and many Communist leaders withdrew into the vast countryside to develop intimate relations with the peasantry.

They gathered in strength in one of the relatively poorer provinces of China, Kiangsi, where they established a Communist republic and ruled the province from 1931 to about 1934. It was at this time that the Red Army, later to become known as the People's Liberation Army, was founded. But through their "Kiangsi experience" the Chinese Communists under Mao learned what they had to do if they were to receive support from the peasants. They realized that they had to relate their strategy and goals to the expectations of the peasantry. "The peasants came to see that the Communists worked for their interest. Their army was perfectly disciplined, neither plundered nor commandeered. What it needed it bought for cash and if it could not be supplied it went elsewhere."[7] Good relations with the peasantry, and the support they gave to the Communists, was an important element of Mao's famous theory of guerrilla warfare.

But the Communist republic in Kiangsi was gradually surrounded by Chiang's forces, while in the northeast Manchuria fell quickly to the invading Japanese. It was at this juncture, aware of Chiang's determination to liquidate the Communists, that Mao made a momentous decision that both saved the Communist party and consolidated its peasant base. The whole Red Army and the Communist party in Kiangsi moved, in what became known as the "Long March," some seven thousand miles across the country to establish its headquarters in the Yenan Province relatively close to Manchuria and Peking. It first moved west, then north, and then east. It was a monumental achievement, and its success was not only due to the perseverance of the leadership and of their followers, but to the general support given to it by the population — by the peasantry. From Yenan, the Communists were able to confront the Japanese between 1936 and the end of World War II, thus emerging as the champions of Chinese nationalism and independence.

The Pillars of Maoism

It was the support of and identification with the peasantry, as well as the increasing assumption by the Communists of a nationalist posture, that accounted for their ultimate victory. But it was to a great extent also due to the development of a new revolutionary strategy — *guerrilla warfare.*

---

7. Fitzgerald. *Mao Tse-tung and China*, p. 39.

Source of inspiration and training for China's Red Army was the Communist stronghold at Yenan. Important army and party councils and assemblies were held in the mountains where the officers and soldiers came for political "revival." (*Photo: Wide World Photos*)

The Peasantry   The peasants invariably play a crucial role in all revolutions, and their grievances have been exploited by conservative, liberal, and communist leaders at different times. Lenin's slogan "land to the peasants" on the eve of the Bolshevik Revolution either directly rallied many of them behind the Communists, or, and even more important, neutralized them. But Marxists believe that while the peasantry could at times be helpful it was only the working class and its leaders, the Communist party, that could develop the proper class and revolutionary consciousness, make the revolution, and establish socialism. Peasants' major preoccupation is the ownership of land: they are considered, therefore, to be fundamentally an obstacle to the building of socialism.

At the second congress of the Third International in 1920 the role of the peasantry had been explicitly recognized as being side by side with the working class. It was Mao who, for the first time, went beyond this to attribute to the peasantry a genuine revolutionary role and to build his revolutionary movement on a peasant basis. The revolution would be made in close association with the peasantry and in great part by the peasantry.

It may be argued that Mao's strategy was dictated by the circumstances. Since the urban centers were controlled by Chiang and the proletarian ranks of the Communist party were decimated, the Communists had no alternative but to turn to the peasants. But there seemed to be more important reasons. Mao, the son of a fairly well-to-do farmer, had spent years in his native province of Hunan studying peasant conditions.[8] He described their miseries, deprivations, and the manner in which they were exploited by the landlords, but he also expressed his admiration for their stoicism, shrewdness, and courage. There was a genuine populist streak in Mao — an admiration for the innate goodness and spontaneity of the peasants. He also saw that the decades of deprivation and exploitation and the constant strife against the hated landlords made the Chinese peasantry a potentially powerful revolutionary force. All that needed to be done was to mobilize it under the proper leadership. Accomplishing this was Mao's major achievement. Without forgetting the importance of the proletariat, he built the Chinese Communist party on the basis of the peasantry and from the peasantry.

Nationalism The slogans of the Bolshevik Revolution were both antinational and anti-war, but they were addressed against the top oligarchy. The Bolsheviks simply overthrew it and replaced it almost overnight. The revolution amounted to a swift replacement of the ruling elite by a revolutionary one. It was almost like a *putsch* though it had the most far-reaching social and economic consequences.

The situation in China was vastly different. First and foremost, the revolution took place over a long period of time in a two-front war against both the Japanese military forces, that had occupied the greater part of Eastern China, and against the Nationalist forces of the Kuomintang led by Chiang. The Communists claimed to be the only truly national force, fighting not only the Japanese but, indirectly, the British and the Americans who were supporting Chiang. Gradually, Chinese nationalism and China's independence became associated with the Communist party and Mao's People's Liberation Army.

The Communist party broadened its appeal to include, in fact, almost all those who were fighting the Japanese but who also favored full and unqualified independence from all former imperialist forces — most notably the British and the Americans. Not only did they dig deep into the rich substratum of the peasantry, but, their appeal was irrespective of class. The base of the revolution was broadened, therefore, to include not only the workers and the peasants but also the middle classes, the intellectuals, and the lower middle classes. The "people" were defined in the broadest possible terms to include virtually all groups. The only "enemies" were the landlords and those who served the interests of the foreign powers, including, of course, those who collaborated with the Japanese.

Mao theorized on "contradictions." He claimed that all contradictions within the people could be resolved; they were supposed to be "nonantagonistic," that is, not inherently leading to conflict. "Antagonistic" con-

---

8. "Report of an Investigation of the Peasant Movement in Hunan" (1927). *In Selected Works of Mao Tse-tung.*

traditions, on the other hand, were limited only to inherently conflictual situations which pitted the people against landlords and collaborators. The first could be reconciled without force; for the second, force was unavoidable. In this way, all Chinese fighting together for their national independence against the common enemies were welcomed into a vast nationalist front led by the Communist party and Mao.

Guerrilla War   In classic Leninist theory and practice the revolution is an act of force made by a trained, organized, and a highly disciplined revolutionary party (the Communist party) acting in the name of the working class. The revolution is ruthless, just as it has to be swift. If successful, it will impose itself upon the society and the Communist party will assume all powers.

The broader definition of the "people" given by Mao, on the other hand, and the particular circumstances of the struggle for power in China, differentiate Maoism from this Leninist model. Mao relied upon popular support, sustained collective effort, and put a premium on the motivation and the initiative of the masses more than on organization and discipline. Furthermore, he could not envisage a revolution in a single uprising replacing the ruling elite in China. The double struggle against both Japanese and Chiang could not be sustained without broad support. The Communist party could not monitor, let alone lead, every skirmish and every confrontation with its enemies. A certain degree of voluntarism and a great degree of decentralization were necessary and, perhaps, unavoidable. (We have noted that the same was the case with the Yugoslav Titoist movement when the partisans fought both against the Germans and the various collaborationist forces.)

Mao and his Communist party relied far more than did the Bolsheviks on shaping "the minds and the souls" of the people, so that they would support his Liberation Army, and provide the fighting forces with shelter, food, information, and new soldiers. In the long struggle which ultimately led to victory, a vast network of connections was built between the Communist party and the People's Liberation Army with the peasants and all other sections of the population. The Communist party spearheaded the movement, but the thrust of the spear depended on the strong links to social groups and the solidarity of supports that had developed.

Under these circumstances, then, the revolution in China was to be made over a long period of time. It was not to be simply the expression of force at a particular moment. To be sure, force is to all revolutionaries what the Bible is to missionaries: Mao's famous statement "Power comes from the barrel of the gun" shows that he had a great respect for force. But his theory of guerrilla warfare shows also that he understood the limitations of force and of the gun when they do not take human factors into account: will, motivation, cooperation, initiative, moral support, and commitment. The barrel is empty without them. This is the basis of Mao's theory of guerrilla warfare; there must be the broadest possible participation, for unless the population is prepared and willing to give its support, fighting is impossible.

Mao's realization that no revolution could really succeed without popular support, derived in part from a teacher of his who admired the British idealists — philosophers who put particular emphasis on the development of individual motivation and purposive action. Without such individual understanding and voluntary participation, no governmental reform or action and, of course, no revolutionary overhaul of the society, could be sustained. A revolution that did not bring forth conscious individual effort was doomed to turn against what it professed to build: collective but conscious and voluntary support and cooperation.

The Communist Regime

It took time after the defeat of the Kuomintang forces under Chiang in 1949 for the Communist regime to take shape. When it did, the major organizational lines were not unusual. First, there was the predominance, or rather the monopoly, of political power and control in the hands of the Communist party; secondly, there was the nationalization of the economy and the collectivization of the land.

As with other communist regimes the three basic organizational pillars of government were: (1) the State and its institutions; (2) the party and its ideology; (3) the army — the People's Liberation Army. Constant modifications of structures and reallocation of powers make anything but some general remarks difficult.[9]

The State   The State is organized along familiar lines. There are the national organs for the whole of the country with some fifty departments and a large civil service. There is a head of state, the Chairman. He directs the activities of the governmental organs and is technically responsible to the National People's Congress, a large assembly meeting infrequently, consisting of over four thousand members. This congress is, only technically again, the supereme legislative and constitution-making body. It consists almost exclusively of Communist party members.

Below the national organs are the provincial and communal organizations. These have varied in size and number over the last twenty years, and are governed by provincial and communal executive bodies — again controlled by the Communist party either directly or through provincial or communal congresses in which the Communist party has a majority.

The Communist Party   The second and supreme pillar of government is the Communist party, consisting today of about forty million members. The principle of democratic centralism applies, with local authorities expected to abide by the decisions of the central organs, while the selection to such organs proceeds, in theory if not in practice, from the lowest level upwards. A National Party Congress consisting of about 1600 party delegates "elects" the central committee, which, in effect, is the supreme collective body of the party. It, in turn, elects the Politburo, consisting of thirty-two members,

9. For a good account of the organization of the State and the Communist party, see Townsend. *Politics in China.* Students are urged to read, in the *New York Times,* the account of the 12th Party Congress held from Sept. 1–10, 1982.

which, in turn, elects the highest authority within the party—the Chairman. In the 12th Party Congress, held in September, 1982, the post of the chairman was established. It is, in effect, the general secretary of the party that assumes the powers of the chairman.

The Army The People's Liberation Army is under the Ministry of National Defense, which in turn is under the Politburo and under the secretary general. It is, of course, thoroughly supervised by political commissars — all of them trusted Communists. For every military unit, from the general staff down to company level, there correspond political departments or officers. Most of the army officers themselves are members of the Communist party.

Every effort has been made to avoid the development of hierarchies within the army. There are no insignia indicating rank; officers have to do, once in a while during the year, the tasks allotted to the soldiers. Morale seems to be high, the organization excellent, and the fighting capabilities high enough to make it difficult for any power, including the Soviet Union, to contemplate an invasion of Chinese territory. In 1951, the Chinese confronted American forces in Korea, drove them back, and were able to hold them off. In border skirmishes with Soviet forces the Chinese have held their ground. There were no defections and no indication of any organizational or morale problems. In 1979, the Chinese were able to move into a strongly fortified area of Vietnam, administering what they termed "a lesson" to an ally of the Soviet Union that was reputed to have a well-organized army.

The Regime in Flux

As some commentators have pointed out, what characterizes the Communist regime in China thus far is a constant tug and pull between "institutionalization" and "transformation." The ideological goals of the regime still remain the transformation of social relations and of the individual by establishing communism. Yet to do so, new institutions must be established in education, governance, the economy, and the army. However, institutionalization slows down change and inertia sets in; quite often vested interests develop which become obstacles to change. How can this be averted? This can be done by once more launching forth in the direction of transforming what is just barely institutionalized! The regime, founded on the commitment to change, becomes endangered by the very change to which it is committed.[10]

To allow a process of institutionalization that fosters and crystallizes hierarchical relations and a bureaucracy that becomes uncompromising towards popular needs, is to abandon hopes for transformation and change. Even more, it is going against the high hopes of Mao that popular participation and the tapping of the ingenuity and spontaneity of the people is the only

10. The thesis of institutionalization versus revolution is developed in Townsend's *Politics in China*. As I mentioned in my preface, I am indebted to the author for many of my observations in this section.

safeguard of socialism. It is also to gradually give in to bureaucratic controls and directions similar to those existing in the Soviet system, and by so doing, to resort increasingly to force rather than to rely on popular support.

There has been a high degree of fluidity, and at times downright instability if not chaos, in the development of the Chinese Communist system. With the death of Mao and the virtual disappearance of all those who were in one way or another associated with the Long March and the civil war, a new generation may put the premium on institutionalization, stability, rapid industrialization, and modernization.

The following main ideological and institutional stages of the Chinese Communist regime since its inception can be outlined:

1. A period of consolidation but also of education and mobilization in the principles of socialism (1949–1953).
2. The move in the direction of economic planning and socialism (1953–1956), followed by a period of liberalization.
3. A massive effort to industrialize — known as the "Great Leap Forward" (1957–1960).
4. A subsequent period of retreat from the goals of rapid industrialization that lasted until 1965, to be followed by
5. The "Cultural Revolution" (1966–1969), again followed by a period of consolidation until 1972.
6. The period since Mao's death when, after a brief conflict between "moderate" leaders and "revolutionaries" (who hailed from the period of the Cultural Revolution and claimed to be Mao's intellectual heirs), the moderates have gained the upper hand. Their emphasis has been upon stability, industrialization, and modernization, with the help of capitalist countries in Western Europe, and even the United States itself.
7. In the 1980s we may again witness a period of flux in which "capitalistic" incentives in the economy and especially in agriculture may be tried side by side with socialist modes of production — a period indeed in which China may alternate between the two. The debate on the pace of industrialization and modernization, and with it, China's economic relations with advanced industrial societies, like Japan and the United States, is likely to continue. At the same time, foreign policy options, including China's relations with the United States and the Soviet Union, will be under constant reexamination. As the debates of the 12th Congress and the leadership that emerged indicate, the accent for future policy will be on pragmatism and not on ideological crusades.

Thus, the unfolding of the Chinese Communist experiment moves in waves that flow and ebb. Socialism began in earnest with the first Five-Year Plan initiated in 1953. Like the first Soviet Five-Year Plan launched more than a decade after the Bolshevik Revolution, its target was to industrialize the country rapidly. Emphasis was put on capital development and on heavy industry. Individual businesses and plants were taken over by the State and, as in Russia, State-centralized bureaucratic planning mechanisms began to develop. Also, as in Russia, a rapid effort was made to collectivize the land by amalgamating peasant households and plots into communes and cooperatives of varying sizes.

But economic planning and the socialization of the economy and the collectivization of agriculture put heavy demands upon the State organization and apparatus. These led to centralization and to State controls that assumed coercive character, and endangered popular support and participation. In 1956, Mao initiated a period of controlled liberalization. He and the party leadership inaugurated what became known as the "Let a Hundred Flowers Bloom" movement, in which an open debate on all matters was encouraged. It revealed that there was discontent among the peasants; that the workers resented centralized management and managerial direction; that bureaucratization was indeed feared; and that many leading party organizers and cadres had abused the powers that centralized planning and direction had put in their hands. Intellectuals began to criticize many aspects of socialism while searching for new formulas that would reconcile communism with freedoms.

Just as suddenly as it began the Hundred Flowers campaign was abandoned. In 1957 Mao returned to the imperatives of industrialization, and seemingly resolved to out-Stalin Stalin's achievements. The new period, known as the "Great Leap Forward," began at the same time as the second Five-Year Plan was introduced in 1958. During the Leap, collectivization moved ahead with the merging of smaller cooperative and communal units into large communes that became the production and administration units in the countryside. They developed their own schools and factories, built mess halls that were used in common, provided for militia, hospitals, roads, and so on. There were about 24,000 such large communes for the whole of China.

The Leap did not prove successful. Within two years progress slowed to a crawl. Central controls were modified in favor of greater local autonomy, work in the communes was made lighter, the size of the communes was reduced, and the total number of communes was increased from about 24,000 to about 75,000. Private plots were returned to the individual peasants and "trade fairs" (another name for free markets) reappeared.

In 1966, a new revolutionary drive was mounted — the Great Proletarian Cultural Revolution. It almost lasted until 1970 and it affected virtually every aspect of the State, the administration, the party, and the economy. It was, in effect, a revolution of the masses and the rank and file of the Communist party — especially strong in the cities, the factories, and the universities — against *their leaders* and *organized by some of them*. Its targets were broad and diffuse, thus providing for as wide a mobilization of the people as was possible. Old ideas, customs, habits, prejudices, selfishness, greed, authority, and hierarchy — all came under a sweeping attack.

The revolution was, characteristically enough, spearheaded by the very young — by high school students who were apparently organized and moved from one place to another by the army. They became known as the Red Guards. In some instances the youthful rebels seized power. Otherwise, they invariably brought down many of the local, State, administrative, and even party officials. More than 30 percent of the members of the central committee fell; many top leaders resigned. All in all there was a vast purge of the State and party cadres that, in contrast with Stalinist methods, did not take place in the dark through the secret police but in the open through powerful pressures from below (even if carefully orchestrated from the top). Its ultimate purpose was to maintain the participatory and popular character of the Maoist regime.

As was the case with the Hundred Flowers and also the Great Leap, the Cultural Revolution came to an end as dramatically and suddenly as it had broken into the open. And as in the past, it was followed by a period of consolidation that lasted well after the death of Mao. The rivalries that followed his death did not affect the regime. Within a relatively short time, the Communist party managed to reestablish its unity and to select a new chairman, who is also now the Head of State and the army.

Conclusion

All regimes that spring from revolutionary ideology, and which take power through revolution, are shaped by the way in which they first managed to acquire power. The Bolshevik Revolution was, in effect, the work of a handful of men and women who believed in organization and for whom the party was a paramilitary instrument for the conquest of power. The Russian Communists, once in power, used the party as an army of a highly centralized political organization, governing the country from the top down through a highly centralized and bureaucratized apparatus.

The Chinese Revolution, on the other hand, and the Communist takeover of power in China, was the work of a vast popular movement of guerrilla warfare that involved, in one form or another, virtually the whole of the countryside and many of the urban populations. Victory was won thanks to popular support and participation. To maintain their leadership, therefore, the Communist leaders and the party have had to go back to the people, so to speak, to mobilize them, organize them, and work with them and for them. Coercion has been widely used but it could not in the long run succeed. It is education in socialism and mobilization for socialism that is best able to bring forth popular support.

This is perhaps the distinctive trait of Chinese communism.[11] Its ultimate goal is to provide and generate incentives and participation — to fashion men and women who ultimately become convinced of the advantages of a communisty society. The building of socialism and the transformation of the individual must go hand in hand. But what if individuals begin to turn away from the socialist framework? And what if individual criticism and dissent begin to question the very citadel of power — the Communist party and its leadership?

The constant shifts and changes underlined by massive appeals to the party rank and file, and the people, together with the frequent attacks against bureaucratization and centralization, indicate that the system is seeking a middle ground between freedoms and constraints, between participation and repression, between orthodoxy and experimentation. It is still going through a period of change and transformation. The Chinese regime is still in flux.

11. For a general discussion of Mao's political ideology and its implications, see Schram. *The Political Thought of Mao Tse-tung*.

Eurocommunism

The term Eurocommunism has been used to describe and identify new common trends, ideological and political, which have appeared since 1975, or earlier, among some European Communist parties within the western democracies, and particularly in France, Italy, and Spain. The term itself suggests that a European type of communism, different in both doctrine and tactics, may be emerging within the Western European democracies that differs from the Soviet one and from that of the Eastern European satellites. The phenomenon, it should be pointed out, is neither comprehensive nor precise. All European communist parties do not act in the same manner, have not agreed on a common doctrine, and do not espouse the same policies. Furthermore, there is no common forum or organization. Meetings between the heads of European communist parties have occasionally taken place, but there is no inter-European machinery for the communist parties to provide for deliberation and to formulate common guidelines.

After 1920, all European communist parties, having seceded from the socialist parties and the Second International, accepted the doctrinal and policy guidelines embodied in the 21 conditions. Notably:

—Class struggle was unavoidable and desirable, with the communists acting on behalf of the working class.
—Revolution was the way to attain power.
—The dictatorship of the proletariat was the necessary instrumentality for the liquidation of the counterrevolutionary forces and the consolidation of the revolution.
—Collectivization and nationalization of the means of production would follow.
—The preservation of the fatherland of socialism — the Soviet Union — against all "imperialist" forces was the duty of all European communists.

The relationship between the national communist parties and the Soviet Union hardened, in practice, into a pattern of subordination to Moscow and control by the Soviets. Many of the tactical switches of the national communist parties could be traced directly to the national and strategic interests of the Soviet Union. Sometimes these called for a revolutionary and militant stance on the part of national communist parties, and sometimes for cooperation with their national governments.

Eurocommunism is supposed to represent a departure from these basic doctrinal and tactical guidelines, particularly with an assertion of an independent stance vis-à-vis the Soviet Union.

Class Struggle

Eurocommunists began to reconsider the principle of class struggle, which, as we saw, is of crucial importance to the thinking of Marx and Lenin. The reasons are many. The distinction between the working class and "capitalists" is not as marked in advanced industrialized societies as it had been in the past. The vast majority of the gainfully employed are salaried — they form a large new middle class. The composition and income of the working class has changed radically to allow for relatively high incomes for skilled and white-collar workers, whose mentality and outlook also became increasingly middle-class. The democratic process also bridges the gap between workers and capitalists, and allows the Communists, in combination with other parties, to seek, and hopefully to obtain, political power. Eurocommunists, therefore, increasingly take a reformist attitude, advocating change, compromise, "advanced democracy," a "popular union" with other left-wing parties — not in order to establish socialism but in order to form a government to prepare the conditions from which socialism will develop.

Revolution

Electoral politics, the agreement of the Communists and other left-wing forces of European countries to seek power peacefully and through the ballot, makes revolution obsolete. Eurocommunists no longer wish to take power by force or to impose one class upon the rest of the society. They prefer to cooperate with other groups to form a majority in parliament. Antonio Gramsci, the Italian Communist leader and theoretician, advocated the tactics of a broad penetration of various socioeconomic groups by the Communists to gain popular support and acceptance. French Communists over recent years abandoned in their pronouncements, their commitment to class, and revolutionary politics, in favor of a broad "popular union." Such efforts may give to the Communists and their allies a majority, or at least adequate parliamentary strength to participate in government, or to cooperate closely with other major parties as coalition partners. In Italy, from 1974 to 1979 the famous "historical compromise" amounted to the political cooperation of the Communists with their archrivals, the Christian Democrats.

Parliamentary Democracy?

Many Eurocommunists therefore seemed to accept the logic of majoritarianism and the principles of democracy. The Italian Communist leader Enrico Berlinguer has even gone beyond this, stating that even if the Italian Communist party got 51 percent of the vote they could not govern against the other 49 percent! He admitted the tactics of compromise and the necessity of getting support from as wide a sector of the population as possible.

French Communists accepted the principle of governmental "alternation," promising that they would accept the popular verdict: there can be no question of dictatorship. The Spanish Communist leader (but not the Portuguese one) committed himself to electoral and democratic politics, and went so far as to accept the monarchy in Spain. They all agree to respect the freedom of association and parties as well as individual and political freedoms.

The principle of democratic centralism, as we noted earlier, makes for hierarchical and leadership control within the Communist party and does not allow the formation of factions. The party thus assumes a paramilitary character, stressing obedience of lower-ranking organs to superior ones, and ultimately, to the leader of the party. It is this democratic centralism that differentiates the Communist party from all other political parties, including the socialists. It is a practice that safeguards unity and militancy, necessary for a party committed to revolution and a dictatorship. The party is the "avant-garde" of the proletariat and the masses, leading them to socialism.

It would have seemed natural, therefore, for the European communist parties with their new profession of faith in democracy to have relaxed a rigorous application of democratic centralism and to allow for an open and free debate within their ranks. This has not come to pass. In fact the French Communist party silences all internal criticisms and does not allow its daily newspaper to publish articles of party members critical of the leadership and suggesting new policies. The same has generally been the case with the Spanish and the Portuguese Communist parties, and even of the Italian Party. The Eurocommunist parties do not seem ready to abandon their tight organization, discipline, and leadership control.

National Communism?

Ever since the death of Stalin the control of the Soviet Communist party over all European communist parties has progressively weakened. National forces, as we have seen first with Tito, weakened Soviet control until it had to be reaffirmed through military intervention — in Hungary in 1956 and again in Czechoslovakia in 1968. But Western European communist parties, the Italian one first and foremost, began to reassert their own intellectual and political independence to develop their program and their course of action. Communism should manifest itself in its national colors, independent of Moscow.

A National Foreign Policy?

Will Eurocommunist parties in the name of the rediscovery of their "national colors" defend foreign policies independent of Soviet ones and even contrary to them? Or will they stay close to their previous line by identifying the interests of communism and the working class with the interests and policies of the Soviet Union? This may well be the ultimate test of the genuineness of the professed independence of the communist parties.

No clear answers can be given as yet. The establishment of a military dictatorship in Poland with the full support of the Soviet leadership in December 1981, however, may give us a clue — especially since the dictatorship had been directed against the newly formed Polish Trade Union, Solidarity. The French Communist party led the way for many European Communist parties — including those of Portugal and Greece — in fully condoning the military coup and in giving its full support to the Soviet Union. (The French Communist leaders had also supported the Soviet military invasion of Afghanistan in December 1980). On the other hand, the Italian Communist party sharply criticized the Soviet Union (as they also had done for the invasion of Afghanistan) and virtually accused the Soviet leadership of imperialist practices. The Spanish Communist party followed the Italian lead. However, it has been going through a severe internal crisis during which its leader and the foremost exponent of Eurocommunism, Santiago Carrillo, was forced to resign. Similarly a pro-Soviet faction is gaining strength within the Italian Communist party. Thus, "Eurocommunism" is still torn between its Soviet attachment and its search for a truly European and independent stance.

Communism and the Third World

It remains now to discuss the appeal of communism and the extent of the adoption of its political and economic organization by the leaders of new nations, mostly in Africa and Asia.

There are a number of reasons which lead one to expect a rapid spread of the Communist model, especially the Leninist, among new nations. It provided a way to rapidly mobilize the population. It suggested a way to industrialize and modernize, as Stalin had done, through collectivization, nationalization, and economic planning. So in the 1950s and 1960s many colonial leaders claimed to be Marxists and Leninists. The revolution was a matter of political organization, they claimed — a matter of leadership capable of exploiting and marshaling the moral indignation of the colonial peoples against their masters. Both Castro and Ché Guevara felt that this should be the basis for revolution in Latin America, where the proximity of the United States and its "colonial" practices, in cooperation with despotic and corrupt regimes, accounted for a spirit of moral indignation and deep resentment. Some of the more sophisticated of the colonial leaders began to look beyond Lenin into some of the early works of Marx where revolution had its sources in a moral protest against deprivation and exploitation.

Emphasis upon will and organization, the appeal to moral imperatives, the support of the peasantry — all these led to the concoction of a "doctrine" in terms of which some colonial revolutionary leaders called themselves Marxist and Leninist and waged war to gain their independence. In so doing they were, of course, cooperating fully with other social and political groups and leaders for whom national independence, not communism, was the primary consideration. The question of the applicability of the Communist model came, therefore, with special urgency *after* independence had been proclaimed and after the colonial powers in India, Burma, Malaysia, Indonesia, the whole of Africa, and most of the Middle East had withdrawn. In some of these countries communism has been a negligible force; in others, lip service has been paid to the Communist doctrine; only in a few has a fairly strong and politically conscious Communist leadership and an organized Communist party developed. In most, the Communist doctrine has been used to hide military authoritarian regimes — as, for instance, in Ethiopia.

A Communist regime that was an approximation of the Soviet model established itself only in very few countries. Vietnam is one; Castro's Cuba is another — but it is only an approximation. So, too, Chinese communism has, as we have seen, basic differences from the Soviet model. In Indonesia, the Communist party came close to assuming a controlling position in the government and establishing a one-party rule, but it was crushed. In the whole of the Middle East, the only country with a legalized Communist party is Israel. In Africa there is hardly anywhere a Communist party, though some political leaders call themselves Marxists. In Burma and Malaysia the Communists have been outlawed.

In most of these countries the doctrine proclaimed favors the establishment of some form of "humanistic" or "democratic" socialism in which the State claims to control the major economic activities without, however, eliminating the market economy. But in virtually all of them there is a one-party system representing, as we pointed out, "democratic" unity and "communitarian" values.

Thus, one might conclude that the Soviet model, important in shaping the doctrine and the organization that led to guerrilla warfare and to independence, has not been adopted by most of the new nations, nor has it been radically modified to suit specific circumstances. The reasons are many. First and foremost was the problem of national integration and consolidation after liberation. The Stalinist model, based upon indoctrination and a well-organized party and force, could not be used. There were, simply, no well-organized communist parties; it was difficult to indoctrinate illiterate and apathetic groups; and, finally, the very use of force might split the population of the new nations into their tribal or ethnic, linguistic, or religious components, rather than uniting it. "Nation-building" can be accomplished by force only when there is a powerful group or party that can use it and impose it.

Secondly, communism as a set of tactics developed by Lenin was welcome to many, but not as a way of life. Most of the African elites viewed their struggle for liberation in moral and religious terms, and sometimes even in the liberal terms in which nationalism had been couched in Europe in the nineteenth century. Marxism-Leninism was "materialist" and "atheistic." But for a good number of Asian, African, and Moslem leaders, it was "another religion" that would not tolerate the existing ones. It was, therefore, unacceptable.

Finally, there were practical considerations stemming from the international political situation and the willingness on the part of the Soviet Union and the United States to offer economic aid. Former colonies maintained ties with the colonial powers: France, for instance, very quickly renegotiated economic, cultural, and military accords after the independence of its African colonies. The same applied to some of the British colonies in Africa in their relations with Britain. American business groups, as well as the American government, had every reason to invest or to give aid so that the new countries would not turn to the Soviet Union. Whatever the affinities were, therefore, between the new leaders of the new nations and the Soviet Union (and there was a debt to the Soviets for the moral and often material support given to them during their independence struggle), it would have been unwise to abandon the ties with the capitalist and democratic west. In fact, as the years went on after independence the Soviet leaders did not show themselves to be particularly generous nor did they provide aid, whether economic or military, without attaching strings. Aid was often clearly subordinated to Soviet strategic considerations.

Ideologies and institutional practices are not easy to import. Democracy has been reinterpreted by the new nations and differs greatly from its original meaning; so, in many instances, has communism. Democratic institutions virtually do not exist in the Third World, but similarly, the one-party system adopted by many of the new states has no resemblance to the Leninist conception of the party nor to Stalinist practice. The new nations are still in the process of developing their own political ideologies by adapting Western ones to their own needs, and their own political culture.

Communism in Crisis

Like the crisis of democracy, and of the democratic and socialist regimes that we discussed, communism and the various communist regimes also seem to be going through a crisis — perhaps an even more serious one. It is a crisis of their economies, a crisis in ideology, and a crisis in their political institutions and structures. To paraphrase the famous battle cry of Marx, today the specter of democracy seems to haunt the Communist world!

By the time Stalin died in 1953 the Soviet economy seemed to have successfully gone through the stages of what might be called primitive industrialization, as they had made massive investment in capital goods to produce steel, iron, cement, oil, coal, and the like. But the technological revolution of the sixties and seventies in Western Europe, Japan, and the United States has left the Soviets behind. Central planning, nationalization of the economy, bureaucratic controls — the Soviet "model" — has not fared well. It has failed in agriculture and in technological modernization and has proven pitifully inadequate in satisfying consumer demand and the production of durable consumer goods. The Soviet Union is beginning to depend on the West not only for wheat and corn, but also for technology. The bureaucratic centralization of the economy has created serious problems of distribution. A number of communist regimes, Hungary, for instance (to say nothing of the efforts that were made in the same direction in Czechoslovakia and Poland), have undertaken extensive decentralization and have introduced individual incentives including the profit motive. China seems to be moving in the same direction, and we have discussed the Yugoslav model briefly.

But even more significant is the crisis in Communist ideology. It is comparable in many ways to the crisis of Marxism in the decades before World War I. In great part it is due to the resurgence of nationalism — a resurgence to which the Soviet Communist leaders contributed. "National-communisms" and various self-styled national Communist regimes have broken from the Communist international movement and its common ideological and political front. After World War II, both the efforts to bring together the Communist regimes and parties under Soviet control and leadership and the efforts to impose the Soviet model of Communism upon all other parties and Communist regimes have failed.

The crisis in communism intensified after the Twentieth Party Congress of the Communist party of the Soviet Union in 1956. It abandoned the commitment to revolution in favor of a commitment to the search for peaceful means to realize socialism and agreed that there were many and different Communist regimes — what is often referred to as "polycentrism." All efforts to maintain the primacy of the Soviet Union were unsuccessful. The same was true in the Third World where, even in the name of Marxism, nonsocialist institutions and practices prevail. Relations with the Soviet Union are based primarily on strategic, economic, and military realities and imperatives rather than on ideological ones.

But for many, it was the political arrangements and institutions in the Soviet Union and Eastern Europe that began to provide the major reason for discontent and disaffection. For a long time Western intellectuals accepted Stalin's rule and the terror associated with it as necessary to bring about economic well-being and equality. Political freedoms were to be put on ice. But with the revelations of what Stalin's dictatorship was — capricious, despotic, and inhuman — even some of the most ardent pro-Soviet Communist ideologues were profoundly shaken. Even the most skilled dialecticians began to doubt that Soviet communism was a one-way ticket to a better world. And most began to fear the journey! Many began to flaunt the Soviet model — even those from the left — and demands for genuine pluralism and democracy, decentralization of power, and accountability of the officeholders became more pronounced. The imposition of a military dictatorship with Soviet support in Poland in 1981 was "the last straw," for many.

The deepening of the political, economic, and ideological crisis in the Communist world, and among all those who professed the Communist ideology and claimed to be united by it, is both sharpened and obscured by one overriding reality — the growth of the Soviet military power. Sheer power in the international arena silences the critics of the Soviet system and stifles the voices of dissenters abroad and at home. As ideological mobilization begins to weaken, Soviet power is used in its place as an instrument of governance and domination. This is the crisis that the Soviet Communist regime faces today — a crisis that may spread far and wide in the communist world. For power without ideology to support it and to mobilize people means, in the last analysis, a crisis in legitimacy and authority that may lead to an increased use of force. The crisis may come to a head when those who give orders and directives find themselves and their orders either ignored or disobeyed. The Soviet leaders and the leaders of communist regimes elsewhere may find themselves in this situation in the near future.

Bibliography

Bicanic, Rudolf. *Economic Policy in Socialist Yugoslavia.* New York: Cambridge U.P., 1973.

Carrillo, Santiago. *Eurocommunism and the State.* New York: Lawrence Hill, 1978.

Dedijer, Vladimir. *Tito Speaks.* London: Weidenfeld and Nicolson, 1953.

Denitch, Bogdan. *The Legitimization of a Revolution: The Yugoslav Case.* New Haven, Conn.: Yale U.P., 1972.

Drachkovitch, Milorad (ed.). *Marxism in the Modern World.* Stanford, Calif.: Stanford U.P., 1965.

Fitzgerald, C. P. *Mao Tse-tung and China.* New York: Homer and Meir, 1976.

Griffith, Samuel B. *Mao Tse-tung: On Guerrilla Warfare.* New York: Praeger, 1961.

Griffith, William E. (ed.). *Communism in Europe.* 2 volumes. Cambridge, Mass.: M.I.T. Press, 1967.

Kaplan, Morton A. *The Many Faces of Communism.* New York: Free Press, 1978.

Lange, Peter and Vannicelli, Maurizio. *The Communist Parties of Italy, France and Spain: Postwar Change and Continuity: A Casebook.* Winchester, Mass.: Allen & Unwin, Inc., 1981.

Mao Tse-tung. *Selected Readings from the Works of Mao Tse-tung.* Peking: Foreign Languages Press, 1971.

Schram, Stuart (ed.). *The Political Thought of Mao Tse-tung.* New York: Praeger, 1963.

Townsend, James R. *Politics in China.* Boston: Little, Brown, 1974.

Ulam, Adam. *Titoism and the Cominform.* Cambridge, Mass.: Harvard U.P., 1952.

Urban, G. R. (ed.). *Eurocommunism: Its Roots and Future in Italy and Elsewhere.* New York: Universe, 1978.

Part Three

Nazism and Fascism: The Totalitarian Right

Preventing the sick from making the healthy sick . . . this ought to be our supreme object in this world . . . . But for this it is above all essential that the healthy should remain separate from the sick, that they should not even associate with the sick . . .

NIETZSCHE   The Genealogy of Morals

Nazism and fascism, like the other totalitarian regimes that developed in Europe and elsewhere after World War I, had deep roots. They did not spring from the wickedness of a leader such as Hitler; they were not the product of deviant personalities; they were not initiated by adventurers and veterans of World War I seeking redemption from defeat or boredom. In fact, they were well-organized and well-structured political movements representing, at one and the same time, a very powerful reaction against both liberal democracy and communism and the communist parties that had developed in the wake of the Bolshevik Revolution. They were movements that reaffirmed, in the strongest possible terms, national solidarity and unity, order and discipline. They drew heavily from the body of anti-democratic and anti-liberal thought, and from the ideology and practice of Leninism.

In other words, right-wing totalitarian movements and regimes cannot be dismissed as exceptions to the democratic norm any more than communist totalitarian systems. They drew their inspiration, whatever the specific historical circumstances that brought them to power, from deep roots that had been planted in fertile soil. These roots have not yet been fully removed. We must not consider Nazism and fascism something that happened in the past and should be forgotten but as a political ideology which is still with us.

8 | *Nazism and Fascism: The Background*

*(Fascism) . . . is the general reaction of modern
times against the flabby materialistic positivism of the
nineteenth century.*

BENITO MUSSOLINI   The Doctrine of Fascism

Right-wing totalitarian movements like those of the Nazis and fascists developed everywhere in Europe soon after World War I. They spread to Central Europe, Portugal, Spain, and the Balkans in the 1930s. They affected countries with strong democratic traditions like France, and even England. Liberal democracy was threatened everywhere.

The new regimes did away with some of the most basic freedoms that the civilized world had built up over many centuries. They proclaimed force at home and war in the international community as the highest of values. Their discrimination against certain races, nations, and creeds was taken to the point of not only advocating, but actually implementing their methodical destruction.

Right-wing totalitarianism, as has often been pointed out, is couched in terms of negative themes — it is "anti" so many things: against liberalism, against individualism, against reason, against equality, against parliamentary institutions, against democracy, against international law, against the bourgeois society and its culture, and against big cities. The twentieth-century right-wing movements signified a culmination and a synthesis of a multiplicity of "antis," most of which were developed throughout the nineteenth century, side by side with the development of liberal democratic thought and democratic regimes. They are also based upon a body of thought that is deeply anti-rational, stressing the importance of emotions and intuition as opposed to scientific inquiry and reason, and seeking to find in communitarian values and solidarity the key to political obligations and stability.

172

The Intellectual Roots

Many authors and philosophers, sociologists, anthropologists, and political scientists contributed to the formulation of an anti-liberal and anti-democratic body of doctrine. Some would have taken pride in the movements and regimes that borrowed from their thinking; others would have rejected them outright as a gross distortion of what they had thought, written, and taught. The major ideas used by the right-wing parties were elitism, racialism, Social Darwinism, irrationalism, the exaltation of violence, the notion that the group has a reality superseding that of the individual, and nationalism. Lenin's conception of a revolutionary party based upon will also played an important role, as did the reaction against industrialization by many social groups who felt threatened by it, and by the impersonality of a mass society.

Elitism

Liberal assumptions of equality and participation had not been accepted by many conservatives. The latter spoke in terms of natural leaders, that is, persons with special endowments and with a special stake in the country due to which they would have special leadership roles. Throughout the nineteenth century a number of authors advanced new arguments to justify the rule of the few, whether by government or by an elite, but the majority was simply incapable of self-government.

Elites derive superiority from intelligence, knowledge, manipulative skills, or from sheer physical courage. One sociologist distinguishes between gifted individuals and the mass of mediocrities who follow them.[1] He asserts that competition takes place only among elites — the people follow like sheep. Democracy, he claims, is nonsense, a better name for it would be "mobocracy." Robert Michels, in a much-quoted book on political parties, has observed and documented the same phenomenon of elitism within socialist parties that claimed to be open, egalitarian, and democratic.[2] They were run by an elite. In all such organizations there is an "iron law" of oligarchy.

The German philosopher Nietzsche reached even more extreme conclusions. He identified leadership with the "heroic man" who has the will to power and the desire to dominate. The "superman," he predicted, would emerge and rise to power to impose his law and his will upon the "spineless multitude" with its Christian "slave morality." The future belonged to heroes unconstrained by law and conventional morality who would set their own morality and make their own law for all to follow. Lenin, too, without subscribing to the "superman" theory, emphasized that only a few, an elite, could organize the Communist party and speak on behalf of the workers and lead them to the promised land of communism.

1. Vilfredo Pareto. *The Mind and Society.* New York: Dowe, 1963.
2. Robert Michels. *Political Parties.* New York: Free Press, 1962.

Irrationalism

Early in the nineteenth century another German philosopher wrote a book characteristically enough entitled *The World as Will and Idea*.[3] It began with the ominous phrase, "The world is my idea. . . ." What this means is that rational and scientific discourse is inadequate to provide us with the understanding of the world surrounding us and that "knowledge" is a matter of intuitive communication that alone can provide full "understanding." Knowledge thus becomes entirely subjective. Much later, the French philosopher Bergson also stressed the intuitive aspects of learning — the mystical communication of the subject with the outside object.[4] It is thanks to intuition that we "know" an object by "entering into it." Science, reason, measurements, observation give us only a relative, partial, and fragmented knowledge; intuition supplies an "absolute" one. . . . "The spirit has never had more violence done to it than when mere numbers made themselves its master," wrote Adolf Hitler.

Myths and Violence

But what is the relevance of intuition or instinct to politics? Simply that logic, persuasion, and argument cannot move people and cannot sustain a political system. In politics the counterpart of intuition is the "myth," that is, an idea, a symbol, a slogan that moves people into action because it appeals to their emotions. They become attached to it and they feel for it. The "crowd" or the "masses" act and can be much more easily moved when their emotions are aroused. They act in terms of stereotypes, prejudices, and instincts, not in terms of reason and proof. The myth unites them and gives purpose and meaning to their lives far better than logical exposition and reasoning. After all, it was the great philosopher Plato who had defined a myth as a "golden lie" to be propagated by the philosopher king in order to keep the people united and under control. All people were to be taught that they were brothers and sisters because they had the same parents, and were to accept inequalities as natural. Myths can take a variety of forms — racial supremacy, racial purity, national superiority and strength, the dictatorship of the proletariat, the resurrection of ancient empires, the reassertion of tribal bonds, the emergence of the superman, and so on.

Georges Sorel, the French revolutionary syndicalist, used the myth explicitly as a vehicle for moral, economic, and social revival.[5] The myth that he considered as potent as the Christian belief in the Second Coming, was that of the general strike, by which he meant the development of a state of mind among the workers favoring the violent destruction of the existing social order. Violence would organize the workers, form the battle lines, and

3. Arthur Schopenhauer. *The World as Will and Idea.* Translated by E. P. Payne, New York: Dover, 1968.
4. Henri Bergson. *The Two Sources of Morality and Religion.* Notre Dame, Ind.: University of Notre Dame Press, p. 177.
5. Georges Sorel. *Reflections on Violence.* New York: Macmillan, 1961.

marshal them to war against the society. Their "sentiments," properly aroused by an elite, would lead to revolution. The myth of the general strike, therefore, called for a state of permanent violence. Violence, Sorel argued, is ennobling in itself, but it also helps people develop the moral courage to distinguish them from bourgeois cowardice and rationality. He wrote:

> Proletarian violence, carried on as pure and simple manifestation of the sentiments of class war, appears . . . a very fine and heroic thing; it is at the service of the immemorial interests of civilization . . . It may . . . save the world from barbarism.[6]

Lenin never accepted Sorel's overall philosophy, but he nonetheless endorsed the need for violence.

Social Darwinism

Charles Darwin's theory of evolution and the notion of the survival of the fittest was quickly, and unwarrantedly, transferred to the social and the international order. In its new setting it became known as Social Darwinism. According to Darwin, "survival" means that some species survive while others perish in the course of adjusting, or failing to adjust, to the environment and to each other. Transposed to human society the term was taken to mean that those who manage to survive or to succeed are superior to those who are unsuccessful or perish. Conflict between individuals and groups, and especially races and nations was declared, therefore, to be a natural and necessary process for the selection of the best and the elimination of the weak and incompetent. The elites in power arrive at their position through struggle; but they are likely to be displaced through struggle if they begin to lose the qualities that brought them to the top. The struggle for survival is likely to affect them just as it affected the dinosaurs.

Social Darwinism had been used by liberals to justify economic competition and economic individualism. Right-wing totalitarianism used it to justify competition and conflict, especially among elite races and nations, and to legitimize the supremacy of some individuals on the grounds of biological superiority. Some nations are considered superior to others and need more territory than others; some races are considered superior to others. Those that are superior are the "master race," while those that are inferior are the "slave races."

Throughout the nineteenth century, sympathy for racial theories was widespread, and Social Darwinism reinforced previously developed racist theories. French and British authors had discoursed on racial differences and were responsible for the establishment of cultural, biological, and moral criteria of superiority and inferiority. They concluded that the white race, and some of its various branches, was superior. The Nazi regime came to a

---

6. Cited in Lane W. Lancaster. *Masters of Political Thought*. Vol. 3. Boston: Houghton Mifflin, p. 296.

Concentration camps; death camps; prisons and cemeteries. This photo
taken at Auschwitz is a poignant reminder of what the "One Thousand
Year Reich" would have meant for all of us. (*Photo: Stock Boston/Berndt*)

most horrifying decision to exterminate the Jews — a fate that was also reserved for other "inferior races."

The Group Mind

As we pointed out, liberalism freed individuals from all attachments to
groups and status that defined and structured their activities. The individual became the driving force within the social and political system. The
formation of associations, and even the existence of the State, was traced
ultimately to contractual and voluntary relations and individual consent.
There was nothing "real" outside of the individual, to whose will, consent,
and rationality all economic, political, and social institutions were traced.
Throughout the nineteenth century, however, this position was strongly contested by those who argued that "individuals," as such, were a mere fiction,
and that their ideas and values, and ultimately their reasoning, derived from
group values. Marx argued, too, that individual attitudes and ideas were
determined by the class to which an individual belonged.

Anthropologists and sociologists claimed to have discovered the "group
mind" in tribal groups. People living in tribal societies could not clearly
distinguish between "I" and "we"; individual morality, value judgments and
attitudes, coincided fully with tribal or collective values and attitudes. In this

way the group was larger than its parts, the individuals, and preceded them. Even more, group and collective ideas had a coercive character: the individuals were constrained by them, and their lives were to be understood only in terms of conformity and compliance to such groups. It was group solidarity, not individual morality, that counted most.

Thus, studying and understanding groups was a better way of understanding society than studying the individual who was nothing else but the sum total of the group images and pressures weighing upon him. Only the group was real. It took but one step to move to larger collectivities, notably the nation. The nation was real and not the individuals who made it; the morality of the nation was the morality of the individual; individual judgments had to yield to national judgments and imperatives. Thus, the nation and nationalism became a superior moral force.

Escape from Freedom

Erich Fromm published a melancholic book in 1941, entitled *Escape from Freedom*. He claimed that there was one basic psychological need that liberalism had ignored. It was the individual's desire to belong, to be attached to groups or to hierarchies that make decisions, and to be part of the whole with fixed obligations to it and fixed rights deriving from it. Feudalism had provided such a setting, and its destruction had uprooted the individuals from their traditional groupings. Individuals found themselves desperately in need of similar ties to anchor their existence — ties that liberalism and industrialization had broken. Totalitarianism was, in essence, a return to group values and to authority; it was a response to the intense need for "belongingness," which, he claimed, was much stronger than reason and self-interest. Liberalism, therefore, and the historical phase of liberalism were nothing but an interlude between the structured life of the feudal society of the past and the subjection to the totalitarian regimes of the future. The latter amounted to a revolt of the individuals against the burdens of freedom and free choice that liberalism had imposed upon them.

Against the Bourgeois Mentality

Bourgeois values were a major target of criticism throughout the nineteenth century. The peaceful but unheroic existence of the citizen; the constant search for material gains and satisfactions; the compromising spirit that democratic liberalism fosters; the smugness of the wealthy and their ability to manipulate representative institutions to their advantage, while paying lip service to equality and freedom; the subordination of all values to material considerations — all this was repugnant to many intellectuals and philosophers, as well as workers. In a reaction, many writers extolled courage, violence, emotions, and instincts. They sought to find new binding ties in common adventures that liberalism downgraded and to help the "true" individual realize himself or herself; to find a way of life that was closer to nature

The "group mind" in action: the Führer arrives at a mass rally, Nuremburg, 1935. (*Photo: Wide World Photos*)

but farther away from reason; closer to instinct and intuition but farther away from material interests; closer to feeling but away from science. It was, in essence, an exaltation of bygone romantic values of valor, adventure and physical strength.

The Historical Setting

As we have pointed out, ideas may hibernate for a long time until the right conditions bring them back to life and transform them into political ideologies and movements. This was the case with the anti-liberal and anti-democratic ideas outlined above. Until World War I, democratic liberalism and democratic liberal regimes remained strong. Even socialist parties had joined, for all practical purposes, democratic parties and regimes. Right-wing extremist movements received only little support.

It took two major upheavals to transform totalitarian ideologies into powerful movements and for liberal democracy to find itself on the defensive almost everywhere.

World War I

World War I accounted for an unprecedented destruction, loss of life, and socioeconomic and political upheavals throughout Europe. It spawned bitterness and distrust in the political institutions of almost all countries involved — both the defeated and the victorious, with the possible exception of England and the United States. In Russia it created the conditions that accounted for the triumph of the Bolshevik Revolution in November 1917. In Germany the semiauthoritarian system collapsed to give place to a democratic constitution, but conditions remained chaotic and democracy was never given a genuine chance to gain respectability. Defeat haunted many Germans, and the democratic constitution established in 1918 was for them the symbol of defeat. In France a strong communist faction emerged and divisions between the left and the right became sharper. Italy (a latecomer in the war on the side of the victorious powers) felt betrayed by its allies when it came to the final settlement at the Treaty of Versailles. In Central and Eastern Europe extreme left-wing radicalism, often supported by Russian communism, alternated for a while with right-wing authoritarian reactions.

The war brought forth new popular demands and had serious political implications. The people of all nations had been mobilized into the war effort. They fought for four years in the trenches where a new spirit of egalitarianism and camaraderie had been fashioned and where distinctions of birth, wealth, and education had been blurred. Wartime sacrifices were translated into demands for a better life and more comforts, and these were pressed hard on national governments. Failure to provide them brought quick political reaction, and more often direct and violent action. Resentment increased and took the form of left- or right-wing extremism. In some countries, as in Russia, the "system" broke down; in others, notably in Germany, inflation deprived a great number of people (particularly the middle classes) of their savings and their pensions, and dislocated economic activity. The liberal democratic states seemed unable to cope.

The Great Depression

It is against this background that the Great Depression of 1929 should be assessed. The depression was particularly severe in Germany, where almost half the labor force found itself without jobs. But throughout the whole of Central Europe, as well as in France and England, unemployment spread.

The faith in liberal economic and political institutions was severely shaken. For the left, depression was a clear indication that Marx had been right in forseeing the collapse of capitalism. For the right wing, the depression was an equally clear manifestation that liberal economic and political institutions could no longer function. A new formula was needed, avoiding both Marxist revolutionary politics and putting an end to economic liberalism.

The remedy suggested was that of a strong State which would overcome internal divisions and cleavages. A new economic system, it would set aside private interests and even private profit in favor of unity and cooperation with common social and national goals. It was the formula used in Italy by the fascists and in Germany by the Nazis, and by all other right-wing nationalist movements throughout Europe.

Because of the depression 'it appealed to a growing number of people and voters. Unemployed workers, farmers, the lower middle classes, and particularly the middle classes, war veterans, university students, found the combination of nationalist and unifying slogans, together with the promise of economic reform, irresistible. Status quo groups, fearing loss of status, joined forces with the disaffected, the romantics, the nationalists, and the unemployed. During the depression, right-wing extremism swelled into powerful political movements everywhere.

Special Reasons

There were other reasons for right-wing totalitarianism's victorious emergence in Italy and Germany. In both countries, but also in many others that followed their example, democracy had never gained legitimacy. Elites, intellectuals, associations, and interest groups never developed a strong working attachment to democratic regimes. They had not become integrated into the system. Neither the educational system nor the family socialized the young into the principles and practices of democracy. As a result, both the Italian Republic and the German democratic constitution were faced with hostility and indifference rather than with affection and support. Nationalism in both countries remained a powerful force. Germany's defeat and the nonrealization of national claims for Italy intensified the two countries' search for nationalist solutions.

The economic difficulties facing these countries right after the war and the inability of their political institutions to cope with them, to provide employment and to arrest inflation, further undermined whatever attachment the people had to democracy.

Similarly, the existence of strong communist parties in both countries played a dominant role. A sharp reaction against them was couched in strong nationalist terms. There was also a strong resentment against the Versailles Treaty that settled the war, imposed heavy preparation payments upon Germany, and gave the victorious powers — England, France and the United States — a dominant position in world affairs.

If we review the various factors that accounted for the coming and spread of right-wing totalitarianism in a number of European countries, we find the following:

1. Defeat or feeling of deprivation in and after World War I.
2. Intensification of nationalism because of the relatively late national unification (Italy and Germany).

3. Inflation, unemployment, and in general, economic depression.
4. Loss of status among low-middle and middle classes or fear of further deterioration of their position.
5. Fear of strong communist and revolutionary movements and parties.
6. Reaction against the international order and the settlement after World War I.
7. Lack of legitimacy of democratic institutions.

Thus the stage had been set for the eruption of powerful anti-democratic and anti-liberal totalitarian mass movements. The individual and the individualistic ethic, which had hardly come into their own, were shoved aside in the name of the group, the party, and the nation. What Aristotle had termed "reason without passion" — the law — to regulate human intercourse and to safeguard peaceful and stable relationships, was to become a laughing stock subject to the whim and caprice of political leaders and tyrants.

Bibliography

Adorno, T. W., et al. *The Authoritarian Personality*. New York: Norton, 1969.

Arendt, Hanna. *The Origins of Totalitarianism*. New York: Harcourt Brace and World, 1968.

Delzell, Charles F. (ed.). *Mediterranean Fascism 1919–1949*. New York: Walker and Co., 1971.

Fromm, Erich. *Escape From Freedom*. New York: Avon Books, 1965.

Gregor, James A. *The Ideology of Fascism*. New York: Free Press, 1969.

Laqueur, Walter (ed.). *Fascism: A Reader's Guide*. Berkeley: University of California Press, 1976.

Mosse, George C. *Crisis of German Ideology: Intellectual Origins of the Third Reich*. New York: Fertig, 1978.

Nietzsche, Friedrich. *Beyond Good and Evil*. New York: Vintage, 1956.

———. *Thus Spoke Zarathustra*. Baltimore: Penguin, 1961.

———. *The Will to Power*. New York: Vintage, 1968.

Oakeshott, Michael. *The Social and Political Doctrines of Contemporary Europe*. New York: Cambridge U.P., 1942.

Talmon, J. L. *The Origins of Totalitarian Democracy*. New York: Norton, 1970.

Weber, Eugen. *Varieties of Fascism*. New York: Van Nostrand, 1964.

Woolf, S. J. (ed.). *European Fascism*. New York: Vintage, 1969.

9 | *Nazism and Fascism: Ideologies and Regimes*

For the Weltanshauung (*the ideology*) *is intolerant
. . . and peremptorily demands its own, exclusive,
and complete recognition as well as the complete
adaptation of public life to its ideas.*

ADOLF HITLER   Mein Kampf

The intellectual background of anti-liberal and anti-democratic thought and the particular historical circumstances of Europe after World War I affected all nations — particularly Germany and Italy. It is in these two countries that the special reasons we mentioned triggered powerful totalitarian movements. It is to these two movements and regimes, the Nazis and the fascists, that we turn now.

The Nazi movement and regime are discussed first, despite the fact that the Italian fascists came to power a decade earlier, because Nazism was far more "successful' in accomplishing what it professed. Italian fascism was less comprehensive and far less effective in mobilizing society. But the Nazis managed to bring virtually all Germans and all elements of German society under their control. Germans were made to "march in step" to the tune of the Nazi party. This was the meaning of the famous term *gleichschaltung* — the "synchronization" of all aspects of social life with the political ideology and objectives of the Nazi party. Not so in fascist Italy. Many did not march at all, while others dragged their feet, and still others marched to different tunes than the one played by the Fascist party. It was said that the Italian fascists made the Italian trains run on time; Hitler and the Nazis led the nation to run in unison into disaster.

German Totalitarianism

A historian of Germany entitles his chapter on German National Socialism "Germany goes berserk."[1] It is only a mild comment on what occurred in one of the most advanced and civilized nations of the world.

Nazism, better than anything else shows the immense power of ideas and the degree to which citizens can be manipulated, not simply into submis-

1. K. S. Pinson. *Modern Germany* 2nd ed. New York: Macmillan, 1966.

sion but also into frenzied action. It should be a constant reminder to all of us — no matter how special the conditions in Germany appear to have been — how fragile the bonds of reason and law are and how vulnerable, under certain circumstances, we *all* may be to political fanaticism.

German totalitarianism became a political reality when the leader of the National Socialist Workers' German party, Adolf Hitler, came to power in January 1933. Hitler immediately set about organizing the new system, the Third Reich,[2] implementing many of the promises he had made. Most notably these included the abolition of the institutions of democracy and the preparation for an expansionist war to establish German world-wide domination.

The Road to Power

The beginnings of the Hitler movement can be traced directly to the aftermath of World War I, and also to the rich background of German anti-democratic literature and right-wing political extremism. Nazism was both nationalistic and racist and also had a strong streak of a populist appeal that was both communitarian and egalitarian. Many nationalists traced the political system they favored to the early German tribes, where direct democracy had been practiced among warriors who were bound together by ties of common blood and common sacrifice and effort.

Defeat in World War I caused a great disillusionment, and in time, a desire for revenge. The discontent was focused on the Versailles Treaty which had stripped Germany of its colonies and imposed a heavy burden of reparations, but there were other factors. First, the galloping inflation of the early 1920s was unprecedented in the economic history of any nation. The inflation wiped out savings, pensions, trust funds, and made salaries and wages dwindle with the passage of every day, week, and month. It created a state of acute panic among the middle classes.

A second important factor was the reaction to Communist revolutionary movements. Revolutions actually took place right after World War I, and Communist regimes were installed temporarily in parts of Germany. Private groups and armies, led by officers and war veterans, took it upon themselves to stop the leftists. Often aided by the police and whatever remained of the German Army, they began to wage war against the Communists and their sympathizers. Many of these veterans and their organizations rallied to the Nazis and formed the hard core of the Nazi party.

The Nazi party was founded in 1921 as the extension of the German Workers' party (DAP) over which Hitler managed to gain control. Its original program included the usual nationalist and racist themes but also promised social and economic reforms that were downright socialist: land reform, nationalizations, and the "breaking of the shackles of capitalism." It also attacked the political and economic elites, and identified the "domestic" and "outside" enemies of Germany as the victorious powers of notably England

---

2. Third Reich was an expression intentionally used to indicate continuity with the German Empire (1871–1918) and the Holy Roman Empire.

Adolf Hitler (1889–1945)

The Führer, ironically enough, was a non-German. Hitler was born in Austria in 1889. A poor student given to prolonged moods of melancholia and daydreaming, he found himself in the army where he served with the rank of a corporal with apparent diligence and courage. Defeat enraged him and he sought scapegoats in the "cowardice" of the civilians and the "conspiracy" of the Jews. Without any formal education — he wanted to be an architect and had tried painting — he had read much of the great nationalist literature.

After World War I he found himself in Munich, capital of Bavaria, where he founded the NDASP (the Nazi party) in 1921. After the abortive effort to seize power in 1923, he received a light sentence and spent the months of his imprisonment writing what became the political bible of Nazism, *Mein Kampf* (My Struggle). It was the Depression and the frustrations and political conflict associated with it that provided the climate for his ascent to power. On January 30, 1933, President Hindenburg asked him to become Chancellor of Germany and he assumed full powers until his "Thousand Year Reich" ended with his suicide in the ruins of Berlin on April 30, 1945.

and France, the Jews and "international Jewry." It was a small party at first — a sect, with not more than a few thousand members as is quite typical of many other extremist nationalist groups. Few paid attention to its founding. When the economic situation improved, it seemed destined to oblivion — particularly so after 1923 when Hitler attempted to take over power by force in Munich. The coup failed dismally and Hitler found himself in jail and the party was outlawed.

In 1924, running in the legislative election under various camouflage labels, the Nazis managed to get thirty-two deputies elected in the legislature and received 6.5 percent of the national vote. Thereafter, its electoral fortunes declined: in the presidential election of 1925 the party's candidate, General Ludendorff, received only 200,000 votes, and in the legislative election of 1928 the party seemed to have been virtually wiped out, receiving only 2.6 percent of the national vote. After 1928, however, and especially after the depression of 1929, the Nazis began to make rapid gains and soon emerged as the strongest single party (see Table 9-1).

TABLE 9-1   Elections and the Nazi Vote

	LEGISLATIVE ELECTIONS	
1924 (May 4)	1,918,300 (32 deputies)	6.0%
1924 (Dec. 7)	907,300 (14 deputies)	3.0%
1928 (May 20)	810,000 (12 deputies)	2.6%
1930 (Sept. 14)	6,409,600 (107 deputies)	18.3%
1932 (July 31)	13,745,800 (230 deputies)	37.4%
1932 (Nov. 1)	11,737,000 (196 deputies)	33.1%
1933 (March 5) (Nazis in power)	17,277,200 (288 deputies)	43.9%
1933 (Nov. 12) (Nazis in control)	39,638,800 (661 deputies)	92.2%
	PRESIDENTIAL ELECTIONS	
1925	200,000 (Ludendorff)	
1932 (March) 1st ballot	11,339,288 (Hitler)	**30.1%**
2nd ballot	13,418,051 (Hitler)	**36.8%**

(From K. S. Pinson. *Modern Germany*, 2nd ed. N.Y.: Macmillan, 1966. By permission.)

There were a number of reasons for the rapid growth of the Nazi party. The party had managed not only to survive but become the sole spokesman of all right-wing extremist groups. Hitler had paid particular attention to its organization and managed to create what amounted to a paramilitary party. Leadership was consolidated in the hands of the leader — the Führer. Uniforms, a special salute, pomp and ritual, and above all, discipline and activism appealed to many, especially the young. In 1931, some 35 percent of the party members were below the age of thirty. Party membership began to grow — especially after 1928–1929 when there were about 100,000 members, to 1,200,000 by 1933, and up to about 2.5 million at the beginning of World War II.

Special shock formations were established. The SA (Brownshirts) and, after 1934, the SS (Black Guards) grew in numbers to almost equal the German army. At the slightest provocation they engaged in street fights or attacks against leftists and opposition leaders whose headquarters they sacked and burned. Anti-Semitic demonstrations and acts of violence were common. All this was testing the will of the Nazis, preparing them for further action and intimidation.

Yet Hitler and his associates pledged to respect "legality" and, in effect, promised not to use violence in order to come to power. Many political leaders believed them, especially among the conservative and centrist groups, thus allowing the Nazi party to operate. They were convinced that it would never receive a majority and that even if allowed to form a government it would abide by the constitution and act according to the rules and procedures of the parliamentary assemblies. After the 1932 election when the Nazis, 196 strong, entered the legislature, Hitler left no doubt at all as to what he meant by "legality." "We come as enemies," he wrote. "Like the wolf coming into a flock of sheep, that is how we come!"[3]

A number of front organizations were created to strengthen the party's appeal and to recruit more members and sympathizers. The Hitler Youth in 1931 numbered only about 100,000. In 1933–1934 it was close to about four million members and at the outbreak of the war almost nine million. In addition there was a Hitler Student League, an Officer's League, a Women's League, a workers' Nazi organization (the Labor Front), and many others representing every academic, social, and professional group in the country. The party gradually became a state within a state with its private army, tribunals, police, and military formations all spreading the Nazi doctrine far and wide and creating within Germany a strong Nazi subculture. It had its own cult, slogans, and morality; they were anti-republican, racist, and nationalist.

With the economic depression and the renewed fear of leftist revolutionary moves, the Nazis made the breakthrough that led them to power in 1933. They became a mass party as the election results show, but they also

---

3. Cited by Bracher. *The German Dictatorship*, p. 142. This, as I note in my preface, is an excellent account of Hitler's Germany, and I am indebted to the author for many of my observations.

attracted the attention and support of the conservative forces and of the army. The business community and the financial elites opened up their purse, and the party's treasury was again full. The Nazis and their leader broadened their appeal to catch, if possible, every group, every section, and every occupation and profession.

Nazi Pledges

To the farmers the Nazis promised "green democracy" and "soil-rooted" pure communitarian values as well as protection and subsidies. They pledged to uphold the rural values and traditions that were menaced by urbanization.

To the workers they promised jobs. Between 1929 and 1932 unemployment had shot up from one million to six million. Many employed and unemployed workers began to join the party and to vote for it. The depression had weakened the trade unions, and left-wing workers were hopelessly divided between socialism and communism.

To the army the Nazis promised rebuilding and an end to the Versailles Treaty.

To the middle classes, they promised special measures to arrest the decline of their income and give them security; above all, they promised to do away with the dangers from the left by eliminating communism. These promises appealed especially to the lower-middle classes — merchants, artisans, shopkeepers, civil service personnel, clerical personnel, and so on.

The Nazi party promised a special place to the young. The future was theirs. "Make room for us, you old ones," was one of their battle cries.

Propaganda was developed into a fine political art along clear-cut lines suggested by Hitler: repetition of the same simple slogans and themes; appeal to the emotions; propositions that clearly distinguished the negative from the positive — "this *is* the truth — *they* lie," "*we* can — *they* cannot"; simple answers to complex problems, i.e. "*we* shall solve unemployment by giving jobs to all": emphasis upon nationalism and national togetherness — *"we"* (Germans) against *"they"* (Jews, plutocrats, capitalists, communists, and so on). These propaganda themes were to be strengthened by direct action taken against opponents. Truth lay not in demonstration but in belief *and* in action. A Nazi was someone who believed and strengthened his belief by acting. Force became the best vindication of belief.

The use of violence by the various party members and by formations among the Hitler Youth, the SA, and the SS, was an integral part of Nazi ideology. Violence, as such, was attractive to some who would be recruited for the sheer pleasure of indulging in acts of terrorism and intimidation. But it was not a negative posture limited to destruction. It provided for psychological outlets; it was considered to be a creative form of expression. It gave an opportunity to the followers to test their courage, and to realize and clarify their ideas by making them prevail through physical force. Violence was the best medium to sharpen the lance of resolution as opposed to reasoning and persuasion. Finally, there was the ennobling experience of camaraderie in joint combat, and of the common sharing in common dangers. It was an

TABLE 9-2   Composition of the Nazi Party

	1930	1934	PERCENTAGE OF POPULATION
Working class	28%	32%	46
White collar	25.6	20.6	12.4
Independent business	20	20	9
Civil service and teachers	8.3	13	5
Farmers	14.7	10.7	9

(From K. Bracher. *The German Dictatorship*, N.Y.: Praeger, 1970, and Weidenfeld Publishers Ltd. Reprinted by permission.)

integral part of the recruitment and the domination of the biologically strong and virile people over their opponents and victims, and ultimately over all others.

The Nazi pledges were powerful. Party membership in 1930 and 1934 clearly shows that the Nazis had a wide appeal among virtually all groups (see Table 9-2). In the 1932 presidential election the Nazi candidate, none other than Hitler himself, received 36.8 percent of the vote. More than one third of German voters wanted him as their president!

Who were the German voters? The great majority of farmers voted for the Nazis as did the majority of the people living in small towns and, in general, in rural areas. Protestants tended to vote for them more than Catholics. A great percentage of the middle and the lower-middle classes voted Nazi. But so did four out of every ten workers and many among the unemployed.

Seymour Martin Lipset wrote that the "ideal type Nazi voter in 1932 was a middle class, self-employed Protestant who lived either on a farm or in a small town and who had previously voted for a centrist or a regionalist political party strongly opposed to the power and influence of big business and big labor."[4] Yet the Nazis received a sizeable working-class vote, even though trade unions, Socialists, and Communists remained, for a while, beyond their reach. The Nazi party had become, in 1932, a truly mass party.

The Nazi Ideology

Nazism as an ideology and a political movement began as a gesture of negation, but there was also the formulation of a number of "positive" themes and propositions on the basis of which the new society would be constructed. Some of them were addressed to the immediate situation, others to long-range social, economic, and political problems created by liberalism and the threat of communism.

Negative Themes   The negative themes were many:

1. *Against class struggle:* The notion of class, developed by Marx and endorsed by all communist parties, was inconsistent with national unity. As

4. Seymour Martin Lipset. *Political Man*. New York: Doubleday, 1963, p. 148.

such, it was only an extension of the idea of conflict and competition developed by liberals and Marxists. The Nazis claimed that the notion of class was incompatible with the communitarian values of the German people and the German nation. Germany was "one"!

2. *Against parliamentary government:* According to the Nazis, parliamentary government leads to the fragmentation of the body politic into parties and groups jockeying for position, compromising their particular interests, and forming unstable governmental coalitions. The "real" national interest was neglected. A common purpose could not develop from such a fragmentation of the national will. "There is no principle which . . . is as false as that of parliamentarianism," wrote Hitler in *Mein Kampf.*

3. *Anti-Trade Union:* Unions express the sectarian and class interests of the working class. However, the workers were also Germans and citizens. They had to be integrated into the community like all others instead of pitting themselves against other Germans.

4. *Against political parties:* Like representative government, political parties expressed special ideological or interest particularisms, splitting the nation. The national purpose called not for parties but for one movement, embodying it. Such a movement, even it it were called a party, should be given monopoly of representation. Hence, all other political parties should be outlawed, and a one-party system instituted.

5. *Against the Treaty of Versailles:* The Versailles Treaty, imposing an inferior status upon Germany that deprived it of its army and required it to pay reparations, had to be eliminated. But more than that, the existing international system that perpetuated the supremacy of some nations — notably England and France — should be drastically altered to give freedom and space to Germany.

There were a number of other comprehensive negative themes that inevitably blend with some of the "positive" formulations of the Nazis.

6. *Anti-Semitism and racialism:* Anti-Semitism had been a common phenomenon in many countries of Europe stemming from religious prejudices, cultural differences, and economic rivalries. The Jews were blamed as responsible for both liberal capitalism *and* for communism. There were extravagant myths attempting to show that the Jews were plotting the domination of the world. This was the case with a document (fabricated by nineteenth-century anti-Semites) called *The Protocols of the Elders of Zion,* in which the Jews were said to set forth their plans to conquer the world. This was widely used by the Nazis. They added a new twist however — that Jews were biologically inferior. They were therefore not only dangerous because of their ideas, their beliefs, and their plans to conquer the world (how inferior people could do it was never explained), but because their very presence within Germany endangered the purity of the German "race." There were only half a million Jews in Germany at the time Hitler assumed power over sixty-five million Germans — that is less than 0.7 percent. More than 200,000 Jews managed to escape the country by 1938. Those who remained were viewed as a germ just as virulent as botulism. It had to be insulated first and then exterminated.

As soon as the Nazis came to power, they began to reduce the German Jews to the status of nonpersons. They could not keep their businesses; they could not receive any social benefits. They were assigned special neighborhoods in which to live; they were constantly harassed and intimidated by the members of the Nazi party, the SA, and its various front organizations; they were arbitrarily arrested, could not engage in any gainful occupation, had their belongings confiscated, and were forced to pay special levies to the state authorities that invariably went to the Nazi party members. Intermarriage was prohibited, and existing intermarriages annulled. The Nazis developed the long-range policy of exterminating all Jews that led actually to the destruction of European Jewry wherever the Nazi armies gained a foothold.

Given its biological basis, German anti-Semitism left no room for compromise. But the same biological discrimination also threatened other groups and nations that the Nazis found dangerous or "impure" — Slavs, Blacks, and so on.

7. Anti-communism: If anti-Semitism derived from racist allegations, anti-communism stemmed primarily from political and international considerations. It was aimed not only against Communists at home, but against the "fatherland of communism," the Soviet Union. It called not only for the elimination of the German Communist party, but also for the elimination of international communism as spear-headed by the Soviet Union. The ideological crusade against communism would thus serve the secular strategic, economic, and geopolitical goals of Germany. It was part and parcel of the *Drag Nach Osten* — the drive eastward.

There were other reasons for anti-communism inherent in the totalitarian ideology of Nazism. The German Communist party was well-organized and disciplined. It also had an ultimate vision of total control, as did Soviet communism. There was an incompatibility, therefore, between two intensely ideological and inherently totalitarian movements. As soon as they came to power, the Nazis outlawed the Communist party, arrested its leaders and jailed and murdered many of them. The party was dismantled. The same fate awaited the Social Democrats, also a Marxist party in name, that had also opposed the Nazis. But it was not until 1941 that the main clash between the Soviet Union and the Nazi Germany took place, when the German armies invaded Russia.

"Positive" Themes Every negation advanced by the Nazis (what they planned to do away with) naturally called for an affirmation (what they planned to do instead). It is only in this sense, therefore, that I am using the term "positive".

Anti-Semitism suggests racialism and the purity of the race; anti-individualism, a communitarian ethic transcending the individual; anti-liberalism, a new political organization; and the anti-Versailles posture, the erection of some new kind of international order. It is the combination of the reasoning behind many of the negations that resulted in the new and dynamic synthesis of social and national life. No matter how morally repugnant, it must be analyzed and discussed if we are to understand the full and ominous implications of the Nazi movement and regime.

1. *Nationalism and racialism:* To understand the character of Nazi German nationalism we must distinguish it from other nationalist movements. There were liberal nationalist movements in the wake of the French Revolution of 1789 identifying with the principle of nationality and demanding that people sharing the same national background — a common history, culture, language, religion — live within a given territory, the nation-state. This is basically the principle of self-determination, allowing peoples to form their own State. There have also been conservative nationalist movements which have extolled national virtues and asserted their superiority over others; they stress national integration and unity at the expense of particularisms, regionalisms and even individual freedoms. But such nationalist movements are content to see the values they assert cultivated and strengthened within the nation-state. They are not expansionist.

Nazi nationalism was both racialist and expansionist. While naturally insisting on the superiority of Germanic values, it also proclaimed the superiority of the German race and the desirability of imposing its superiority upon others. Aryans were superior not only to Jews but also to Slavs, Turks, Greeks, French, and so on. And among the Aryans, the Germans were the superior race because they had managed and, thanks to the Nazis, forever intended, to keep their race "pure." They would not allow for a "mongrelization" similar to what they claimed had occurred in the United States. They were the *master race* destined to dominate all others. This racialist doctrine, coupled with extreme nationalism, led to the inevitability of war.

2. *Expansionism:* The valor of the race could not be proven by assertion only. It had to be demonstrated on the proving ground of war and conquest. The master race was to be a race of warriors subduing lesser races. Germany was to conquer and Berlin would become the capital of the world. But, in addition to racism, there were ideological, economic, and strategic reasons to justify an expansionist and warlike policy. A totalitarian system is "total" at home, in that it tries to subordinate everything to its ideology and control. It cannot allow competing units to exist. But the same is true in international terms. The logic of totalitarianism calls for the elimination of competing centers of power everywhere.

Economic reasons were also advanced. One was the notion of "proletarian" nations; another that of "living space." According to the former, World War I had allowed some nations to control the world's wealth — e.g., England, the United States, France — while other nations like Germany, Italy, and even Japan were poor, "proletarian," without colonies, raw materials, and resources. Similarly, some nations had ample space at their disposal: the French, British, and Dutch had their colonial empires. The Soviet Union and United States had immense land at their disposal. Other nations did not, however, and Germany, without colonies, was squeezed into the center of Europe, while its population was growing and its needs increasing. Land, therefore, would have to be reapportioned to meet the German needs. To this argument yet another one was added — the distinction between "young" and "old" nations, suggesting growth against decay. Germany, in historical terms, was "young" compared to England or France, and needed "living space" and land into which to grow.

Thus, the conquest of territory and the destruction of neighboring nation-states became an essential element of the Nazi ideology, and a long-range policy goal. It could not be attained overnight. The elimination of Soviet Russia (an old bulwark against German expansion to the east, but also an ideological foe), and of France (the spearhead of the plutocracies, especially England and the United States), would have to come first. The Japanese and the Italians were offered only tactical alliances in the expansionist German ambitions. Their position in the international order that the Nazis would build would have to be settled later.

3. *Communitarianism:* The elimination of all freedoms, and their replacement by a single "freedom" — that of obeying the party that represented the German community, and the leader of that party — was the essence of German totalitarianism. It was central to the building of a new political system that would replace liberalism and capitalism. All parties, all organizations, all associations, all religious groups, and churches would become subordinated to the communitarian will. After the Nazis came to power, freedom of press, of association, and of speech, ceased to exist. All parties were abolished. The individual — alone, free, independent, thinking his or her own thoughts — would give place to the "new individual" imbued with communitarian and nationalist beliefs as dictated by the leader and the party. The individual and the community would become one. Dissenters were, of course, not to be tolerated; they were executed or sent to concentration camps. But individuals who tried to remain aloof and distant from the national community were declared to be "asocial." They had failed to respond to the demands of the party and the community; they were not fully mobilized; they were not one with the nation.

Communitarianism called, therefore, for constant participation; it aimed to inculcate a spirit of individual attachment to the whole and a readiness not only to obey, but also to sacrifice everything for the general interest as defined by the Nazis. But communitarianism also suggested the need to subordinate private interest in the economic sphere to general social goals and, thereby, the subordination of the market economy to the party, and the leader. The early Nazi ideology was distinctly anti-capitalist, and it advocated the supremacy of national goals over all economic interests.

4. *Leadership ("Führerprinzip") and the party:* In what ways do communitarian values manifest themselves? One way is the direct participation of all in decision making — claimed to be the practice of the early Germanic tribes. A second way is for the community to select its representatives. This notion of representation was given a particular twist by the Nazis. They accepted it but they rejected free elections. The Nazi party "represented" the German people because it was in tune with the people and expressed directly the desires of the nation. Within the party its leader instinctively, and intuitively, acted for the whole. It is the leader, therefore, who best expresses the communitarian values.

Within six months after it came to power the "monopoly" of the Nazi party was legalized. The National Socialist Workers' party constituted the *only* political party in Germany . . . Whoever undertook to maintain the organizational structure of another political party or to form another political party was to be punished with penal servitude up to three years.

Communitarian aspirations gave a populist trait to Nazism. It claimed to embody values and principles that stemmed directly from the people — the *volk*. It was the "people's spirit" — the *volksgeist* — that was tapped by the party and was represented by it. Hence the party, in the name of this unique representative quality, claimed to be the only vehicle of representation and the very essence of direct democracy. But because of this, it claimed also to be an entity above the State and to control the State while acting on behalf of the community. The State was nothing, in the last analysis, but an agency, an instrumentality of the party, and all its offices and officials were subordinate to the party.

The leadership principle is the cornerstone of Nazism and the institution that best combines authority and control with "representation." It is a principle that cannot be easily defined since it can be only "understood" by those who experience it. The leader decides everything and everybody must obey. He can delegate his authority to others but can never give it up. He is the law, and hence above the law. He can legislate and then change that legislation overnight. His will is arbitrary, absolute, and superior. He can set procedures and can change them at will. He is free to appoint his successor just as a Roman emperor could make his horse a consul — and send it to the slaughterhouse!

Yet the question remains: from where does the leader derive his representative quality? The answer is very difficult. First, it is his capacity to speak on behalf of the national and popular spirit. It is also his special ability to persuade his followers: he has a special charisma that convinces the many to obey. It is also his intuition: his ability to sense what is right and wrong; what must be done and what must not be done; his feeling for what is good for all.

But what about the leader's authority? Why do people obey? The link is the mystical and intuitive link between leader and followers. He speaks for the people and the people agree with him because he speaks for them! And where his authority does not quite prevail, the leader has, at his disposal, formidable instruments of coercion, intimidation, and downright terror to elicit obedience.

While it is relatively easy to describe the omnipotence and omnicompetence of the Führer, it is far more difficult to explain it. How would a civilized nation, even one in which democratic values and institutions had not gained roots, accept it? And how can one explain the German people's fealty to the Führer until Germany had been reduced to ruins? In the last analysis, there can be no explanation except the very trite one. Hitler, his totalitarian regime, and his leadership principle combined with nationalism, racism, and expansionism, must have had, under the particular circumstances, a strong appeal to some prominent traits of German political culture.

Nazism and the German Political Culture

Much thought has been given to discovering the particular traits of the German political history and culture that made it so receptive to Nazism.[5] Foremost among them is the weakness of liberal and pluralistic democracy. The middle classes had not made a liberal revolution; they did not develop (as in England, the United States, and France), a network of associations and interest groups through which they could influence the State and interact with it. In contrast, many authoritarian social and political structures survived — in the army, in the landed aristocracy, in the civil service, and even in industry. These had developed rapidly in the last quarter of the nineteenth century in the form of large-scale monopolistic organizations. Authority and authoritarian structures were valued more than individual freedoms, equalities, and pluralism.

Respect for the authority of elite groups — the army officer, the top civil servant, the industrialist, the Prussian landowner — inculcated both discipline and deference. There is a well-known story according to which a German mob, during an uprising in the early 1920s, prepared to storm a post office whose front lawn had a "Keep off" sign. The mob swerved and attacked through the back door! Respect for authority and all symbols of authority accounted for the high prestige of the army — even after defeat. It was a state within a state, and socialist and liberal political leaders trembled before the presence of an army officer in the years of the republic. The army was a socializing force inculcating authoritarian not democratic values that would preserve it against the intrusions of parliamentarians, liberals, and leftists. The universities, remained the preserve of the upper classes and there, too, abject deference to academic authority was the rule. Education from bottom up was centered on passive learning of what was being offered — not on critical examination and creative individual effort.

For a long time, Germany had remained a prey to Romanticism, in its letters, art, philosophy, and politics. Abstract and general ideas were developed to solve or to answer the most transcendental questions of justice and knowledge through imagination rather than empirical examination and experimentation. Philosophy and theology, the studies of fundamental questions and of God, and not the study of society and social interrelationships, was the hallmark of the German intellectual. It inculcated a state of mind that was attracted by what appeared to be absolute and definitive and not by what was problem-solving and pragmatic.

Nationalism as an end in itself remained a powerful force, and when the German nation and the State were considered to be the ultimate vehicle for the realization of justice and goodness on earth there could be no limits to the scope and aspirations of the nationalists. Perhaps because the unification of Germany into a national state came so late, nationalism took the most integrative and absolutist form, bringing all Germans together into one State and reasserting their superiority and the superiority of what they stood for over all others.

5. See Ralf Dahrendorf. *Society and Democracy in Germany*. New York: Doubleday, 1969.

The vast majority of Germans acquiesced in the Nazi takeover, often with enthusiasm. They showed remarkable loyalty throughout Hitler's stay in power. Many did so out of self-interest; how many submitted out of fear is difficult to tell. Let us see how the various "social groups" reacted to the coming to power of the Nazis and their regime.

The Army   Diminished in status, reduced in numbers, bearing the brunt of defeat, and hostile to communism and to left-wing movements, army officers saw, in the coming of the Nazis, the prospects of their rehabilitation. Never at ease with republican institutions, the army's position was that it either should be a dominant force in the society or a separate and distinct entity for training soldiers, maintaining order and making war. It would not play a subordinate role. After World War I, many of its officers joined right-wing vigilante organizations against Communists and leftists. Throughout Hitler's rise to power, prominent officers cooperated with him or gave him indirect helping hands. He promised the rehabilitation of the nation and saw in war an answer for past failures. As General Blomberg testified at the Nuremburg trials: "Before 1938–1939 the German generals were not opposed to Hitler. There was no ground for opposition since he brought them the success they desired."[6] It was only when the fortunes of the war began to turn against Germany that a number of generals became impatient with Hitler and even conspired to assassinate him.

Civil Service   German civil servants, federal and state, responded with satisfaction to Hitler's program and supported his regime. The Nazis seemed to them to represent the basic values of order, centralized authority, and national integrity to which they were accustomed. Once it became clear that party members would not replace them, the support of the bureaucracy was overwhelming. It was strengthened by generous promotions and increases in salaries.

Yet bureaucracies are accustomed to an orderly way of doing things. They accept hierarchical relationships and a careful structuring of inferior-superior lines of command. They are committed to a rational, detached, and impartial way of reaching decisions and of implementing them; they are concerned with efficiency. The Prussian, and later on German, bureaucracy was always considered to be both well-organized and efficient. As a result, the frequent intrusions into it of the Nazi leaders, and the ultimate power they had to intervene and make decisions themselves, alienated some civil servants, forced the resignation of others, and often created confusion. However, at no time during the Hitler regime was there an open defiance on the part of the civil service.

The Church   Religious groups tried to maintain a certain distance from the Nazis, but an effort was made to eliminate some and to bring the two major churches, Catholic and Lutheran, under control. Jews were quickly isolated

6. Cited in Pinson, op. cit. p. 508.

and their synagogues burned; Jehovah's Witnesses were persecuted. A Concordat was signed with the Vatican giving the Catholic Church some autonomy — the right to hold services, raise funds, and to distribute pastoral letters to the faithful. But the Concordat also legitimized the Nazi State in the eyes of many Catholics. They were particularly receptive to the Nazi anti-communist pledges and during the war they considered it their patriotic duty to support the fatherland, especially when at war against the Soviet Union.

The Lutheran Church maintained a distance from the State, distinguishing political from spiritual matters. Political obedience was one thing, and the worship of God another, but the Lutherans gave their support to the Nazis as citizens, whatever their innermost thoughts might have been. Even to those for whom Hitler was a tyrant, obedience to the State was an obligation and prayer the only answer.

Individual Catholic prelates and Lutheran pastors occasionally raised their voices against the Nazi regime and its atrocities, but they were the exceptions to the general passivity of the churches.

Business Groups   As for business groups, they gave their full support and cooperation once the "socialist" pledges that were in the original platform of the party were abandoned. Neither private property nor business profits were tampered with, and the anti-labor and anti-trade-union measures satisfied them fully. Business elites cooperated closely with the Nazi leaders, trading favors and benefits with them.

The Middle Class, Farmers, and Workers   Germany had never experienced a genuine middle-class liberal movement as had England, France, and the United States. Rapid industrialization was grafted upon semi-feudal and authoritarian social structures. Paternalistic and hierarchical relationships were the rule. The middle classes *fitted* themselves into these structures instead of creating their own kind of political and social relationships — egalitarian and participatory. They felt more at home with authoritarian solutions and hierarchical relationships, and hence, they were inclined to accept Nazism and the authoritarian and nationalist philosophy it represented. Furthermore, the Nazi anti-communist ideology and their intention of doing away with trade unions reflected the middle-class fear of the working class and their political parties. The overwhelming majority of the middle-class voters voted for the Nazis and supported them throughout their stay in power. The lower middle classes — the petite bourgeoisie — insecure, patriotic, and anti-socialist — gave them their full support as they sought a niche in the Nazi order.

Similarly, the farmers gave the Nazis overwhelming support. The rustic virtues the Nazis extolled were also theirs: protection, in the form of higher tariffs, provided them with added revenue; anti-communism appealed to their traditional nationalism and conservatism. Small towns and rural communities voted overwhelmingly Nazi.

It was only the workers, then, who seemed to demur. But even among them it was only the politically and ideologically organized and committed, those who belonged to trade unions or were in the Communist and Socialist parties, who provided the opposition. The unemployed, as we pointed out,

tended to join the party in return for promises of employment. With the
coming of World War II in 1939, full employment was attained and the labor
force was by and large materially better off than it had been at any time since
before World War I. There was no organized opposition, and no spirit of
resistance. The majority of the workers, too, rallied to the Nazis.

The Economy

The Nazis failed to implement their original economic program. They did not
nationalize the monopolies; on the contrary, every effort was made to encourage concentration and cartelization; they did not confiscate war profits or
unearned income; they did not undertake land reform, and they did not take
over uncultivated lands and transform them into peasant cooperatives.
Populist and socialist promises were forgotten when they came to power. The
Nazi Party's socialist leaders, many of whom had taken these promises seriously, were massacred in 1934.

Nazi economic policy consisted of a series of improvisations to meet the
political objectives of rearmament and war. There is no doubt that the economy was subordinated not only to political and ideological exigencies, but
also to the necessity of planning or waging war. From the very start, controls
were put on foreign exchange. Special efforts were made to promote investment and direct it to key areas of economic activity; to secure raw materials
and, when it became necessary, to produce them at home (as, for instance,
with synthetic gas and rubber). In general, the emphasis was put on reducing
imports and promoting self-sufficiency. Priorities were established, wages
controlled, and labor scarcities met through the importation of foreign, often
slave labor — especially in the war period. However, cartelization proceeded
through the amalgamation of firms or the takeover of smaller ones, and
profits remained secure, even during the war. Property, both individual and
corporate, was respected.

Political imperatives prevailed. But the economy was not absorbed by
the State; it was not nationalized. It became subordinate to the State and the
party — a subordination that most other countries had experienced in time of
war. There was nothing distinct about the Nazi economy — it produced no
new blueprint for production, trade, growth, or consumption. It made no
effort to establish a new framework for labor-capital relations, other than to
disband all trade unions.

Conclusion

With an ideology that appealed, at least in part, to some of the basic cultural
traits of the German people, with a militant party to mobilize the people
behind it, with a magnetic political leader trying to resurrect the national
demons of the Germanic racial and national superiority while exploiting all
the weakness of a deadlocked parliamentary government, the totalitarian
state came to Germany with far greater support than anywhere else.

The Nazis were a mass party — far more so than the Russian Bolsheviks in 1917, the Italian fascists in 1922, or the Spanish Falange from 1936

to 1938. They received, in free and open elections, a greater percentage of votes than any other totalitarian party in Europe, or for that matter, than any other party in Germany. They were welcomed by most social groups and classes, including an appreciable part of the workers, and by the important elite groups, including the churches and the military. Nazism was a homemade product. It was "made in Germany" by the Germans.

Italian Fascism

Totalitarian political systems must be judged, like all other political systems, in terms of their ability to fulfill their objectives. Italian fascism did not achieve the degree of control that German Nazism achieved. Its objectives were very similar, but the resources — political, social, and economic — were not present. Italy's industrial development could not compare with that of Germany; national integration was still incomplete and civic discipline inadequate; the elites never gave their full support to the new system, or they gave it with many reservations and conditions. The fascist regime was not strong enough to destroy them or to supplant them.

When it came to an expansionist effort, first in Ethiopia (1936), then in Albania (1938) and in Greece (1941), the Italians proved to be woefully inadequate. They had to be supported and ultimately replaced by German soldiers almost everywhere they fought. Thus, while German Nazism showed the terrifying capabilities of a totalitarian system, Italian fascism failed to generate the power which is needed to realize doctrinal goals and aspirations.

The Road to Power

The Fascist party emerged in Italy at just about the same time as the Nazis did in Germany. But the Fascist State came into being much earlier. The fascists took over power on October 28, 1922 — a decade before Hitler. By 1923, when Mussolini was setting the foundations of the new Italian order, Hitler was still a political upstart and in jail for the abortive Munich *putsch*.

The similarities in the way by which the fascists and the Nazis took power are striking:

1. Fascism capitalized on the nationalistic fervor which followed World War I because Italy did not receive the territorial compensation for the war effort that the Italians thought they deserved.
2. Italy's parliamentary institutions could not cope with the problems facing the country. There were many political parties, sharply divided on ideological and policy matters. Governments consisted of short-lived coalitions, and cabinet instability was the rule.
3. Democratic institutions were not valued by major sections of the population, and Italy's experience with democracy and representative government had been limited. A small elite consisting of the northern industrialists, landowners, and the Catholic hierarchy ruled the country. The middle classes, the lower-middle classes, and the peasantry were

THE BETTMAN ARCHIVE, INC.

Benito Mussolini (1883–1945)

The son of a socialist blacksmith and a Catholic schoolteacher, Mussolini broke with the Italian Socialist party over his support for World War I, and became editor of the nationalist *Il Popolo d'Italia*. In 1919, he founded the Fascist party, and on October 22, 1922, King Victor Emmanuel IV asked him to become prime minister. Mussolini began to put into effect his philosophy of a totalitarian one-party state by abolishing republican institutions. He also attempted to realize plans for a "new Roman empire" by embarking on a series of military adventures, including the conquest of Ethiopia (1935–1936), support of Franco in Spain (1936–1938), and the occupation of Albania (1939). In June 1940 Italy entered into World War II on the side of the Germans, but its forces were unable to make any genuine contribution to the German war effort. Expelled from office on July 25, 1943, after the invasion of Sicily by allied forces, he was arrested and subsequently executed by partisans on April 28, 1945.

Mussolini provided some good formulations of the fascist ideology, notably in his *The Doctrine of Fascism; Fascism: Doctrine and Institutions;* and in his *Autobiography*.

either weak or unable to exercise political influence and bring about necessary reforms.

4. The workers joined powerful leftist movements, some led by the Socialist party, some by anarchists and syndicalists, and some by the Communists, who, after 1920 began to assume an important position in many trade unions. A strong minority endorsed extremist programs and direct action. They were organized for a revolutionary takeover and used the strike as a vehicle for weakening the State. They occupied factories and led the farmers to the occupation of land. Socialists showed remarkable strength at the polls, gaining 1,834,792 votes and 156 deputies in the legislature in the election of 1919. Again, in the election of 1921, their respective strength was 1,631,435 votes and 138 deputies. This "red menace" threatened not only the conservative forces, the Church, the industrial elites, and the monarchy, but also the middle classes, the lower-middle classes, and the peasants in regions where the Church was particularly influential.

5. In this context, as in Germany, vigilante nationalist groups began to mushroom. They were led by former army officers and veterans. They took the law into their own hands in fighting the leftists, with the complicity of national and local governmental authorities. Gang wars developed in the cities and the countryside. The newly formed Fascist party began to play the leading role in combating "the reds."

6. Inflation, and the relative success of trade unions in maintaining their real wages through collective action while the middle and lower-middle classes suffered, accounted for a sharp right-wing reaction on the part of the latter. They were losing income and status, and they were increasingly forced down to the economic and social levels of the workers.

7. Mussolini, the founder of the Fascist party, was not, in contrast to Hitler, a newcomer to politics. But the similarities with Hitler are remarkable. They both came from the lower-middle classes; both had read what they found congenial to their activist and romantic dispositions and admired the many writers who had criticized liberalism and extolled will-power and communitarian nationalist values. Mussolini, too, had fought in World War I and had been wounded. He, too, was a great orator. Like Hitler, Mussolini at first propounded ideas that had strong socialist overtones: confiscation of war profits, socialization of industries, workers' participation in the running of firms, the utilization of unused land by those who could work it, and appeal to the poor and the workers with promises of social and economic equity.

8. As with Hitler, Mussolini did not have to shoot his way into power. He was received by the King and was appointed by him.

The Fascist Party

The term fascist comes from the Latin word *fasces,* which was an emblem carried by ancient Roman magistrates as a symbol of their authority. It consisted of many rods tightly banded together, with an axe protruding on top. It conveyed remarkably well the underlying philosophy of the fascists: the combining of individuals together, in order to generate both power and authority.

The Italian Fascist party was founded in 1919. At that time it was but one of many extremist nationalist groups. Only one hundred persons attended the founding meeting. Its program was both nationalist and socialist. It endorsed workers' revolutionary movements and strikes and demanded the expropriation of land and the nationalization of industries such as mines and transport. Mussolini tried to straddle right-wing nationalist themes and extreme leftist demands, hoping to gain support from both the left and the right. His early appeal was so similar to Hitler's that his party could have been easily called the National Socialist Workers' party of Italy.

At first the fascists did not fare well. In the election of 1919, in which the socialists gained 156 seats in the Chamber of Deputies, the fascists failed to gain a single seat. Mussolini himself, a candidate in Milan, received less than 5,000 votes out of 346,000 cast. The program of his party contained the socialist slogans to which we have referred: an eight-hour working day, minimum wage policy, participation of workers in the management of industries, welfare measures with comprehensive sickness and old age protection, a capital tax leading to the expropriation of the wealthy, and the confiscation of the property of religious organizations and of war profits.

Within two years of the founding of the party its membership had grown to 300,000. In the 1921 election, the Fascist party secured thirty-five seats in the legislature and 19.6 percent of the vote (1,289,556). But what strengthened them even more was the private war they began to wage against all leftists. Left-wing clubs, newspapers, trade unions, and party headquarters were sacked. Agricultural cooperative societies were destroyed. The fascists, like the Nazis, appeared the strong men of "law and order" where government failed to provide protection. Their program also began to swing to the right. Mussolini now attacked the "Russian myth" of communism, spoke of rural democracy as opposed to collectivization, rejected class war in favor of national unity, and promised to protect the workers but only in accordance "with the interests of production." Subsequently, in a party congress, the concepts of both economic liberalism and a strong State were endorsed. The party declared itself neutral on the question of the monarchy, which it had previously opposed. There was no mention of confiscation of lands held by religious organizations. Thus, both the monarchy and the Church were placated.

The decision by the Socialists, in cooperation with the Communists, many other leftist organizations, and the trade unions, to organize a general strike late in 1922 gave Mussolini the opportunity for his "March on Rome" and takeover of power. Actually he did not march; he simply took the train from Milan! His fascist squads, however, had occupied various localities and tens of thousands had moved into Rome and its outskirts. The King received Mussolini and asked him to take office. Thus, the Fascist State was born.

Fascism, like Nazism, was to be the answer to liberal democracy, doing away with competition, individualism, the quest for profit and material gain, divisions, fragmentations, and particularisms. Instead, a new regime would be established to create unity and cooperation, discipline and joint effort for the realization of collective purpose under the State. "Believe; Obey; Work; Fight" was one of the mottos of fascism. "Everything within the State; everything for the State; nothing outside the State," was another.

The argument favoring the inclusiveness and the primacy of the State is, as we know, an old one. For the fascists it meant the subordination of all social activities and organizations, all individual interests, all cultural manifestations (including religion), and all rights — material, political, and moral — to the State. Without the collectivity of the group, there can be no individual life and freedom and, of course, no common purpose. The State expresses them all. Morality can no longer be based on individual rational calculations: it exists when we share fully the collective purpose of the State and we obey the State. "Fascism is for liberty," wrote Mussolini, but " . . . for the only liberty that can be taken seriously, the liberty of the State. In this sense fascism is totalitarian and the Fascist State the synthesis and unity of all values . . . [It] interprets, develops and gives power to every aspect of the life of the people."[7] The State, therefore, is a truly moral creative force.

Mussolini went beyond even this by saying that the Fascist State is truly democratic, for democracy in its purest form is "what ought to be." Fascism provides this kind of morality by substituting for the will of the many that of the few, and by subordinating the few to the will of one. The will of the leader becomes their will and, in turn, the will of all.

At this point, the student should note a subtle but important difference between Nazism and fascism. The first was as we noted a "populist" movement claiming to represent the German *volk* from which the Nazi party emanated. As a result, the party claimed to be above the State. The fascist doctrine, on the other hand, influenced by the legacy of Roman law, was statist and authoritarian. It presumed a hierarchy of institutions and functions all organized by the State and operating under the State. The Fascist party, through its national, regional, and local organizations, played an important role as an adjunct of the Fascist State. Good fascists obeyed the Fascist State and their loyalty was to the State above all. One of the better exponents of the theory of the Fascist State wrote:

> The idea of the State as a force (which as a result of the general state of ignorance is seen as a German-Prussian idea) is plainly a Latin and Italian one. It is directly linked with the intellectual tradition of Rome . . . It is Italy's duty to reclaim it as a part of

---

7. Cited by Herman Finer. *Mussolini's Italy*. New York: Henry Holt, 1935, p. 201. As I noted in my preface, this book, though written in the 1930s, retains a remarkable freshness. I acknowledge my thanks to the late author.

our natural heritage, in its genuine form, and translate it into action with the political wisdom that over the centuries has always been part of the genius of our race.[8]

Side by side with the concept of State, and often used interchangeably with it, is the nation. In fact, it is the combination of the two — a combination that is "indissolubly" cemented — that the fascists stressed. The nation and nationalism provide the ultimate spiritual focus to bind people together within the State that embodies it. Nationalism "is the central inspiration of the human personality living in the civil community; [it] descends into . . . and makes its home in the heart of the man of action as of the thinker, of the artist, as of the scientists." Nationalism "becomes the very soul of the soul" of all of us.[9]

Nationalism and statism, the quest for the absolute ethical ideal, theoretically divests fascism of material considerations. To live dangerously, to navigate on the high and perilous seas, to be able and prepared to fight at any time at any risk, gives to life a heroic quality which the drudgery of the "economic man," constantly concerned about his insurance, his wage, and his benefits, is incapable of showing. The rational man must give place to the heroic man and material considerations to dreams of great exploits. The real man must replace the mechanical man produced by liberalism. This rationale, in part, accounts for the influx of younger people and university students into the fascist movement.

The Leader (Il Duce)   This effort to fashion a new society and a "fascist man" called for leadership and for the right kind of institutions to organize it and lead it. The Fascist party and the leader (Il Duce) play the key roles. The leader speaks for the party and the State. He combines in his person the highest offices of the State and of the party. The party represents the movement that speaks for the leader and the State and acts on their behalf. Party officials occupy virtually all the important posts in the State. In fact, almost all civil service positions were reserved by law for party members and officials, which assured the party of patronage. The party also organized and structured all social activities and mobilized the rank and file to provide for support and watch out for deviant manifestations. Finally, the leader, with top party officials, controlled the economy, which, like everything else, was supposed to be subordinate to the State and to its ideology.

Thus, the leader is the responsible chief of government. Mussolini allowed the King to stay in office as the formal head of state in order to get the support of monarchists and conservatives. But throughout the fascist regime the King was a mere shadow and many forgot that he existed. Mussolini was in charge of the Cabinet and often held a number of Cabinet posts at the same time. Parliament continued to meet and to legislate, but all bills came from the leader. The fascists controlled the elections and enjoyed wide

8. Alfredo Rocco in Adrian Lyttelton (ed.). *Italian Fascism*. New York: Harper & Row, 1973, p. 262.
9. Finer, op. cit., p. 222.

popular support until the beginning of World War II. At election time there was only one slate of candidates — all proposed by the fascists. There was no opposition.

The Development of the Party   The Fascist party held the monopoly of representation, the virtual monopoly of officeholding, and the monopoly of mobilization and recruitment, but it did not develop a private army as the Nazis did through the SS and SA formations. Throughout the fascist period the army and the officer-corps maintained their autonomy. The fascist militia remained relatively unimportant.

From the days when it took power, the party grew rapidly. From about 300,000 in 1922–1923, it grew to about one million by 1931 and to over two and a half million in the years before World War II. It controlled the legislature. In the last contested and relatively free election in 1923, the Fascist party received 4,671,555 votes — 65.3 percent of the total. Thereafter it amounted to 100 percent!

The party also controlled a number of "front organizations" among civil servants, retired officers, fascist trade unions, teachers, students, and so on. A total of at least four million people were involved in these organizations. Thus, about six to seven million Italians were members of the Fascist

---

The Ten Commandments of the Fascist Fighter[10]

1. God and Fatherland: all other affections and duties come after these.
2. Whoever is not ready to give himself body and soul for his country and to serve the Duce without discussion, is not worthy of wearing the Black Shirt.
3. Use your intelligence to understand the orders that you receive and all your enthusiasm for obedience.
4. Discipline is not only a virtue of the soldiers in the ranks, it must also be the practice of everyday.
5. A bad child and a negligent student are not Fascists.
6. Organize your time in such a way that work will be a joy and your games, work.
7. Learn to suffer without complaining . . .
8. In actual circumstances, remember that the good lies in audacity.
9. Good actions, like actions in war, must not be done by halves: carry them to their extreme consequence.
10. And thank God every day for having made you Fascist and Italian.

---

10. Adapted from Tannenbaum. *The Fascist Experience.* This is one of the better books on Italian fascism and I am indebted to the author for some of my observations and figures in this section. Also Finer, op. cit., pp. 426–54 contains a survey of fascist youth organizations.

party or of party front organizations. In sheer numbers the fascists permeated the whole of Italian society.

Of particular significance were the youth organizations, aimed at six to twenty-one year olds, that were sponsored and controlled by the fascists. Recruitment began at a tender age, and at least one boy or girl out of every two was in some youth organization. But there were many other organizations. For intellectuals, the *Academia d'Italia* was the source of many fascist publications; for Catholics, the *Centro Nazionale Italiano;* for army leaders, the *Istituto Nazionale di Culture Fasciste* (numbering in 1941 200,000 members). There was also a youth movement for children who had completed school, the *Fasci Giovalini de Combattimente,* while a very active fascist organization recruited many of the university students — the *Gioventi Universitario Fasciste.* A mass front organization was developed to provide various cultural and athletic activities for employees and workers — the *Dopolavoro* (literally "after work"), which had over two million members by the late 1930s.

The picture of fascist control, then, is fairly clear. The party controlled opinion, the education of the youth, and all the media; it outlawed all opposition and, through its various agencies, intimidated those who were of a different mind. All agencies of the State were in the hands of party members. One is tempted to say that fascism had become the only dominant force in the Italian society. But this is not quite true.

Pockets of Resistance

The aspirations for totalitarian control under the leadership of one person or one group always meet obstacles. There is an inherent diversity and pluralism in all societies made up of individuals, families, groups, associations, regions, interests, professions, political ideologies, and cultural differences, and no system can ever reduce all these forces to absolute subordination. Often this is because many of these smaller social entities refuse to be reduced to conformity. They prefer to hear their own drummer instead of marching in step to a dictated tune. But just as often it is because, despite its efforts, a totalitarian state cannot develop enough resources to control and to intimidate *everybody.* This was more true in the case of Italy than of Germany.

The Church First and foremost among the various groups that fascism failed to control was the Catholic Church — both a powerful spiritual and social and political force. It had given its support to the conservatives and to Mussolini's coming to power for fear, among other reasons, that the Marxists, materialist and atheist, might come to power first. Mussolini was its bulwark.

It soon became apparent, however, that the totalitarian claims of the Fascist State to encompass and control every social and cultural activity — the very assertion that the State was the highest moral force within society and focus of all loyalties — could not be reconciled with the spiritual claims of the Church. The Church claimed control over education and the spiritual

Mussolini is shown leading his fascists on their "March on Rome," 1922.
(*Photo: Brown Brothers*)

guidance of all members of society and refused to become subordinate to the
State — any State. Yet education was central to the fascist philosophy. It was
the means for the development of a new citizen, the mobilization and indoctrination of the young, and the inculcation of absolute loyalty. Conflict was
inevitable and the fascists had to move very cautiously.

Their first move was to placate the Church. In 1929, a treaty was signed
between the Fascist State and the Papacy. It recognized Catholicism as the
official religion of Italy, and gave the Pope full sovereignty over the Vatican.
The Church also received from the State a lump sum and an annual subsidy.
In return, the Papacy recognized the Italian State — i.e., the Fascist State.
In a separate agreement, the Concordat, the Church secured freedom to the
public exercise of all rites, ceremonies, and sacraments. Religious marriages
were given civil recognition, religious instruction in Catholicism was made
mandatory in all elementary and secondary schools. Hence, the Church was
given special and autonomous functions within the State.

Most important of all, Catholic Action, a lay organization with more
than a million members for disseminating Catholicism through various social
and public undertakings, was given the freedom to diffuse and encourage

religious principles. It was precisely over this role that conflicts emerged. The fascists claimed primacy over education; the Church refused it. It would not allow anybody to interfere with its prerogative to infuse the spiritual teachings of Christ. But the Fascist State could not allow the Church to become a rival organization, with Catholic Action countering its own efforts to indoctrinate youth in fascist political morality and loyalty. In an encyclical, the Pope refused to let the young and the faithful submit to "the cult of the State," nor to allow the State to monopolize the education of the young in their formative years. Particularly obnoxious to the Church was an oath required of the citizens asking them to obey the Facist State "without discussion." If that oath was to be required, the Pope instructed Catholics to take it "with mental reservations" that proved their loyalty to God.

After months of polemic, a compromise was reached. The Catholic Action was allowed to operate, but on condition that it would limit its activities to religious work. "God" was reintroduced in the fascist oath so that citizens would swear allegiance to *both* State and God. In this manner, the Church hoped to maintain some of its spiritual autonomy. It did not outwardly oppose fascism, but it refused to be absorbed into it. It gave its support, especially in the years of war, but the fascists could never take it for granted. Thus, the Church remained throughout the fascist era a powerful and separate organization. It maintained control over the Catholic Action; constantly prodded the fascist leaders, including Mussolini, to take action on certain matters or to refrain from acting on others; it maintained parallel youth organizations, schools, and universities, and had the monopoly of religious education.

Many have argued that the top Catholic hierarchy, including the Pope, followed a "wait and see" policy. The fascist regime was a positive force in their eyes in eliminating communism and in establishing order. A Catholic intellectual wrote: "Fascism can be proud of the fact that its institutions, its laws and its works are realizing for the first time in history . . . the eternal truth of Catholic and Latin political thought."[11] There was a genuine hope on the part of the Church that its own spiritual dominance would eventually assert itself and that it would be able to harness the Fascist State to the spiritual and political values espoused by Italian Catholicism — humane and social, but paternalistic and authoritarian.

On the other hand, there were many leading Catholics who, from the very start, opposed fascism, declaring its secular character as well as its political doctrine to be contrary to the spirit of the Church, and asking the believers to resist it. Whatever our appreciation of the policies and the role of the Catholic Church may be — an ally of fascism, a benevolent neutral, a neutral bystander, a spiritual opponent, a political opposition force — what counts most for the purpose of our discussion is that the Church remained a *visible* and *organized* separate force within a regime that claimed to be totalitarian. Fascism was not strong enough to bring the Church within the State. And the Church was strong enough to maintain its aloofness.

11. In Tannenbaum, op. cit., p. 200.

Other Groups Business groups and landowners gave their support to fascism the moment it spoke out in favor of private property, and the profit motive, and against agrarian reforms and the redistribution of land. The destruction of the trade unions and of all political parties, especially the left-wing ones, gave to the northern industrialists what they most wanted. Similarly, the middle classes and the lower middle classes, delivered from the "red peril," saw in fascism the opportunities for the maintenance and even the improvement of their material conditions and social status. They became the staunchest supporters of the regime. As in Germany, the only group to maintain its distance was that of the workers, despite efforts by the fascists to entice them into controlled unions. However, it was primarily among the more organized and politically involved workers — those who had belonged to trade unions and had been politically active in the Socialist and Communist parties — that this was true. Unemployed, unskilled, and migrant workers were easily mobilized into the system. The peasantry remained generally apathetic.

One group that maintained its autonomy was the army. There was no direct interference with the high command and the officer corps from the Fascist party or the State, which was not the case in Germany. Promotions and higher pay satisfied the army officers. As for the King, he remained, as we have seen, in office but without power. Yet he symbolized for many conservatives an autonomous force that could provide, in time, a rallying point for opposition.

The Corporate State

We have left the discussion of the economic organization of Italy under fascism till last. It took the form of corporatism — used to denote cooperation between capital and labor as opposed to class conflict. Corporatism comes from the word *corpus*, body, and its institutions are designed to bring workers and owners together into "one body," in which there is a cooperation and consultation before decisions are made. It is an old theory, stressing the organic relationships between two groups or classes which according to Marx are inherently antagonistic. It suggests harmony and common interest.

In his famous encyclical, "Rerum Novarum" (1891), the Pope had declared:

> . . . Employers and workmen may themselves [establish] . . .
> institutions and organizations which afford opportune assistance
> to those in need and which may draw the two orders to-
> gether . . .[12]

Forty years later, in 1931, in another encyclical, "Quadregissimo Anno," the Pope came out fully for corporatism:

> The Corporations are composed of representatives of the unions
> . . . of workingmen and employers of the same trade and profes-

12. Text from *Seven Great Encyclicals*. Glen Rock, N.J.: Paulist Press, 1939, p. 23.

sion and as genuine and exclusive instruments and institutions of the State they direct and coordinate the activities of the syndicates in all matters of common interest. Strikes and lockouts are forbidden . . . Little reflection is required to perceive the advantages in the institution thus summarily described: peaceful collaboration of the classes, repression of socialist organization and efforts, the moderating authority of a special ministry.[13]

"We have created the Corporate State," Mussolini proudly announced in 1927. However, constant modifications of the corporate structure, changes in the powers of the "corporations" and in their numbers make it very difficult to identify exactly what the Corporate State was and whether it existed at all, except on paper.

The regime established twenty-two corporations. Among them, the most important were those for cereals, fruit, vegetables and flour, beet and sugar, lumber and wood, chemical trades, textiles and engineering, credit and insurance, building trades, sea and air, inland communications. Every such corporation, corresponding to a broad area of economic activity, included representatives of all interests involved in all the branches of economic activity included in it — employers, employees, managers, owners, and so on. All corporations in turn elected the General Corporate Assembly consisting of eight hundred members. This was the Corporate Chamber. In each corporation, employers and employees were equally represented, but in each one also there were members of the Fascist party representing "the public." The trade unions from which representatives of the employees were selected were, of course, fascist trade unions. A corporation was declared to be an organ of the State, an official body.

What were the functions of the corporations? They were mostly to reconcile conflicts among the various branches of activity that were included in it, to better coordinate their respective activities, and to regulate employment and the technical training of its members. They were expected also to provide for discipline in production, and, with the approval of the State, to fix prices for goods, services, and wages and supervise the working conditions in various firms and services.

The Fascist State had the first and last word. "The corporations were the links in the chain which bound the citizens tightly to the State."[14] They were presided over by a fascist minister, and most decisions could be made only with the approval of the State. The old trade unions had been destroyed and the fascist unions guaranteed the domination of the fascists. Thus, the corporative mechanism turned out to be an instrument to control the workers and provide a link between the Fascist State and the business and industrial elites. This was a far cry from what corporatism was meant to be. It forced the workers underground and did nothing to alleviate class conflict.[15]

13. Ibid., p. 151.
14. Lyttelton, op. cit., p. 31.
15. Finer, op. cit., describes in detail the corporations and the structure of the Corporate State.

There was a great distance between fascist ideology and practice, as there was between the fascist movement and the system of government the fascists built. The original ideology was anti-bourgeois, anti-liberal, antiestablishment, and championed extensive structural reforms of the society in favor of the workers and the poor and against the privileged elite groups and their institutions — landowners, industrialists, the Church, the monarchy.

In practice, and even before the fascists came to power, there was a shift in favor of these powerful groups. The middle classes, the landowners, the Church, the industrial elites, the civil servants, the monarchy and the bourgeoisie all gave their support and their money. By 1928, the Fascist State had eliminated free trade unions. By 1931, it fully normalized its relations with the Church. Corporatism never developed into a genuine form of cooperation between capital and labor; at best, it represented a form of state capitalism in which all business groups, manufacturers and landowners cooperated under the supervision of the State.

In a curious way the Fascist State that roared upon the scene of Italian history in order to capture and renovate society became the captive and the instrument of the very power elites that it promised to subordinate. Italian fascism was unable to destroy the existing structural elite of society as the Bolsheviks did, and as the Nazis tried and succeeded in great part in doing. It was unable to dominate all society as the Nazis unquestionably did. The much-vaunted unity of the nation under the Fascist State disintegrated during World War II. The old political forces and particularisms reasserted themselves when the war was over.

Nazism and Fascism: Interpretations

In discussing Nazism and fascism we alluded to some of the underlying causes of right-wing totalitarian movements. It is time now to restate briefly some of the interpretations that have been advanced, and to raise some questions about the present status of right-wing totalitarian ideologies. Were Nazism and fascism passing phenomena or, on the contrary, can they be considered as ideologies that are likely to endure?

The Abnormality and Uniqueness Theories

A widely held notion a few decades ago was that totalitarianism and its specific manifestations in Germany, Italy, and elsewhere, were deviations from the democratic liberal norm. It was a disease, like measles. It could not affect the normal and inevitable progress of societies in the direction of open and democratic politics, any more than contagious diseases normally affect children's growth.

An equally widely held belief holds that Italian and German fascism were unique phenomena which correspond to the particular histories of these countries (late unification, and defeat or dissatisfaction in World War I) or their particular political cultures (primarily the lack of democratic political tradition and institutions and the corresponding development of powerful left-wing revolutionary movements). In both cases the inference drawn was that the right-wing extremist totalitarian phenomenon was self-contained. It would not spread elsewhere.

The Marxist Theory

A classic interpretation widely used by many authors was the Marxist one, formally endorsed by the Communist Third International. According to it, fascism or Nazism correspond to the "last stage of monopolistic capitalism." It is spearheaded by the most racist and expansionist elements of the capitalist class in an effort to maintain its rule at home and subjugate other peoples and their economies. Expansionism and war are two of the remaining means available to the capitalists faced with economic depression and the growing contradictions of their system that Marx had anticipated. The evidence was considered clear: both Nazism and fascism geared the economy to war, distracting the people from their economic problems by appealing to their nationalism and by preparing them for war. They maintained private property and profits and destroyed the trade unions and working class parties.

The Modernization Theory

Another theory views totalitarianism as a movement that corresponds to a stage of economic modernization. As the industrial and, in general, nonagricultural sectors gradually gain, there is a shift of power from the traditional landed and commercial elites to industrial and banking groups. Rapid industrialization accounts for an influx of farmers into the cities and for urbanization, and, in general, for a rapid growth in the numbers of industrial workers. These shifts bring about a new type of political mobilization and new political parties that attempt to recruit the new workers, the urban masses, and also the disgruntled peasants. Invariably, such a mobilization frightens the middle classes and the industrial elite groups who begin to favor repressive and integrative solutions. One author considers the optimal condition for the development of fascism to be when the nonagricultural occupational groups have increased, at the expense of agriculture, to the point where they represent about 40 to 50 percent of the gainfully employed. This is, of course, not an assertion that all such societies will develop fascism, simply that it is one of the many conditions propitious for its emergence.[16]

It is precisely the many other conditions that account for fascism, that are missing both from the Marxist theory and the modernization theory. For instance, if the highest and last stage of capitalism accounts for fascism, why did it develop in Germany but not in equally or even more advanced econo-

16. A. F. K. Organski. "Fascism and Modernization" in S. J. Woolf (ed.). *The Nature of Fascism.* New York: Random House, 1968.

mies? Similarly, if we take the theory of modernization to explain Italian fascism, what accounted for its absence in other countries going through roughly a parallel stage?

Psychological Interpretations

Totalitarianism has been viewed by many authors as a psychological mass phenomenon. People react to a "threat" or to "alienation," both of which occur during the development of industrialization and the concomitant creation of a "mass society." The first accounts for large-scale, impersonal organizations with a high degree of division of labor and specialization. A mass society corresponds to the breakup of most intermediate social structures — village, family, neighborhoods — and many traditional institutions which structure and shape individual values, attitudes, and life. The ultimate result is the "atomization" of society, all the old group disintegrated, the individual now alone and lonely. A reaction sets in, as we saw in discussing Fromm's *Escape from Freedom*, in favor of communal and integrative ideologies.

The perception of threat strengthens totalitarian appeals when the threatened individuals belong to groups that are comfortable, relatively well-off, and satisfied with their lot. Such is the case with the middle classes that enjoy a higher income and a better status than farmers or workers or low-middle class people. They are, according to some authors, the key to the door to power for right-wing totalitarian movements. They can keep the door closed or they can open it when special economic conditions begin to account for a loss of income and when special social conditions make them feel that they are in danger of losing their position in society.

There is hardly any doubt, as we have seen, that the middle classes, both in Germany and Italy, gave their full support to the Nazis and the fascists in order to protect themselves against threats to their income and status. They sought protection against trade unions and workers, and found it.

Yet, as with the previous theories, this psychological interpretation fails to provide a satisfactory and general explanation. If Germany was a mass society in 1933, so were the United States and England. Why did right-wing extremism gain the upper hand in one country but not in the others? Similarly, if the middle classes were "threatened" in Germany, so were they threatened in other industrialized systems, including the United States, during the Great Depression. Why did they seek defense in a totalitarian system in Germany but not elsewhere? Why were anti-democratic solutions sought in some countries and not in others? A theory that does not provide us with the explanation of as many occurrences as possible is not satisfactory.

Managerial Revolution?

Totalitarianism and totalitarian regimes have been viewed by some as representing a "managerial revolution" to replace the inept political leadership of democratic regimes. The economic structure of capitalism, they argue, has changed. Property is not in the hands of only a few; it is widely dispersed among stockholders. Property owners cannot and do not make decisions: their managers do. Decision making, therefore, is increasingly concentrated in the hands of a managerial elite that enters into close contact with other elites, not only in the economy but also in the army and the civil service; it even enters into close cooperation with labor leaders. It is a coalition, in other words, of persons with technical skills in production, management, administration, and group organization.

It is this new managerial elite, then, that makes the major decisions in the economy (often through planning): production levels, the establishment of economic priorities, the utilization of resources, the supply of money, income distribution, wage policy, and so on. Gradually the democratic institutions become an obstacle to this *de facto* government of experts and managers who control the heights of the economy and society.[17] Totalitarianism in the form of fascism or Nazism have been viewed accordingly as the triumph of the technocrat and the expert — of a power elite which finally does away with democracy for the sake of efficiency and organization.

The difficulty with this interpretation is that it assigns a role to rationality, knowledge, and technical expertise that neither the fascists nor the Nazis valued. On the contrary, in both systems there was a constant struggle between the political ideological propositions, utopian or downright irrational, and the imperatives of rational management. There were constant conflicts between the economic managers and the party or the State, between the army officers and the State, and between the economic planners and the party leaders. Fascism and Nazism amounted, in fact, to the predominance of politics over technical spheres such as competence, organization, management, and efficiency.

Personality Theory

Considerable ingenuity has gone into efforts to show that totalitarianism appeals to and receives widespread support from individuals with a particular type of personality — the "authoritarian" or "potentially authoritarian." A number of attitudinal traits combined constitutes a "syndrome" or a "pattern" of the authoritarian personality: anti-Semitism, nationalism, fear of outsiders or aliens, conservative political outlook, strict family upbringing. Persons showing this syndrome are likely to be found among the lower-middle classes, the workers, and the uneducated. Similarly, persons suffering from various types of anxiety, even paranoia, who are unable to make decisions and choices and often are afraid of the outside world, divest themselves easily of their freedoms in favor of authoritarian leadership which provides some degree of fixity and stability in their lives.

But there is no adequate evidence to attribute fascism or Nazism and membership in and support for totalitarian movements to particular personal-

17. James Burnham. *The Managerial Revolution*. Bloomington: Indiana U.P., 1973.

ity types. To begin with, both Nazi and fascist movements received strong support from the middle classes, to say nothing of university students — persons, that is, with relatively comfortable backgrounds and higher education. Support was lowest from the working classes, where many of the traits associated with an authoritarian personality would be found. Secondly, even if we concede that there is an authoritarian upbringing in German and Italian families, a random distribution of political attitudes, ranging from authoritarian to democratic, would show only marginal differences for various countries of Europe and elsewhere. To assume that there was a preponderance of authoritarian personality types and syndromes among the Germans and the Italians, as compared to other nationalities, requires statistical proof that is not available and is unlikely to be found. "Personality" may in some instances be a contributing factor, but it is a very marginal one.

Conclusion

All the interpretations given of totalitarian movements provide us with only parts of an explanation. In some cases it may well be that levels of modernization provided a setting; in other cases, the lonely uprooted individual may have sought shelter in unity and communitarian effort; in others, authoritarian solutions were sought by business and financial groups to defend the economic system that provided them with profits; in still others, the middle classes and the lower middle classes, confronted with loss of income and status, revolted against democracy and liberal institutions.

No single interpretation will do; and even if all of them are put together they do not point to the set of conditions that will *inevitably* lead to totalitarianism. They do help us, however, in identifying the conditions under which political systems may be susceptible to totalitarian assault. The study of right-wing totalitarian movements, therefore, becomes not the study of unique manifestations but the comparative study of a potentially universal phenomenon.

Is Fascism Dead?

As we have noted, ideologies often go through a process of ebb and flow. Right-wing extremism and totalitarianism has deep roots, and it is not at all unlikely that, given certain conditions, they may surface again. This does not mean that they will take a form identical to that taken in either Italy or Germany, only that they will follow the same general themes of nationalism, anti-liberalism, and anti-individualism in order to impose a national, communitarian and integrative ideology.

Many of the conditions for the rise of totalitarian movements and regimes continue to be present. The mass society has become even more impersonal and atomized because of rapid modernization and technological development. Individuals are very much alone, and their discontents and frustrations may lead them to espouse unifying and communitarian themes.

The liberal ethic that continues to emphasize individual effort and to promise material well-being has raised high expectations for abundance. But it has also undermined some of the basic control mechanisms of society — the Church, the class, elite groups, the structure of deference, and mutuality of respect. Even the modern political party seems unable to hold people together around common programs, and to pattern and regulate their expectations accordingly. The democratic society has been reduced to a myriad of competing and conflicting groups (some refer to them as molecular groups) each one of which tries to maximize its benefits and advantages. It is not unlikely, therefore, that new ideological and totalitarian parties may try to capture the frustrations and discontents of the many that are not satisfied with their position and material well-being.

International tensions may cause a revival of nationalism, defensive or expansionist, that will be used to subordinate individual and group demands, and also result in a loss of freedoms to absolutist nationalist myths and ends. Lastly, the ruling elites seem to have regrouped into a more coherent "power elite," consisting of the major decision-makers in society — economic, political, labor, and military — and the temptation to safeguard their positions through repressive measures cannot be excluded. As for the middle classes, the rate of inflation and the prospects of an economic depression in many societies may cause the same threat and panic that it caused in pre-Nazi Germany.

All that may be needed for virulent extremist movements to emerge may well be a severe international crisis or another serious economic crisis. It may account for a resurgence of revolutionary leftist parties, of one denomination or another, that would put the elites and the middle classes on the defensive. It may bring forth a movement or a system that would attempt to control group particularisms, to replace representative institutions, to set aside political competition, and to manipulate public opinion around nationalist and communitarian themes. Force will replace consent, even if only to a degree, and propaganda will replace persuasion. The prospect of totalitarianism, in other words, remains very much alive. So does the rich ideological background from which it can draw.

Bibliography

Allen, William Sheridan. *The Nazi Seizure of Power: The Experience of a Single German Town.* New York: New Viewpoints, 1973.

Aycoberry, Pierre. *The Nazi Question.* New York: Pantheon Books, 1981.

Bracher, K. Dietrich. *The German Dictatorship.* New York: Praeger, 1970.

Bullock, Alan. *Hitler: A Study in Tyranny.* New York: Harper & Row, 1971.

Carsten, F. F. *The Rise of Fascism.* Berkeley: University of California Press, 1967.

DeFelice, Renzo. *Interpretations of Fascism.* Cambridge, Mass.: Harvard U.P., 1977.

Gallo, Max. *Mussolini's Italy.* New York: Macmillan, 1973.

Gregor, James A. *Fascism: The Contemporary Interpretations*. Morristown, N.J.: General Learning Press, 1975.

Heiden, Konrad. *Der Fuehrer*. Boston: Beacon, 1969.

Hitler, Adolf. *Mein Kampf*. Boston: Houghton Mifflin, 1962.

Mussolini, Benito. *My Autobiography*. New York: Charles Scribner's Sons, 1928.

Neumann, Franz. *Behemoth: The Structure and Practice of National Socialism* 2nd ed. New York: Oxford U.P., 1944.

Shirer, William L. *The Rise and Fall of the Third Reich*. New York: Fawcett-World, 1978.

Smith, Dennis Mack. *Mussolini's Roman Empire*. New York: Viking, 1976.

Tannenbaum, Edward R. *The Fascist Experience*. New York: Basic Books, 1972.

10 | *The Authoritarian Right*

*And in him consisteth the Essence of the
Commonwealth; which (to define it) is One Person of
whose Acts a great Multitude . . . have made . . .
the Author, to the end he may use the strength and
means of them all, as he shall think expedient, for
their Peace and Common Defense*
THOMAS HOBBES Leviathan

Authoritarianism is much more a form of governance than a political ideology, and it must be sharply distinguished both from conservative ideology and from totalitarianism. A conservative ideology, as we have noted, is basically consistent with the tenets of democracy, constitutionalism and the rule of law, representative government, and individual freedoms. Authoritarian regimes are not. They are forms of government which rely upon force, eliminate oppositions and freedoms, and often stress nationalism at the risk of becoming expansionist.

Similarly, despite some important resemblances, a sharp distinction should be made between authoritarian and totalitarian regimes. Totalitarian systems stress the mobilization and the participation of the citizenry; authoritarian systems try to keep the citizen in a state of passive obedience. Authoritarian rulers are satisfied when the citizenry remains apathetic and does not oppose the government. The official political ideology in totalitarian systems is "total" — it affects every aspect of social life, economic, political, religious, family, and so on. The aim is to create "new" men and women. Authoritarian systems, on the other hand, have no such all-embracing ideology; they are satisfied to leave social groupings alone — whether Church, family, economic groups, sports, or individual and cultural activities.

In totalitaritan systems the single party is the most dynamic vehicle of change and control; in authoritarian systems that have a single party, the party has far less power and is not important as a vehicle of control and governance. The party yields to the government and to powerful socioeconomic groups. These distinctions must be kept in mind. The reach and grasp of totalitarian systems is longer and firmer — that of authoritarian ones

217

shorter and relatively weak. The goals of totalitarian regimes are comprehensive; those of authoritarian ones are specific. Totalitarian systems try to dig deep roots in the society and manage to endure against many adversities — even military defeat; authoritarian systems have no strong supports and are very fragile — adversity easily topples them. Finally, though personal rule is common to both systems, the party plays a far more important role in institutionalizing and organizing power in totalitarian systems. The death of the leader is almost always fatal in authoritarian systems; totalitarian ones have managed to survive it.

Thus, what distinguishes authoritarian regimes from totalitarian ones is: the ideology of totalitarianism regimes is broader in scope and more intense; totalitarianism regimes have an established well-organized party; totalitarian regimes effect a mass mobilization. All totalitarian regimes have authoritarian traits: they use force, and they control all media and communications as well as all organizations and associations, including economic ones. But authoritarian regimes are not totalitarian — the authority of the state is selective and limited; mobilization is not intense. Indeed, very often no mobilization takes place; if there is a political party, it is small and it competes with other State and private organizations; competing ideologies are sometimes allowed to coexist with the authoritarian state.

Particular forms of authoritarian systems are many. They may be *traditional, bureaucratic, charismatic* or *military*. In traditional systems authority stems from historical rules and customs and rulership is hereditary; in charismatic systems leadership stems from the popularity of the leader and the support he or she manages to elicit; bureaucratic authoritarian systems rely upon respect for the authority of the State and its agents, the bureaucracy, and authority is neither personal nor hereditary but statist. Military authoritarian regimes, finally, are based on either the coercive power of the army or the respect and deference the citizens develop for it, or on both. Its cornerstone is the army's discipline and organization, but leadership generally is personal — it comes from one of the army's officers. "Collegial" military dictatorships do not last long if they do not acknowledge the predominant position of one officer or another.

Bonapartism is a term that represents, historically, a good approximation of authoritarianism. We find in it the charisma of the leader, bureaucratic organization (what we called statism), and a strong military basis. Napoleon Bonaparte was a young French general before he became First Consul in 1801. Even elements of traditionalism were injected when Napoleon was crowned Emperor, in 1804 by the Pope, in the Cathedral of Reims where the French kings had been crowned. His nephew Louis Bonaparte established the second Empire, using the legacy that Napoleon had bequeathed from the first Empire and Louis ruled from 1851 to 1879, also an Emperor.

We find in Bonapartism four basic traits: (a) personal government, (b) centralized bureaucratic authority and organization — i.e., statism, (c) nationalism, and (d) the bypassing of the representative assemblies and institutions in favor of direct popular consultations in the form of plebiscites. There was no mass party to mobilize the people, and although the police used coercive practices, and there was widespread intimidation, opposition was never eliminated.

Franquismo

As with Bonapartism, Spanish authoritarianism became intimately linked with one man — General Francisco Franco (1892–1975), otherwise called the Caudillo (the leader). The governance he established lasted only as long as he lived. Franco never called himself or his regime fascist, even if he admitted to admiring many aspects of the Italian fascist regime. He combined, through his personal rule, forces that were outright fascist, others that were ultraconservative and monarchist, and some that came from the various conservative political parties. He appealed to the military, the Church, the landowners, and the economic and industrial elites, the middle classes, and many of the peasants, especially in the areas where the Church was a dominant force.

Authoritarianism in one form or another was hardly new for Spain, which did not have a genuine republican tradition. Moreover, the economic

Franco inspects the battlefront prior to his insurgent army's assault on Valencia in 1938. (*Wide World Photos*)

and social profile of the country made it particularly receptive to authoritarianism. The majority of the people were illiterate; modernization and economic growth had lagged way behind Western Europe; the Church had opposed republican institutions and governments, and the economic and landed oligarchy favored repression rather than reform. The lower classes — workers, but many farmers too — were in a state of constant defiance and revolt. Many workers joined anarchist syndicalist organizations committed to direct action rather than political participation and party politics. The Communist party, weak at first, managed to gain strength during the Spanish Civil War (1936–1939). At the same time, powerful separatist movements in Catalonia and the Basque region often joined forces with the left wing against the centralization that the right-wing forces and the army tried to impose. The middle classes, which might have been able to exert a moderating influence, were weak. When they were faced with the danger from the left they went, as middle classes almost always do, to the side of the right-wing forces, and, eventually, to Franco.

In the 1930s all the elements of a civil war were present. As in Italy and Germany, there were strikes, occupations of factories, and takeovers by farmers of land belonging to absentee landowners and the Church. Again, as in Italy and Germany, "nationalist" bands and organizations began to take the law into their own hands and to indulge in direct action and intimidation. Fascist organizations developed; notable among them was the Falange, which claimed to be a genuine totalitarian party. Yet, unlike Italy and Germany, the Spanish "revolution" began as a classic military uprising among the officers and special troops in Spanish Morocco. Franco marched into Spain and into political power behind his troops. There was no equivalent of the "March on Rome" and nobody formally invited Franco to form a government. It was a military and not a political uprising, designed to crush the communists and their republican allies. It was a pragmatic and on the spot solution. Franquismo never became a genuine political doctrine with a comprehensive political ideology.

The same pragmatic and opportunistic stance was followed by Franco from his takeover of power in 1936 and until his death in 1975. He followed a policy of compromise and adjustment, both at home and abroad, changing policies as the fortunes of World War II changed and reconciling and neutralizing conflicting forces at home so as to keep his hand free. With most of the communist and left-wing leaders eliminated during and immediately after the civil war, he had little to fear from the left. To the right he had to contend with and try to balance a number of forces: there were the loyalists who considered Franco only a temporary interlude before the restoration of the monarchy; there was the Catholic Church that maintained control over education and insisted on imposing its ultra-conservative doctrine upon the State; and there were the genuine fascists — the falangists — highly ideological, and pushing for revolutionary changes, for a Corporatist State, and for social justice. The Falange was also anti-clerical. There were, of course, the military, the pillar of Franco's regime, interested particularly in order and in their own autonomy and privileges. There were, finally, the economic elites who were wary of both the Falange and the Church. The one was an obstacle to their own privileges and profits, the other an obstacle to economic modernization.

At no time did Franco allow any of these forces to become dominant over the others. But at no time did he envisage the subordination of any one of them or some of them to a combination of others. He played a balancing act that could well be called "controlled pluralism" — which, of course, is another way of saying that the system never assumed an encompassing and dominant role by subordinating all forces under it. At best it played a mediating role. A historian of Spain writes that the regime, by 1950, had adopted the posture of "a pragmatic, middle of the road authoritarian state, not fascist but resolutely anti-Communist, with stress on domestic development and survival."[1]

The Falange

Franco's Spain had a Fascist party but in contrast to Germany and Italy it never became a mass party and never played an influential role in the regime.[2] Founded in 1934 by a number of young intellectuals, some of whom were deeply influenced by the social doctrine of the Catholic Church, and others, even more, by the secular aspirations of the Nazis, the Falange became the only political party in Franco's Spain. Its name (literally "phalanx," after the phalanx of the ancient Macedonian army, which deployed its soldiers in close ranks in depth, providing both for strength and quick movement) was chosen to symbolize mass, organization, and power. As with other right-wing totalitarian parties, its aim was to assume control of the State, to create a comprehensive ideology, to mobilize the masses and bring under it even the Church and the army. It was anti-capitalist, corporatist, stressed egalitarianism and popular participation and mobilization; it was nationalist and, of course, intensely anti-Communist. Among the twenty-five points of its original program the following are of particular significance:

—Political unity for Spain and elimination of regional separatism
—Abolution of political parties
—Establishment of a national dictatorship led by one party
—Use of violence in the regeneration of Spain
—Development of Spanish imperial power
—Expansion and strengthening of the armed forces
—Recognition and support of Catholicism as the official religion of Spain, but rejection of any clerical influence in government

In economic and social matters the Falange promised an economic revolution to include:

—Establishment of national syndicates embracing employers and employees.

1. Payne. *Franco's Spain*. pp. 38–39.
2. Parts of my account of the Spanish Falange comes from Stanley Payne's excellent monograph *Falange* (Stanford U.P., 1961) and I owe thanks to the author.

—Sweeping agrarian reforms to reclaim wasteland, to improve techniques, to concentrate scattered holdings and to reorganize the large landed estates (*latifundia*)

—Industrial expansion

—Respect of private property but nationalization of credit facilities

Personal Government

In its aspirations the Falange soon began to clash with the Church hierarchy, the army, and the bureaucracy, and to frighten the economic elites. The party was kept carefully under control by Franco. Its membership remained small. By the end of 1945 party officials began to reconsider their doctrine, asserting now that totalitarianism was incompatible with moral values (i.e., religion). It dropped all corporatist ideas, especially pronouncements favoring joint decision making by workers and owners. Eventually it ceased to be an important force.

The fundamental reason for the failure of the Falange was Franco and his authoritarian regime. The party had an ideology and wanted to politicize and mobilize the masses. Franco was opposed to both. Franco would have preferred to depoliticize his regime as much as possible and to let the mass of the people acquiesce to its control out of ignorance, rather than having them involved in political crusades. When the Falange was useful Franco used it in his balancing act against other political forces; otherwise he gave it no support nor did he allow it to become a dominant political force.

Franquismo continued in the direction of statism and personal government, concerned after the 1950s with economic development and modernization, but maintained the same hard repressive and exclusive policies with regard to leftist parties. The trade unions remained under the control of the State thanks to the device of the Corporate State and the establishment of vertically organized corporations consisting of managers and workers in the same industry, as had been the case with Italy and neighboring Portugal.

Limited efforts in the direction of liberalization were made — the abolition of prior censorship of press and books; the election of some of the members of the legislature (many of whom continued to be appointed); a broadening of educational opportunities; economic reforms; but above all industrialization and urbanization, which began to move forward at an accelerated pace. The active population engaged in agriculture declined between 1950 and 1970 from over 50 percent to not more than 30 percent. What is more, new political elites emerged. As Richard Herr points out, they were "made up of high government officials, bankers, technocrats, and corporation managers, as in Germany and France and other industrial nations."[3] They began to influence the regime. But this was not incompatible with Franquismo since it had never developed a strong ideological position and had never allowed a mass party to develop and overshadow all other groups.

3. Richard Herr. *An Historical Essay on Modern Spain.* Berkeley: University of California Press, p. 260.

Franco's Spain tells us something about the flexibility and the pragmatism of authoritarian regimes. Franco adjusted both at home and abroad to changing circumstances; he allowed representative assemblies to operate as long as he could manipulate them; he framed constitutional documents; he provided for laws of succession — but he himself remained the highest law. When international circumstances changed, he, like the second Bonaparte, began to liberalize the regime without ever abandoning the political control he held. Like Louis Bonaparte, he began to make room for new elites and to press for economic development and modernization. But the flexibility of the regime and its pragmatism also indicate its inherent fragility. Without an ideology and a strong mass political party, it had to rely on an intensely personal element of leadership, and when the leader died there were no institutions to carry on the governance that had been established.

The Authoritarian Right in the United States

"Extremism," writes Seymour Martin Lipset with particular reference to American political history, "describes the violation, through action or advocacy, of the democratic political process."[4] Despite sporadic flare-ups from what has come to be called the American "extreme" or "radical" right, the democratic process in the United States has held remarkably well. Extremist movements hardly ever succeeded in synthesizing their various negations into a program or an ideology or in transforming them into some kind of positive political formula in order to seek, let alone gain, broad national support and political power.

The strains and stresses of American society have, inevitably, spawned extremist movements. Most but not all of these have come from the right. They have been movements of disaffection appearing in "periods of incipient change"; they are addressed to groups that "feel deprived" or feel "that they have been deprived of something they consider important" but also to particular groups whose "rising aspirations lead them to realize that they have always been deprived of something they now want."[5] Under such circumstances, and unless there is a deep commitment to democracy, the success of authoritarian movements becomes a distinct possibility.

Underlying economic factors have always played a crucial role in the rise of extremist movements, but in the American experience ethnic, racial, and religious factors have been more important. Only since World War II have economic as well as international and genuinely ideological political factors begun to gain prominence.

The Know-Nothings

One of the earliest extremist movements was the Know-Nothing party that developed in New England, with particular strength in Massachusetts, in the 1820s. It was primarily composed of workers and artisans who feared that the

4. Seymour Martin Lipset and Earl Raab. *The Politics of Unreason.* p. 428.
5. Ibid.

influx of immigrants would depress their wages and drive them out of work. They advocated the exclusion of immigrants and wanted to prevent their participation in politics. Direct action was often taken against foreigners: members were supposed to "know nothing" about such action. Even if wages appeared to be the central issue, psychological factors played an important role. In an expanding economy, there could be work both for immigrant workers and also for the indigenous Anglo-Saxons. But the very fact that "foreigners" would attain the income of the native workers appeared to the latter an affront to their position and status within the community.

The Ku Klux Klan

The Ku Klux Klan (KKK) emerged in the South right after the Civil War, to intimidate blacks and thwart the federal measures taken to give them citizenship and extend constitutional rights after they had been freed. It was a regional movement based on community and vigilante organizations, and gangs, designed to keep blacks out of politics and the economy, to deprive them of access to property, and to keep them at the level of farmhands and unskilled workers. It also kept a tight control upon all whites suspected of showing tolerance and sympathy to blacks. In the years following World War I the Klan had a particularly strong revival, emerging not only as the advocate of white supremacy but also as the champion of "Protestant" and native superiority over all immigrant and non-Protestant religious groups. It became the proponent of the purity of Americans — against Italians, Jews, Mexicans, Japanese, and so on. At one point in the 1920s, it numbered more than four million members and extended beyond the South into the Southwest and California. It exerted a strong influence over the Southern state legislatures.

The Klan did not directly challenge the Constitution. It gave it, however, a special interpretation favoring state rights and state autonomy. It was unwilling to see individual protection and civil rights extended to the groups and to the minorities it had singled out. It favored restrictive and repressive legislation, and when they were not forthcoming, resorted to direct violence with burnings, intimidation, evictions, and not infrequently, lynchings.

Like the Know-Nothings, the Ku Klux Klan's membership consisted of low-income and low-status groups: artisans, shopkeepers, unskilled workers, and farmers who had moved from the farm to small towns. Their leadership came from petty officials — police officers, for example, small-town businessmen, realtors, and an assortment of veterans. Local ministers of various Protestant denominations played an important role and added biblical zest and justification to the movement, especially in the campaign against Catholics and Jews. In general, the movement preached religious orthodoxy and conformity, the simple values of rural life and of the small town against the big city, and was against American entanglements abroad. It was fearful of industrialization and modernization because they were changing American society and shifting the weight of population and of economic and political power into the cities and away from the countryside. The movement against the immigrant was a desperate effort to vindicate the position of white, small-town, low- and middle-class Protestant America, and to maintain their economic, social, and political status in a changing world.

Father Coughlin

The first genuine ideological and national extremist right-wing movement was developed by Father Coughlin, a Catholic priest, between 1928 and 1940 — the years of the Great Depression. Unemployment peaked at a level of about nine to ten million until 1939, despite the New Deal measures. Not only did blue-collar and white-collar workers suffer, but also the farmers, the middle classes, and many of the manufacturing and trading groups. Fascism had triumphed in Italy, and the Hitler movement had begun the upward climb in Germany. Democracy, as we have seen, was on the defensive, and socioeconomic conditions in the United States were ripe for a strong movement against it. Father Coughlin tried to exploit all this.

His movement had many of the characteristics of a totalitarian right-wing movement similar to those of Italy and Germany. First, it purported to be a mass movement. According to surveys conducted at the time, almost one-third of the American people "approved" of what Father Coughlin said. What he said was not addressed to native Americans. It did not pit them against immigrants: it almost did the reverse. It struck at the major American institutions and the elites, pitting the "small man" against the "establishment."

A second important feature of the movement was its anti-Semitism. It endorsed the racist doctrines of the Nazis and described Jews in the same racist terms. But there were other special reasons — one of them manifestly religious, exploiting the Catholic bias against the Jewish faith. It viewed the Jews as an "internationalist element," distinct from the American melting pot. The infamous and malicious *Protocols of the Elders of Zion*, which, as we have seen, Hitler had publicized, were frequently broadcast and printed by spokesmen in the various pamphlets of the movement.

Its third feature was anti-communism. Communism was a threat both because of its anti-religious appeal, and also because of its emphasis upon class. This was in opposition to the national and communitarian philosophy Father Coughlin wished to impart.

Finally, while a staunch nationalist and an isolationist, Father Coughlin began to lean increasingly in the direction of the Nazi and the Italian models, favoring the support of both countries. Just before the demise of his movement in 1940 (by this time its popularity had waned, and at the beginning of the war it was outlawed) he identified fully with the cause of the Nazis to the point of declaring himself to be a "fascist."

His program had all the familiar "antis": it was anti-elite, anti-Semitic, anti-internationalist (but with a growing sympathy for Hitler and Mussolini that in the years before the war became outright support), anti-democratic, anti-liberal, anti-capitalist and anti-Constitution. It was one of the first movements to directly advocate the overhaul of the Constitution of the United States. It also suggested a new social order against *both* big capital and big labor. The name of the movement, characteristically enough, was The Union Party for Social Justice, and it merged with other extremist groups to form the National Union. It preached unifying and communitarian themes.

The social configuration of its support was not dissimilar from the one found in the early stages of Nazism and fascism. It came from low middle-class groups, and from rural areas and small towns; there was considerable support among the middle classes, and higher support from among Catholics and the unemployed.

Joseph McCarthy

It was a convergence of many factors that both sharpened and deepened the content and the thrust of the American extreme right in the 1950s. The major ones were similar to those that accounted for the emergence of fascism in Italy after World War I: profound discontent with the settlement that followed World War II. Many in the United States felt that the Russians had strengthened their position, and began to search for scapegoats. Senator Joseph McCarthy found one in "international communism" and its agents in the United States. Single-handedly, he began to mount a campaign against not only Communists, but also their sympathizers — left-wingers and liberals — the so-called "fellow travelers." The term included intellectuals, university professors, members of the "Northeastern establishment" and bankers, and supporters of the United Nations. Not only Democrats, but also Republican leaders — even President Eisenhower — were accused. McCarthy, in many highly publicized appearances and through investigations conducted by his Senate Committee, discovered "hundreds" of card-carrying communists in the State Department. He claimed that agreements at Yalta and Potsdam during and after World War II were engineered by the fellow travelers to give undue benefits and advantages to the Soviet Union. The United States had been cheated by them from its victory.

While McCarthy never managed to organize a national movement, national response was widespread and positive. This was the period of "The Great Fear,"[6] when wholesale purges of "crypto-Communists" occurred in the federal government, in universities, the army, and the trade unions. It was also a movement which began to show clearly the impact that the media of communication, especially TV, can have in creating a "national" state of mind. McCarthy and his activities were widely publicized.

Conspiracy theories are common in extremist movements. With Hitler it was the conspiracy of the Jews and the failure of the civilians to support their soldiers in war that played an important role. The conspiracy of the Communists against the United States was a notion that satisfied many conservatives and appealed to others who felt that the international position of the United States was slipping. In a peculiar way the McCarthy crusade

---

6. David Caute. *The Great Fear: The Anti-Communist Purge Under Truman and Eisenhower.*

Senator McCarthy, whipping up an anti-communist terror in New York, 1954. (*Photo: UPI*)

appealed also to the forces of nativism that we found in the Know-Nothings and the Klan. There were the "ins," the good Americans, and the "outs," the Communists, fellow travelers, crypto-Communists, left-wing liberals, and so on.

The 1960s

With the demise of McCarthyism in the middle 1950s, a number of new extremist right-wing organizations and "third parties" mushroomed. They all followed the same basic themes — anti-communism, a bellicose attitude towards the Soviet Union, and a blanket endorsement of nationalist ideals. But right-wing extremism also assumed a blatantly conservative posture with regard to domestic issues — social and economic ones. It began also to broaden its attack against the major American political and economic elites, and to criticize the American system of constitutional democracy. Many organizations assumed the posture of the minuscule nationalist organizations that had developed in Germany before the Nazis managed to bring them together. They urged direct action and formed vigilante groups.

The John Birch Society, founded in 1958, became in a sense the intellectual inspiration for these movements. It kept a check of "Communist penetration" and "communist control" of the United States. This ranged from as low as 30 percent to as high as 60 percent! President Eisenhower and John Foster Dulles, the Secretary of State, were considered to be "communist agents." Its membership in the late 1960s was almost 100,000, but it appears that it has declined since. It had about four thousand local chapters, some of which are now inactive. It publishes the *American Opinion,* a monthly review, and its official ideology can be found in the John Birch Society *Blue Book.* It owns a publishing company and several bookstores through which it disseminates its material.

The Minutemen

"Minutemen" was an extremist vigilante organization founded in 1960 by Robert DePugh, a Missouri businessman, with the purpose of training Americans in guerrilla warfare. This group would be used to fight the Communists once they had conquered the United States, an event which the Minutemen saw as highly probable, either through internal subversion or invasion. Membership estimates ranged from DePugh's claim of a high of 25,000 to a low of 500. In the late 1960s, the Patriotic party was established as the political branch of the Minutemen. Both groups have had links to various neo-Nazi and rightist paramilitary groups, as well as the KKK.

Several groups of Minutemen have been seized with illegal arms caches which have included rifles, submachine guns, explosives, mortars, and anti-tank weapons. In August 1968, members were arrested after a gun battle with state police as the result of an armed attack on a farm run by the New England Committee of Nonviolent Action at Voluntown, Conn., in which several people were wounded. DePugh himself was implicated in a plot to rob a Seattle bank. He was arrested in July 1969 and subsequently sentenced to a ten-year prison term.

The Prospects of American Extremism

American right-wingers can be identified in terms of their "antis." They are against the United Nations and all its international organizations, against NATO, against diplomatic relations with the Soviet Union, against the social legislation of the New Deal, against capital gains taxes, against income tax, against the Rural Electrification Administration, against the National Relations Labor Board, against federal wage and price controls, against the Federal Reserve System, against urban renewal, and against all forms of federal regulatory controls and federal intervention in the economy. What they favor is a free enterprise system. They represent the extreme right of the neo-conservatives. What distinguishes them sharply from all those who call themselves conservative is that they have raised questions about the democratic process itself, urging constitutional revision, direct action, and repression. Extremists show little respect for constitutional individual guarantees. Yet aside from the commitment to economic liberalism, they have developed no positive ideology other than an exclusive form of nationalism in which Communists, "collectivists," "liberals," and New Dealers can have no place.

At least two particular circumstances have strengthened the extreme right and have provided it with considerable popular support. The first, and perhaps most important, was the "black movement." In the beginning this took the form of urban riots, and later desegregation when the Supreme Court, in 1954, and various federal district courts enforced equal opportunities and integration. Non-discriminatory provisions for blacks in buying houses, in employment, and in education, caused a backlash among many workers, low income groups, and white immigrants. A new "Know-Nothing" mentality developed. A militant and "preservative" (to use Lipset's term) posture emerged. Deep-set psychological forces came together in the late 1960s to enhance this posture. According to David Rieseman, one generation had already gone by since the New Deal legislation had been in force, and its impact was now causing a feeling of threat and frustration among many in the middle classes and many other groups. What was the threat?

The "old middle class" of the 1930s — the independent physician, homebuilder, farm owner, small-town lawyer, realtor, automobile dealer, gasoline station owner, small businessman and the like — were definitely being shoved aside. The small town, and its ways of life, were perishing as urbanization gained momentum. The coming of the immigrant groups to full political power, and even to social status, intensified the feeling of threat on the part of "middle America."

But the new elites found themselves in danger too, and on the defensive. The managerial elites that replaced the family-owned enterprise or a small corporation were without roots and property. They were self-made men or women. Success alternated with failure in the fast-moving and highly impersonal large organizations, firms, and corporations. The military themselves found their traditional claims to authority challenged by the experts — from universities, various think-tanks, business and technical schools. A new intelligentsia, well-versed in military, technical, and international problems, began to supersede the military establishment. It was Secretary McNamara, a president of the Ford Motor Corporation, who under President Kennedy and Johnson directed the Pentagon with the help of civilians. And it was Henry Kissinger who became secretary of state.

So, while the "old middle classes" were in a state of frustration, the "new middle classes" — technicians, engineers, teachers and professors, white-collar workers, middle managerial groups, the bureacracy — which had been steadily growing in numbers, income, social status, and position, began, too, to experience the same predicament. New groups, notably the blacks, began to make their bid for power and income. At the same time, inflation began to endanger all middle-class groups old and new. Finally, an intractable international situation, and what amounted to defeat in the war in Vietnam, shook the myth of American supremacy. In a fast-changing world at home and abroad the traditional landmarks that spelled security and confidence for the American public were being washed away.

A feeling of frustration, resentment, and impotence has always provided the best climate for the growth of extremist movements — with simple answers to complex problems and nationalist solutions to deepset social and economic difficulties. Almost half a century after the New Deal, and more than a generation after victory in World War II, this is the spirit that may be prevalent today. The foundations of American democracy and constitutional government may be tested as never before.

Bibliography

Bell, Daniel (ed.). *The Radical Right.* New York: Doubleday, 1964.

Caute, David. *The Great Fear.* New York: Simon and Schuster, 1978.

Collier, David (ed.). *The New Authoritarianism in Latin America.* Princeton, N.J.: Princeton University Press, 1979.

Epstein, Benjamin, and Forster, Arnold. *The Radical Right.* New York: Vintage, 1967.

Hobbes, Thomas. *Leviathan.* Baltimore, Md.: Penguin, 1968.

Linz, Juan. "Totalitarian and Authoritarian Regimes" in *Handbook* of Political Science, vol. 3. Reading, Mass.: Addison-Wesley, 1975.

Lipset, Seymour Martin, and Raab, Earl. *The Politics of Unreason: Right Wing Extremism in America 1790–1970,* Chicago: University of Chicago Press, 1978.

Payne, Stanley. *Falange: A History of Spanish Fascism.* Stanford, Calif.: Stanford U.P., 1961.

———. *Franco's Spain.* New York: Cromwell, 1967.

Perlmutter, Amos. *Modern Authoritarianism: A Comparative Institutional Analysis.* New Haven, Conn.: Yale University Press, 1981.

Rogger, Hans, and Weber, Eugen (eds.) *The European Right: A Historical Profile.* Berkeley: University of California Press, 1965.

Part Four

Old Wine in New Bottles: Revolutions and Nationalisms

What is truth? said jesting Pilate, and would not stay for an answer.

FRANCIS BACON   "Of Truth"

The most powerful ideologies in our world today seem to revolve around "nationalism" and "revolution." Somewhere in a corner of the Sahara, the Polisario are fighting for their national independence; in Iran, it was in the name of independence that a populist movement erupted; in Central America, revolutionaries and guerrillas claim to be fighting for their independence against "Yankee imperialism"; the Corsicans, the Welsh, the Scots, the Catalanians, the Basques have been on the move; the Arabs seem to be on the verge of a Holy War in the name of the "Arab nation" and Islam. The Palestinian Liberation Organization claims a home in the Holy Land, while the Prime Minister of Israel asks all Jews — wherever they may be — to stand up for the land of their forefathers. Is there a black nationalism in the United States — people ask.

At the same time — and often linked with various nationalist movements — claims for economic well-being, social justice, and equality continue to mobilize the poor and the wretched into revolutionary movements in all corners of the world. The North-South dialogue — between the rich and the poor nations — is about a more equitable distribution of our planet's resources. But even within rich nations revolutionary movements demand a better distribution of the national wealth. The "revolution of rising expectations" may have peaked, but it remains a powerful force that has to be reckoned. In many countries military and authoritarian regimes defend the wealth and privilege of the few or try, in the name of the people, to improve the economy. Politics, in fact, seems to have given place to revolutionary

233

strife — or to put the same idea differently, the use of force to make a revolution or to avert it has become an alternative to politics.

In contrast to liberalism and Marxism that we discussed earlier — both of them powerful revolutionary ideologies — the revolutionary ideologies to be discussed in this chapter are intensive and unstructured ideological movements. Not only do they appeal to powerful ethical imperatives but they pay little attention to history and circumstances in order to develop a coherent body of theory and to suggest tactics. They seem to have these things in common — to change by an effort of will and organization what has been deeply traced over many centuries, to reshape social, economic, and political life, and to refashion even human nature. Like the Commissar in Orwell's *1984,* many of the contemporary revolutionaries would say "Forget all these notions about human nature; WE make human nature." All of them are committed to action — revolutionary action — even when the theory behind it is uncertain and the goals unclear. Action by itself and in itself will provide the experience that will guide the revolutionary leaders to reform and change. The revolutionary is expected to learn from the revolution. As with the anarchists — that we discuss briefly — contemporary revolutionaries put the accent on will and action.

I have tried in this part to separate "revolution" and "nationalism," and the ideologies from which they spring, as they grip the minds and the hearts of so many throughout the world. Both borrow a great deal from past ideologies, from Marxism and Leninism that we have discussed, and also from anarchism and liberalism. So do national independence movements. The wine is the same old heady wine — the bottles and the labels are new.

11 | *Ideologies and Revolutionary Movements*

If men cannot refer to a common value, recognized by all as existing in each one, then man is incomprehensible to man. The rebel demands that this value should be clearly recognized in himself because he knows or suspects, that without this principle, crime and disorder would reign throughout the world.
ALBERT CAMUS   The Rebel

I am nothing and I should be everything.
KARL MARX   Critique of Hegel's Philosophy

Most people have romantic notions about revolutions — the mob storming the Bastille, the tea thrown into the Boston Harbor, the Bolsheviks storming the Winter Palace, Gandhi and his followers lying on the railroad tracks in a movement of civil disobedience that paralyzed the British rule in India. Heroic statements come to our minds: "Give me liberty, or give me death"; "the despotism of liberty against tyranny"; "workers of the world arise: you have nothing to lose but your chains."

The Nature of Revolutions

There is much more than rhetoric and romantic imagery to a revolution! It is a grim business. A revolution is an act of organized violence to bring about radical changes in the economic, social, and political relations within a given system. It uses force to destroy (sometimes physically) and replace those who hold power.

Protests, civil disobedience, turmoil, demonstrations, and acts of violence are not revolutions, as such, though they may precede them. All depends on the degree of mobilization and organization and on the ideas people share when they commit acts of violence.

Gandhi's disobedience in India was aimed at driving out the British and replacing colonial rule with an Indian government — it was a revolutionary movement. Martin Luther King, on the other hand, simply wanted to force concessions that would allow the blacks to participate (as they were entitled to do) in the American system. In the past, periodic peasants' rebellions in Germany, France, Italy, and Eastern Europe aimed to reclaim the land from the nobility. These rebellions did not have broad political goals such as changing the political regime.

Major revolutions have been associated with: (a) a national or a colonial independence movement against a foreign occupying power — a phenomenon common in Europe in the nineteenth century and throughout most of the colonial world in the twentieth century; (b) separatist movements mobilizing ethnic or religious groups to secede from the state in which they live; (c) a movement organized by some social groups or classes against those that hold power within a given regime. The Puritan Revolution under Cromwell, the French Revolution, the Bolshevik Revolution in 1917, and the Chinese Communist Revolution in 1949 are the archetypal cases. But the national independence movements in the nineteenth century, and the guerrilla warfare in Vietnam, Algeria, and elsewhere only a decade or so ago, and in some of the Latin American countries today, are also revolutions.

The Role of Ideology

People do not revolt unless they first get the idea that organized force is a remedy for their situation. Some philosophers have suggested that conflict and revolutions lie in the interstices of the historical process — and we have noted that both Hegel and Marx assumed that a dialectic process (involving conflict between opposing forces) was historically inevitable. According to this notion, history itself is what counts — the actors, individuals, and groups act in accord with "its laws." Conflict and revolutions are, in a sense, predetermined; and so are the ideologies related to them.

Marx developed the most complete ideology *of* a revolution and *for* a revolution. It is the material conditions that by and large shape ideology. The ruling class — the bourgeoisie — tries to impose its ideology upon all others. But the workers, though not immune to it, ultimately reject it in order to develop a revolutionary ideology — a "counter-ideology." We saw that Lenin claimed that only a small elite could act for the workers in leading them against their masters.

If circumstances (the material conditions) shape ideologies, what role do ideologies play in shaping circumstances? It is an endless argument. Determinists tend to look primarily at the circumstances and claim that ideologies cannot arise or function independently. Marxists, as we have seen, perform a balancing act between the two — there is interplay between *both* the circumstances *and* the ideology. Other revolutionaries tend to emphasize both *will* and *ideas* — so much as to attribute to them an independent role. For these revolutionaries ideology is primary — what Marx called the "theory that becomes a material force when it grips the masses."

As for the substance of a revolutionary ideology, a number of elements shape it. A distinction is often made by some between an "inherent" and a "derived" ideology. The first is another name for the culture of a people — the sum total of their experiences and customs, their oral traditions, their habits, and their common memories of past rights, privileges, and claims. The "inherent" ideology usually provides the context for the development of a revolutionary consciousness, but this is not enough. What is needed is a theory — a "derived ideology" — that will spell out, in a structured and organized manner, the reasons why force is necessary and will outline the goals that force will realize.

"Derived ideologies" comes from political theorists — say Marx, Rousseau, Tom Paine, Herbert Marcuse, and many others. The transmission belt between "derived" and "inherent" consists of the intellectuals. They blend theory, popular culture, and traditions in order to shape a revolutionary ideology and a revolutionary movement. Theory will write the grammar of the revolution, leaving it to the organizers to do the spelling.

An Italian Communist theoretician, Antonio Gramsci, emphasized the independent and creative role of ideology. There are many areas of indeterminancy in the society; there are many groups that do not belong either to the bourgeoisie or to the proletariat. They float in limbo. Ideology, he claimed, if it blended theory and popular culture and was developed and propagated by the intellectuals and organizers — the "organic intellectuals" as he called them — would sufficiently mobilize and organize these groups. The intellectuals distill the new ideology drop by drop to conquer the masses slowly and to build ideological pockets and bastions that are immune to the prevailing ideology. It is not an exaggeration to say that the revolution was, for Gramsci, primarily a vast educational and organizational effort, that did not necessarily need to rely on the use of force (though never excluding it) against the ruling class. Force would come in handy, but only to enhance the ideological awareness and preparedness of the masses. Revolution was a matter of the mind — the transformation of the ideology held by the people.

The Circumstances: Structural Factors

When does the "theory . . . grip the masses" — to become a revolutionary movement? Crane Britton, after a survey of the major revolutions (the Puritan Revolution, the French Revolution, the Bolshevik Revolution, and the American Revolution), found some common structural characteristics.[1] They are the following:

1. The political societies in which revolutions occurred were "on the whole on the upgrade economically before the revolution." In most cases they were revolutions of hope and not despair; the actors were not downtrodden, starving, poor, or slaves. The ideology they shared was one of optimism. There was an expectation of better opportunities . . .

2. In all cases — although perhaps less so with the American Revolution — there were strong class antagonisms, but revolutions cannot be explained in terms of one class fighting against another. In fact, revolutions

1. Crane, Brinton, "The Anatomy of Revolution," *Passim.* New Jersey: Prentice-Hall, 1938.

occur when social classes come closer together, so that the privileges and power of some appears intolerable. As de Tocqueville had noted, people resent inequalities only when they become a little more equal! Untouchables and slaves rarely revolt. The idea of revolution comes in the minds of men and women who become relatively better-off, whose wants and expectations are on the rise.

3. Another phenomenon associated with revolution is the "desertion of the intellectuals" — of those who write and preach, of the clerks and the teachers. They shift their allegiance from the regime in search of alternatives. By doing so, they sap its strength. Revolution, then, "begins" in the minds of the intellectuals — those we called in our first chapter the "ideologues." They think and germinate the thoughts of revolution long before these thoughts trickle down to the hovel of the peasant or the artisan's basement or the slums or the workshops.

4. Before a revolution there is a breakdown in the efficiency and performance of the government. This is due to the fact that economic changes occur, such as industrialization with new technological innovations. The government is unable to take these economic changes into account, to respond to new needs and demands, and to adjust to them. The government officials lose faith in their ability to control events and to govern. Relatedly, the finances and the administration of the government suffer. The "organized discontented groups" press their demands at this juncture and the governmental apparatus is unable to react. In almost all cases, the government and the regime are in a state of virtual collapse *before* the revolution succeeds! A crucial factor in a revolution is the weakness shown at the top of the existing structure, not the strength mustered at the bottom.

Is it possible, then, to say that a revolution as a process seems to start at the top? That there are structural societal factors that can best explain it? All one can say is that they play a very important role. Marx was clearly aware of it because the timing of the workers' revolution, as we have seen, was related to major structural changes in the capitalistic economy and the political regime that reflected it. This was not so for Lenin and many of his followers who emphasized will and leadership.

The Individual: Subjective Factors

Even if revolution is a mass organized movement, it is the individual who must be mobilized. Nobody will leave home and family, job, or farm, unless prompted by powerful reasons to do so. Only a handful of individuals are "born radicals" — their personalities propel them to radical action to change things; most people, however, venture into the unknown world of revolution and violence only because they feel, or are made to feel, that their lives are in danger.

The feeling of threat — particularly the threat of deprivation — is the most common psychological motivation for a revolution. The most common threat is to one's livelihood, one's expectations, and one's position in the society — his or her status. Rising material opportunities provide for the hope of more, and when for one reason or another opportunities do not materialize, people become apprehensive. Even more, *they feel deprived* in two ways: (a) their expectations of what they believe they are worth — of what they should be getting — do not materialize; (b) their standard of living falls behind others. This is often referred to as "relative deprivation." The threat to status is generally shared more or less among well-established groups that find their position, income, and importance in the society threatened by other groups. Revolutions motivated by such threat to status have been common among middle-class and lower-middle class groups and are considered, as we have seen, the major reasons for fascism and Nazism. Direct deprivation of one's livelihood and expectations is commonly associated with revolutions by peasantry, working classes, and often lower-middle-class groups.

Will and Revolution: The Meaning of Praxis

Historical, economic, psychological, and structural conditions and circumstances prepare men and women for a revolution; they do not make it! Will, leadership, organization, mass involvement and support, or even acquiescence are needed. Revolutionaries emphasize will; they stress the voluntaristic, organizational, and elitist nature of a revolution. They want "praxis" — they want action! Praxis can refer to an act in a play. There are so many acts in a play — three, or four, or five — and we must see them all before we know what the players will do and what will be done to them. A praxis is, then, a time category within which planned actions take place. It combines revolutionary theory and action.

Proponents of praxis, however, put action first. There are two reasons: first, revolutionary action trains, educates, prepares, and above all, mobilizes groups such as students and the intelligentsia into a revolutionary formation that propagates its own ideology — a counter-ideology; second, praxis, the action of the revolution, appeals to what we called the "inherent ideology" — to all the discontents and the claims inherited by the culture, the history, and the traditions of a society.

Through praxis, the discontent of the farmers may blend with the frustration of the unemployed and the resentment of ethnic or racial minority groups. In this manner, the "counter-ideology" gradually gains momentum and the "official ideology," along with the State and its various institutions, are rendered impotent. The important thing is to begin — to move into action. "We engage the enemy and then we shall see" — both Napoleon, a great general, and Lenin, a great revolutionary, were fond of this expression.

There is a subtle and an unpredictable interplay between the revolutionary movement and its leadership on the one hand and the evolving circumstances on the other. The circumstances cannot be reshaped easily and the powerholders do not give in readily. Revolutionaries may have to improvise; new revolutionary institutions spring from nowhere — as was the case in the Paris Commune in 1870, in the Bolshevik Revolution in 1917, or with guerrilla warfare in many areas of the colonial world. The revolution goes on. It is, to use the term of a French revolutionary, "A revolution inside the Revolution." The constant interplay between revolutionary will and circumstances educates and refines both the method and the objectives of the revolutionaries.

Praxis, then, is the starting point of a revolution to reshape society. But it is also a vast effort consisting of a series of multiple acts of violence and defiance that may stretch over a long period of time, to create the conditions for a revolution — to shape the "counter-ideology." Praxis, gradually and cumulatively, prepares the society for a new way of life with new institutions in accord with the counter-ideology that is gaining roots.

However, both as a frontal revolutionary act and as a gradual process to develop a new revolutionary consciousness, praxis displays the same characteristic — the emphasis on political will and leadership and the importance it gives to ideology. Praxis gives a lot of room to "subjective" as opposed to "objective" factors.

In considering the notion of praxis there is one more difficult point — one that we touched upon in our introductory chapter. If philosophy without action or an invitation to action is idle contemplation, action without theory is blind. How can the philosophers save the world — how can they become kings — without action? The revolutionaries that are committed to praxis are informed, or at least are supposed to be informed, by theory, by philosophy — mostly by Marxism. But even the most sophisticated among them admit that the theory is but a guideline and that only in the course of their revolutionary action will the truth and moral superiority of their endeavors be revealed. Many of the revolutionaries of the twentieth century both from the right and the left, seem to have taken praxis to mean willed action based on subjective criteria of right and wrong, but this implies that the actor is more important than the author and that he can change the play to suit his will! So can the revolutionary while the revolution goes on.

Anarchism

As with the terrorists today, anarchists stalked the earth in the latter part of the nineteenth century and continued until the 1930s. Of all revolutionaries they have been and are the most committed to direct action — to praxis. Anarchism as a doctrine was inspired by some of the greatest philosophers and was steeped profoundly in moral idealism. A number of powerful intellectual forces shaped the doctrine of anarchism: Christianity, liberalism, socialism, and idealism were among the most important.

Christianity

Christianity (despite the fact that most anarchists were against religion and the Church) provided a strong ingredient for the development of anarchist thought. The individual as God's creature, and endowed with rationality, should be free to live his or her temporal life. He or she should not be subject to any secular powers. Christianity pitted moral individual consciousness against temporal authority and, in so doing, promoted an attitude of defiance and insubordination.

Liberalism

Anarchism also followed the "moral core" of liberalism and the first priority was to maintain the moral autonomy of the individual. To do so the anarchists proposed to eliminate the State, democratic or not, and to do away with all the coercive traits of political authority and to replace them with free and spontaneously formed associations. This was only a step beyond classic liberalism according to which, as we saw earlier, the state is formed by a voluntary contract among the citizens. Since any contract involves some degree of alienation of one's freedom, anarchists wish, in effect, to revoke the contract and put an end to all obligations undertaken by the citizen. But the same was true for society and societal relations; they, too, must be purged of everything that allows some people to dominate others — everything and anything that allows for subordination and inequalities. The major institution that makes for inequalities is property, and some anarchists, notably Michael Bakunin (1814–1876), favored communism as a solution. Others, however, especially P. J. Proudhon (1809–1864), would allow for some individual property but favored economic democracy with the control and organization of production and productive forces lodged in voluntary "associations."

Socialism

Most anarchists shared the attitudes of the Utopian Socialists that we discussed briefly in Chapter 3. They favored the elimination of private property — or at least of large-scale private holdings in land, industry, or finances. They also favored collectivism and socialism in various forms. The extent to which private property was to be allowed by some anarchists related only to small holdings and to property held by voluntary associations. For all of them the destruction of the propertied classes was necessary for the liberation of the individual.

Idealism

Anarchism in the nineteenth century received a powerful infusion of intellectual life from the German idealist philosophy, notably that of Hegel. His scheme of history embodied the gradual unfolding of the Spirit in our world. Anarchists concluded that the spirit manifested itself through individuals who, after all, *are* the agents of history. It was the individual as an individual that embodied truth, and it was up to the individual to assert it even against the prevailing circumstances. The individual is unique as a rational and sentient being. To remain so it was imperative, first of all, to destroy all coercive institutions, including the state, and put an end to everything that the individual had given up (alienated) to others. Only then would he or she recover what Max Stirner (1806–1856) called full "personal gratification" — the reaffirmation of one's ego — the "Unique I." The only appropriate institutions for such a reaffirmation were the spontaneous associations into which people would gather voluntarily.

Anarchism as a Movement

The many intellectual roots of anarchism also account for the fragmentation of the movement as it appeared within the First International in 1864. Some anarchists became fully committed to socialism — to the collective ownership of the means of production — while others insisted that some degree of private property should be permitted. Those who argued for collectivization, however, were opposed to State ownership. Indeed, Bakunin and his followers were in favor of the destruction of the State. They had no patience with bureaucracy even if it were to be controlled by the workers as the Marxists favored. The collective property would be handled by associations formed on a voluntary basis. Those who favored some degree of private property were, too, opposed to the State. But in contrast to the Marxists, they favored direct workers' action — what became known as anarcho-syndicalism. The workers by their own efforts, not through political and party action, would undertake to destroy the dominant position of the capitalists and emancipate themselves.

Finally, some anarchists became committed to personal direct action, including assassination, against all agents of authority. In the reaffirmation of their moral autonomy they became known as Nihilist — accepting nothing and committed to the rejection of everything.

Violence Unable to organize a movement, fragmented in many sects, and often propelled by sheer individual determination, the anarchists began to rely more and more on what we might call individual praxis — individual acts of violence to undermine authority, to disrupt order, and even to physically exterminate the "enemy." Assassinations and bombings became widespread. Terrorism was often directed against persons in authority irrespective of any consideration of responsibility or guilt. The more innocent and the more respected the victim and the more senseless the crime, the greater was the damage to the legal order. Random acts of terror such as theft, fire, bombings, and assassination became ennobling in themselves. Destruction wrought for its own sake — the rejection of anything and everything — became the political credo and practice of anarchists according to the *Catechism of an Anarchist*, attributed to Bakunin. The Tsar of Russia and some of his ministers, the Emperor of Germany, the President of the French Republic, and the King of Italy, received special attention — such "attention" often resulted in death. In 1893 a bomb, with hundreds of nails, exploded in the French Parliament.[2] In 1901 President McKinley was assassinated as some of

2. The anarchist impulse was not without appeal, as is the case with terrorists today, to the romantics and the discontented. Many of the anarchists became heroes before they were sentenced to death and after they were executed. In some cases their burial places became the objects of pilgrimages. "What a magnificent gesture" said a French poet in commenting on the explosion of the bomb. "Who cares about the victims!"

the anarchists by then had moved to the United States. The "Unique I"

243

Ideologies and Revolutionary Movements

seemed to be on the rampage.

Ever since the 1960s there has been a return to terrorism that resembles the anarchist actions of the past. Small bands in Germany, France, Italy, and Spain have been responsible for the daily commission of crimes. Heads of State, prime ministers, army officials, judges, police officers, and ambassadors have been assassinated. The Red Brigade in Italy, the Baader-Meinhof band in Germany, the Weathermen and extremist groups in the United States, and others in Japan and Holland have been particularly active. Often there are identifiable political motives and reasons. Acts of violence are committed in the name of separatism as in Spain, or in Corsica, and in the name of some kind of national identification and autonomy as among the Palestinians. But generally the philosophy today is not very different from what it was in the past — to discredit the established order and to prepare for a revolutionary change whose goals are unclear.

The New Left

The term New Left or Radical Left is used to describe the general movement of agitation, protest, and revolt organized and led, in great part, by young people and university students in the 1960s. The system under attack was, and continues to be, that of the modern industrialized societies — democratic or not. As seen by its opponents, the system's major characteristics are repressiveness and comprehensiveness; it is bureaucratic, impersonal, and authoritarian. Everything is subordinated to management, thanks to the advances of technology; production is geared to material gain and profit; and standards of measurement and evaluation become exclusively quantitative. The State, hand in hand with the huge industrial organizations, socializes people to accept the values the system manufactures — the ideology of consumerism, wasteful production, and the inculcation of work discipline. The individual becomes an empty shell, losing all capacity for pleasure, joy, and fulfillment. He or she becomes "dehumanized." This is "the system" the New Left paints in order to call for its destruction.

Different manifestations of the New Left movement appeared at approximately the same time, throughout the 1960s,[3] in democratic industrialized countries such as Japan, England, France, Germany, Italy, Holland, and the United States. While varying in intensity from country to country, there were a number of common characteristics in the movement: it occurred in rich countries where the standard of living was high; it rejected the whole scheme of values, organization, and structure of authority in these societies; it was not and is not Communist (indeed it sharply criticized the Soviet political, social, and economic system and ridiculed the various national Communist parties). "Please leave the Communist party as clean on leaving as you find it on entering" was one of the slogans of leftist French students.

---

3. For an overall account of the various left-wing student movements, see Lipset and Altbach. *Students in Revolt.*

"Under the cobblestones, the beach!" This is a street scene from the 1968 student uprising in Paris. (*Photo: Wide World Photos*)

The revolt of the students was addressed at first against university and university life — the dry knowledge it imparted, the overcrowding of classes, the impersonality of instruction, the lack of adequate financial supports, and the emphasis upon natural sciences and rational discourse, tests, and examinations. "When examined, answer with questions" was another motto of the French students. But the university reflected the values of society, and was meant to educate and prepare the young people to live in the society; it is society's major socializing force. By attacking the university, the whole society also came under attack. Criticism of the university was essentially social and political criticism, and the revolt spilled out of the campuses to appeal to everybody who was dissatisfied and unhappy.

One of the high points of the New Left movement was the uprising of May and June 1968 in Paris and many other French cities. The students led the way by striking, occupying the universities, throwing out their professors, deriding the meaning and validity of what they were being taught, and asking for a new university — the "anti-university." The revolt spread to workers, public servants, and salaried personnel. Public buildings were occupied, TV and radio stations taken over, barricades built, battles with the "forces of order" fought, and the students seemed on the verge of taking power. In an unprecedented show of spontaneity, and against the instructions of their trade-union and political leaders, the French workers began to join. They went on strike, occupied factories, and brought the whole economy to a standstill. One firm after another, one organization after another, one administration after another, and one service after another, were "taken over" by those who worked in them. Theaters, newspapers, the opera, the ballet, and even soccer teams were taken over by actors, reporters, singers, dancers, and players. The only organization that was not taken over seemed to be the Paris Stock Exchange — it was set on fire!

Another high point in the political and revolutionary activity of the New Left took place in the United States at the Democratic party convention held in Chicago at the end of August 1968. Demonstrations against the war in Vietnam had already reached a peak, forcing Lyndon Johnson to announce that he would not seek renomination. A number of students and leftist organizations decided to demonstrate at the Chicago convention and to force a peace candidate upon the Democratic party. But their demands were broader, and the participants ranged from those who favored peace and were against the military draft to genuine revolutionaries who were driven by the vision of a new society. The National Mobilization Committee to End the War in Vietnam (a loose organization which appealed to all people who were against the war) played an important role. In addition, there were the Committee for an Open Convention, seeking the nomination of Eugene McCarthy; the Students for Democratic Society; and the Youth International Party (Yippies), advocates of the "counterculture."

The New Left and the student uprisings should be put in their proper historical and intellectual context. Like anarchism, the New Left represented the long-standing grievances against industrialization and the impersonality and coerciveness of modern society with its complexity — all of which were seen to distort human nature and account for "alienation."

Alienation

Use of the term "alienation" to describe the state of mind of the people living in an industrialized society appears more often in the literature of the New Left than the word "spirit" in the Bible. To be alienated is to be a stranger (alien); in French, the word means insane (*aliené*). In Roman law the term

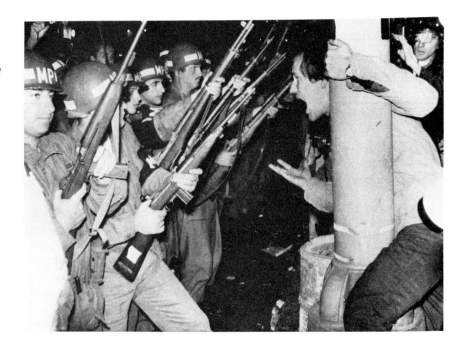

The New Left in America. Confrontation with the National Guard, Chicago, 1968. (*Photo: UPI*)

applied to those who could not legally make decisions: the *alieni juris* (women, slaves, minors) were under the jurisdiction of somebody else who made decisions for them and about them. Another word for alienation is "estrangement" — being or feeling like a stranger. Its opposite is "integration" or "participation," wherein an individual feels like part of a whole — whether family, neighborhood, university, factory, city, State, and so on. How to make individuals feel part of the whole, how to make them into social beings without depriving them of their freedoms, individuality, and spontaneity, and how to reconcile the "natural" person with the "social" being has been one of the major and most difficult problems in political philosophy.

No matter how you look at it, alienation, with its consequences, is very serious. To be a stranger in your own home, village, town, or factory is not only to be alone, but also to be without means to reach out into the world and to the people surrounding you, and to be unable to communicate with them. Even worse, it is a state of mind that makes it difficult for the alienated individual to receive messages and communications from others. He or she shuts them off: the individual is literally "spaced out." The more the society develops new and rapid mechanisms of communication, the more individual loneliness becomes unbearable. There is boredom at first, then frustration, and then sheer anger. The individual searches for an outlet to find togetherness, love, and fellowship, but in vain. Most other individuals are in the same state of mind, and whatever communication there is among them is superficial — skin deep. All share the same feeling of estrangement. The mass society is a state of "collective loneliness" — a lonely crowd[4] — as anybody who walks the streets of a big city or drives a car during the rush hour can tell. The social person has devoured the individual. Spontaneity, creativity, desire, pleasure are gone. What has brought this situation about?

Types of Alienation   There are at least three basic types of alienation. Firstly, there is the phenomenon of uprootedness — the severance of the individual from a primary group — family, village, and the simple values of rural traditional life to which the individual was attached. Such a phenomenon occurs at first in the early stages of industrialization but recurs in waves as industrialization develops. Individuals move from the country to the city in search for jobs in new surroundings that are alien. Emigration is essentially the same phenomenon and is characterized by the same feeling of alienation. It was clearly the situation of many immigrant groups that came to the United States, as some of the books of the noted historian Oscar Handlin portray so well.[5]

Alienation is also present when an individual severs ties with his or her natural environment: the soil, the simple uncomplicated life which one has some control over and can understand, the freedom to dispose of one's time and leisure, the satisfaction of simple needs through the performance of simple tasks such as fishing, hunting, and farming. With industrialization, division of labor, specialization and interdependence, the individual's ability to control the environment and to understand it diminishes. New economic and social relations are built upon which we become increasingly dependent for our livelihood and way of life. We are no longer our own masters; impersonal forces and relationships are at work that shape us and our lives.

A second type of alienation appears when technology, and more particularly rational and scientific thought, advance. The New Left considers "objectivity," — science, the search for laws — to be a major cause of alienation. The scientific method claims to be limited only in what can be shown to be valid and what can be proven through measurement and empirical verification. This scientific outlook, however, misses the very essence of the individual — emotions, feelings, and intuition — and subordinates truth to demonstrable correlations. Scientists commit themselves to explaining how things work in order to control the environment better and make it work more efficiently. They gradually lose the ability to think in terms of moral values. They never ask the crucial question as to whether things that work efficiently should be allowed to work at all.

Scientific inquiry provides only a partial, if at all valid, explanation of existence. It never attains what the French philosopher Henri Bergson called "the ultimate reality" (*les realités profondes*), which can be grasped only

4. The term is the title of David Reisman's path-breaking book, *The Lonely Crowd*. New Haven, Conn.: Yale U.P., 1950.
5. Oscar Handlin. *The Uprooted*. Boston: Little Brown, 1951.

intuitively. It deals with the external manifestations of reality, never with its essence. Even worse, the scientific mind ultimately associates the individual with "things," to be correlated, aggregated, classified, and "explained." It leads, therefore, to the manipulation of the individual in the same way in which various chemical elements can be manipulated to manufacture a product.

Finally, a third, perhaps the classic type of alienation, as suggested by Adam Smith and fully developed by Karl Marx, is the separation of the workers from what they produce. In industrial society, the workers have no control, no physical hold of what they produce, and naturally, no freedom to decide what to produce and how to dispose of what they produce. Part of their produce is taken away from them in the form of surplus value that is translated into profit for the capitalists; the rest becomes merchandise, a commodity to be sold at the market. The worker does not recognize it as his or her own. Furthermore, a product is produced not because the workers need it, or want it, or will be able to buy and enjoy it. It is something that others want and can buy. Finally, the workers find no fulfillment in the performance of routine tasks that the specialization of labor requires; work is no longer creative.

For the Marxists this type of alienation will end when the means of production are socialized so that the working class as a whole will be free to decide what and how to produce and how to allocate the product. They will become masters of themselves again by mastering production. Their alienation will end. From nothing, they will become "everything."

It is characteristic of their indictment of our industrialized society that the New Left not only emphasizes all three types of alienation, as outlined above, but that they propose to reintegrate the individuals back into the three ways of life that they have been deprived of. Their purpose is to bring them back into the "natural life" and into some of the primary associations they had to abandon; to replace science and rationality with feeling, imagination, and intuition, and to give back to the workers their products and their freedom to decide upon *what* to produce.

The Subjection of the Individual

It was the assertion of the individual conscience — of the "inner man" — as distinguished from the outside world and the social group, that represented the early awakening of freedom. The tribal individual mentally broke away from the tribe to develop his ways and to liberate himself from the repressive conformity it imposed. The "we" — the group, or the tribe — gradually became "I," the individual. Stoics and Christians asserted the claims of individual conscience against the awesome power of the Roman emperors. The liberals, much later, confronted the power of monarchs.

Liberalism, therefore, was originally a great liberating force. Social and economic development throughout the nineteenth century and into the twentieth, produced, however, some unanticipated changes. The individual entrepreneur was replaced by the big corporation; concentration led to the increase of power and decision making for some, while producing a large number of salaried without power. Big firms began to dominate the economy. At the same time, advanced technology spread not only to production but to all forms of social life. Big organizations and new organizational techniques of management created new forms of control that subordinated the individual. Mechanization became the rule. Mario Savio, one of the leaders of the New Left in the United States, wrote:

> There is a time when the operation of the machine becomes so odious, makes you so sick at heart that you can't take part; you can't even tacitly take part, and you've got to put your bodies upon the levers, upon all the apparatus and you've got to make it stop.[6]

The demand for efficiency and profit develops its own logic, which leads to the production of goods as an end in itself without reference to social goals. Herbert Marcuse, philosopher of the New Left, claims that in advanced industrialized societies:

> the technical apparatus of production and distribution (with an increased sector of automation) functions not as the sum total of mere instruments which can be isolated from their social and political effects, but rather as a system that determines . . . the product of the apparatus as well as the operations of servicing and extending it. . . . The productive apparatus, tends *to become totalitarian to the extent to which it determines not only the socially needed occupations and skills and attitudes but also individual needs and aspirations.*[7]

Thus, the productive forces obliterate the line that separates the society from the individual, between private and public existence, between the "I" and the "we," and between the inner self and the social whole. This is the crux of the problem. The individual is invaded by the outside forces and values of organization and production.

To put this idea quite simply: society as a whole is supposed to be run by a managerial and technologic elite which, in the name of efficiency and profit, develops methods of organization and coordination that propagate a conformist ideology to its methods and goals. All individuals are required to "march in step." Production is geared to those needs that will keep the industrial apparatus working, even if production is not geared to real needs. Ideology, however, will be used to make the objects produced *seem* desirable and "real." The individual is made to conform to the needs of management, organization, and technology. Thus, social man leaves behind him inner man, and his own freedom to choose and decide. The technological rationality of the industrialized society:

6. Massimo Teodori (ed.). *The New Left: A Documentary History.* New York: Bobbs-Merrill. 1969, p. 156.
7. Marcuse. *One Dimensional Man.* p. xv.

reveals its political character as it becomes the great vehicle of better domination, creating a truly totalitarian universe in which society and nature, mind and body, are kept in a permanent state of mobilization for the defense of their universe[8]

There can be no better definition of the Nazi principle of "synchronization" which we discussed earlier.

The Role of Ideology

The absorption of the individual into the system of the advanced industrialized societies is a gradual process, and ideology plays the crucial role. It rationalizes and legitimizes production and efficiency; socializes the young people in the school and the university to accept them; and sets the tone for their preparation to play special roles within the system. It is primarily in the ideology of production that consumerism and material satisfactions predominate. Modernization and growth are viewed exclusively in quantitative terms. It is a materialist ethic that gradually invades our lives until we can no longer refute or avoid it. It affects our moral judgments, our tastes, our pleasures, and our leisure time. Political and ethical considerations are subordinated to it. Education, performance, and life-styles are reduced to pure material considerations that can be checked, double-checked, and tabulated.

It is an ideology that becomes all-encompassing. People are free — but only to accept it and live by it; they are equal — but only to participate in it; they can compete with each other — but only on its terms; there is pluralism and group life — but only among the associations and groups that conform to it. The crucial point, then, according to the advocates of the New Left, is that individuals are free within the framework of this ideology but cannot declare their freedom *against it* or *against* the political system that sustains it. Industrialized advanced societies have created a consensus through the wholesale inculcation of the values of technology, material abundance, efficiency, and consumption. Democracies manage, without repressive tactics, precisely because the ideology they have fashioned has permeated all of us. Soviet totalitarianism still relies on repression, according to Marcuse, simply because the values of its industrial society have not as yet been thoroughly assimilated and internalized.

The student will notice here the sharp departure of the New Left from the classic Marxist critique. The argument against capitalism is not that it fails to produce enough but that it produces a great deal! The indictment made by the New Left is that capitalism has created abundance and continues to be capable of producing an ever-growing variety of material goods. It has become dangerous to all of us precisely because of its efficiency and its ability to give to all of us a relative degree of well-being. It is because of this efficiency that democratic capitalism has managed to integrate everybody, or virtually everybody, within its own logic and ideology. Its tentacles have

8. Marcuse, op. cit.

spread into every home, and into every social, economic, political, or religious group. It is a threat to all of us because it has proven so successful.

But what is the nature of the threat? I believe the answer lies primarily in the distinction between "false" and "true" consciousness that Marx elaborated from a somewhat different perspective.

False and True Consciousness   The industrial and technological society of today has managed to bring together hitherto antagonistic forces. Business and organized labor; Democrats and Republicans in the United States; Labourites and Conservatives in England; Christian Democrats and Social Democrats in Germany; Communists and Christian Democrats in Italy; Gaullists and Communists in France — all accept it. They compete within an economic and industrial system that they all want to maintain. Genuine revolutionary movements aimed at transcending the system and replacing it with a different one exist virtually nowhere in any of the advanced industrialized societies. In fact, it is difficult to envisage revolution in societies where the vast majority of men and women fully accept the prevalent values. The only possibility is that there are still forces in society which may, as Marcuse puts it, "explode the society."

From where, then, will the explosion come? Only from a realization by the citizens, or some of them, that the ideology they have accepted, and the consciousness of the social world that it has imparted to them, is false. Explosion will then result from the outright rejection of what is false; it will be the assertion of the real consciousness of individuals — of real interests against fabricated interests. Ultimately, it will be the explosion of the individual's inner or moral self against the ideology of the industrial society.

The terms "false" and "true," "real" and "fabricated" are not new. Rousseau had argued that it is possible for all the people to be fooled and to lose sight of their real interests. Marx and Lenin feared that the workers would accept reformist policies dealing with their material conditions and thus lose sight of their real interest, which was to make a revolution and socialize the means of production. Even alienated individuals can be made to think that their alienated status is normal and in accord with their individuality. "Alienation" may, in other words, through advertising propaganda and socialization, be so rationalized as to become acceptable. In a frightening passage, Marcuse identifies the situation and the predicament: "the subject which is alienated . . . is swallowed by his alienated existence."[9] This simply means that we have all been made to accept the values that account for our alienation, *which are false and contrary to our real interests*, and take them to be true. We have been made to believe that we are free when in fact we are slaves. Our "false" and "fabricated" consciousness has swallowed up our "true" and "innermost" self. We think we are "I" when, in fact, we all have become "they." The "manufactured" social individual has destroyed the true and moral self.

9. Op. cit., p. 11.

Nothing could be more frightening than the notion that alienation has become socialized and accepted and that what we all believe is false. It amounts to saying that we take shadows to be real things, and that our false consciousness has replaced truth. It is almost as if in the name of rationality, to which we all pay lip service, we have established a society that is collectively insane. Yet we do not know it, we have no means at our disposal to show it, and there is no doctor to diagnose our case!

The Explosion

The explosion can come only in the form of a moral outburst — a moral rejection of the existing society. It will stem from moral indignation, and its objective will be moral rehabilitation. It will not spring from deprivation, nor will it come from the workers. It will come from all those who have maintained their inner self intact from the ideological contamination the advanced industrial societies spread. It will come from all those who have not been swallowed up by their alienated self, the men and women who have somehow managed to maintain their true consciousness and who will defy the society that tries to mold and shape them.

But defiance is not an explosion. An explosion suggests destruction, not simply a change in the management or leadership of society, nor just the replacement of one class by another as in Marxism. An explosion is the destruction of the dominant ideology, the fundamental values of society, and of the social relations and working practices that its ideology legitimizes.

What are they to be replaced with? Although the New Left makes a number of suggestions, there is no blueprint; many among its supporters would argue that none is needed. A prisoner, they would say, must escape from the jail first before he begins to think of where he will go.

Revolutions follow careful guidelines, which revolutionaries provide. They spell out organization, discipline, leadership, and specific procedures. The New Left has produced virtually no such guidelines. By appealing directly to the individual conscience they neglect the requirements of common organized effort. In fact, they seem to rely to a great degree upon anarchy as the only creative response to organization and totalitarian control. But even so, an explosion requires, as any student of physics or chemistry knows, the bringing together of some ingredients, substances, or chemicals. The explosion of society also requires some such social and human ingredients. What are they?

The three essential elements are *imagination, action,* and *rejection.* All three are linked together in terms of a deeply moral disavowal, almost religious in its fervor, of the ways of life of our contemporary industrialized societies.

Imagination. The French sociologist Alain Touraine points out that the revolution of the students and the New Left in general was "the revolution of the imagination," and that, perhaps because of it, it turned out to be "an imaginary revolution."[10] "Be realistic; think of the impossible"; "Under the

10. Touraine. *The May Movement.*

cobblestones, the beach" — these were two recurring slogans of the French students during their uprising in 1968. Imagination is clearly seen as the outlet for the enslaved self. It is the vision of a new world, without police officers, coercion, rules, roles, and duties; where time will not be measured by minutes and hours; material needs will no longer weigh on our minds; desires will be fulfilled almost instantly; where intuition will provide for truth that can be "understood" and not measured and verified; where there will be no masters, no bosses, no hierarchies; where struggle, domestic, and international, will give place to peace; where, finally, everything that separates us from each other — walls, rooms, offices, blocks, and national boundaries — will be erased. There will be no "No Trespass" signs anywhere: this will be the world of the "real self," of the natural self — spontaneous, creative, intuitive, and almost instinctual. It is the exact opposite of the alienated self: the real "I," not the fabricated and collective "they."

Action. Imagination must be coupled with action. To be "engaged" is essential not only to promoting one's ends but to understanding them better. "Being" should not be, and cannot be, separated from "doing." Theory must lead to action and action will refine theory. For it is only in action, and only by acting, that an individual can "enter into the essence of things" and understand them fully. The New Left discards objectivity and the separation between the actor and the object. The actor must "enter into" the object. To think of something in a detached way is meaningless, but to think of something and to do it is the essence of comprehension. The New Left is, therefore, activist, but action is not an instrument to attain predetermined objectives. It is, rather, essential to the understanding and the refining of objectives. We learn while we act, and we act in order to learn! Praxis becomes all-important.

Rejection. Imagination and action, however, must both be inspired by a powerful personal and moral rejection of the existing order of things. In the philosophy of the New Left there are many powerful negations — as many as in the totalitarian movements we discussed earlier. The New Left, however, is distinctly anti-State, anti-nationalist, anti-authoritarian, anti-liberal, anti-intellectual and against democratic and parliamentary institutions.

The Counterculture

What will the world be like after the explosion? The revolution of the imagination will result in a Utopia. Even if there is no comprehensive blueprint, and even if the New Left assumes that once the revolution is started it will gain momentum and shape as the people gain knowledge from the revolutionary experience, there are enough bits and pieces that we can put together. What emerges from them, as Theodore Roszak points out, is a "vision."[11]

It is a vision of a communal society divided into small neighborhoods and groups; of a simple, almost pastoral life, where the complexities and ugliness of city life are done away with; of a free and egalitarian society

11. Roszak. *The Making of a Counter-Culture.*

without hierarchies, authorities, and coercive agencies; of an intensely individualistic society cultivating individual freedom and spontaneity. It is also a participatory society: people within different groups take charge of their own affairs. Finally, it is a world-wide society — or rather a world-wide community — without national boundaries, armies and states, and without customs officials.

The New Left contends that each of the three forms of alienation we discussed earlier must be taken into account and eliminated. Small groups and a simple life will give individuals a sense of belongingness, and bring them back closer to nature and to their primary organizations — the family and the village. The control and ownership of production by the producers will do away with the workers' alienation; the full participation in decision making of all those affected by the work done or the decisions to be made will do away with the impersonality of bureaucratic organizations and their coercive character. Finally, the establishment of working and living conditions based upon individual inclinations will make work pleasurable again and life joyful.

Some of the principles of the New Left were spelled out during the 1968 uprisings in France, and were elaborated by the spontaneously formed Action Committees:

1. Take collective responsibility for one's own affairs, that is, self-government.
2. Destroy all hierarchies which merely serve to paralyze the initiative of all groups and individuals.
3. Make all those in whom authority is vested permanently responsible to the people.
4. Spread information and ideas throughout the movement.
5. Put an end to the division of labor and of knowledge which only serves to isolate people one from another.
6. Open the university to all who are at present excluded.
7. Defend maximum political and intellectual freedom as a basic democratic right.[12]

One American leader put the goals of the New Left very succinctly:

> I think it has to do with two types of goals. One which we might call "existential humanism" is expressed by the desire to change the way we, as individuals, actually live and deal with other people. We speak of the attempt to achieve "community," to reach levels of intimacy and directiveness with others unencumbered by the conventional barriers of race, status, class, etc. . . . . Second, we say that we seek a radical transformation of the social order. Thus we say that we want a redistribution of wealth and power in the society; that we want to develop new centers of power as a basis for such a redistribution; that we look forward

---

12. Cohen-Bendit. *Obsolete Communism: The Left-Wing Alternative*, p. 90.

toward the emergence of new political and social institutions which can authentically provide the conditions for freedom.[13]

In the vision of the future new society three elements predominate: *anarchism, participation,* and the *quality of life.*

Anarchism   The proponents of the New Left echo some of the same anarchist themes: rejection of bigness; destruction of authority and of political and economic organizational hierarchies and, of course, of the State. They emphasize work and living in small groups — communes and associations through which the individuals control their environment, organize their work, and take charge of their own affairs. The New Left shares with the anarchists the same quest for individualization, for spontaneity and creativity, and for free play. They, too, reject private property in favor of communal or associational collectivism. The New Left, finally, like the anarchists, believes in the use of force and direct action and shares the anarchists' outright moral rejections of existing society. A small number of activists among the New Left have joined conspiratorial and terroristic organizations bent upon destruction and political assassination.

Participation   Participation of all in the management of common affairs is, for the New Left, one of the most potent instruments for putting an end to alienation. Limited forms of participation, especially of the workers in industrial firms, have been practiced in many countries. They involve consultations, profit-sharing, and the autonomy of the workers to determine their working conditions. They do not question, however, the basic rules of the capitalistic economy with regard to property ownership and the managerial and hierarchical organization of the firms.

The demands of the New Left are far more comprehensive. First, they apply not only to industrial firms and to economic activities, but to all others, political, social, and cultural; all those involved in a given activity and in any organization that makes decisions that affect them should participate in making them. Secondly, the New Left has specific notions about organizational structures, advocating their reduction in size and complexity. Finally, it proposes the socialization of all economic units that are privately owned. Participation is, in effect, equivalent to socialism plus internal democracy.

The Quality of Life   One of the recurrent themes of the New Left is the degradation (past, present, and future) of the quality of our lives in the industrially advanced societies. Our environment has been used and abused for the sake of immediate benefits and profits. Our forests have been spoiled, lakes and rivers polluted, neighborhoods uprooted in the name of urban renewal, mountains have been deformed by ugly mining scars, and millions of Americans (and even larger numbers of Europeans) live in areas where the

13. David Flack. "Some Problems, Issues and Proposals," in Jacobs and Landau. *The New Radicals,* p. 163.

air is fast becoming unbreathable. Cities themselves grow, as population growth continues unchecked, without any consideration to health and beauty and without the realization that cities are for people to live together. High structures have replaced neighborhoods, and neighborly amenities have given place to supermarkets, super-hospitals, and multi-universities. Life in the city has become as impersonal as life is in the big organizations where people work. The private motor vehicle, given its appetite for roads and fuel, begins to dominate our lives and our economy.

The New Left stands resolutely for quality. It advocates, in effect, a totally new way of life. In substance it wishes to extirpate the evils of materialism and replace them with the purity of spirituality. Its world will assert the kingdom of the spirit (but not of reason) over material concerns; imagination and feeling, intuition and insights will take the precedence they had before the Enlightenment and the Industrial Revolution. To accomplish this, a vast change in attitudes and beliefs, methods of learning and consumption habits are needed.

This is, then, the new world of the New Left. It is the exact reverse of what the New Left sees in our contemporary industrial societies. For collectivity, read individualism; for bigness, smallness; for complexity, simplicity; for imposition, self-government; for coercion, freedom; for hierarchy, equality; for private property, socialism; for profit, social need; for materialism, spirituality; for war, peace; for competition, cooperation; for science and technology, intuition and spontaneity; for knowledge, experience; for reason, feeling. It is a different, new, and shiny world. One of its advocates states that the first step of the revolution will be "to proclaim a new heaven and a new earth so vast, so marvelous that the inordinate claims of technical expertise must of necessity withdraw in the presence of such a splendor to a subordinate and marginal status in the lives of men."[14] This is a call for religious and moral reawakening rather than for political action.

The Wretched of the Earth[15]

"If poverty was the cause of revolutions, we would all be sitting on a powder keg," wrote Leon Trotsky, one of the foremost practitioners of the art of revolution. One needs only to take the United Nations Statistical Year Book and look at a world map to identify vast areas of our globe where hundreds of millions of poor live — with an annual income that is less than seventy-five to one hundred dollars. In relatively prosperous nations the distribution of wealth and well-being is skewed with millions of people deprived of the amenities of life — housing, warmth, health care, and even food. But though ready to give a hand to riots and to demonstrations and looting, the poor do

14. Roszak, op. cit., p. 240.
15. This is the title of Frantz Fanon's book, in his own words, "the handbook for the Black Revolution that is changing the shape of the world."

not develop a revolutionary consciousness; they do not make revolutions. Even the theory of "deprivation" does not readily apply to them — they do not have a clear awareness of what they are worth and what they should be entitled to in order to feel deprived.

George Orwell, in his book *1984*, discusses the possibility of revolution against the established power-holders, Big Brother and the Inner Brotherhood and the Party, that have a tight grip over the "proles," — the poor, wretched, and disregarded masses, that account for 85 percent of the population of his imaginary state. They could destroy the party that has enslaved them. If they could become conscious of their own strength they would rise up "and shake them like a horse shaking off flies." But Orwell quickly stifles all hope . . . "Until (the proles) become conscious, they will never rebel, and until after they have rebelled, they cannot become conscious." The poor, the underprivileged, the slaves, and the wretched of the earth seem to be in a box.

It is only recently that anti-colonialism (pitting the poor blacks in Africa against the white colonial powers) has been associated with some very strong revolutionary doctrines and movements that are addressed to the poor and the wretched.

Concern with the situation of the African, and also all other blacks, dates from the turn of the century and before. Pan-Africanism as an ideology and a movement expressed the solidarity and brotherhood, notably among the Caribbean and the United States blacks. One of the major promoters was W. E. Burghard DuBois (1868–1963), a professor of sociology at the University of Atlanta, who had a doctorate from the University of Heidelberg. Deeply concerned with the status of the American blacks, DuBois stressed civil and political rights and political action. Gradually, he saw the problem of American blacks in broader terms and sought the recognition of their rights through a world-wide movement that would bring them together. The ultimate objective was the liberation of all blacks — in the United States, Latin America, Africa, and, of course, the Caribbean, along with the development of a pan-African consciousness. He urged American blacks to develop intimate contacts with their African brothers.

The first formal step in the direction of pan-Africanism was the organization of the Congress of Paris in 1919, immediately after World War I. Other conferences followed in London, in 1921 and 1923, and in New York, in 1927 — the last with over two hundred delegates. They asked for equal treatment and the right to be consulted in the decisions made for them by the colonial government.

Pan-Africanism remained, however, an elite movement. It maintained and, in fact, sought an open dialogue with the colonial powers and the white elites. Gradually, with the appearance of new leaders in the 1950s and 1960s, the quest for equality and independence became more intransigent and the poverty that plagued the whole continent led to revolutionary movements that mobilized the poor and the downtrodden. New African intellectuals, and some American blacks, began to move restlessly towards a redefinition of their own identity and of their relations between Africans and whites.

Frantz Fanon (1925–1961) merits special mention. An Algerian psychiatrist (trained in France) he reconciled elements of Marxism with Freudian psychology to develop a theory of colonial and racial revolutions. He put all the emphasis on *praxis* — on the act of rebelling and on the use of violence by the black "subjects" against their white colonial "masters."

He rejected the "liberal" model of revolution in which the more developed and middle-class native groups using Western institutions such as political parties, representative government, lobbying, trade unions, and the like, would put pressure upon the colonial governments to gain reforms leading to national independence. This had been, in substance, the tactics of the pan-African movement and conferences. Fanon believed that the native middle classes were parasitic and lived off their colonial masters. They could not be relied upon, nor could they be expected to gain independence for their peoples. They have "black skins but wear white masks!" Many from among them had come in contact with the Western civilization, studied in Western universities, and had become "assimilated" in the Western culture.

Fanon, though paying lip service to it, also rejected Marxism. As we noted, Marxism called for some degree of industrial development and the existence even of a small working class, such as dock workers, transport workers, and workers in manufacturing. As late as 1960, more than 90 percent of the Africans were peasants. In Algeria — the most developed African "colony" — the figure was 85 percent. They were peasants in almost the feudal sense of the term, with the land often owned by the white colonizers or otherwise cultivated in communal arrangements. African private farmers were virtually nonexistent. Without a working class — and given the argument previously discussed that even in more developed countries the working class could not, by itself, develop a revolutionary consciousness — how could one fit the Marxist scheme in Africa?

Fanon chose a third way. This was to use the mass of the peasantry and their abject poverty in order to bring about an "explosion" — in Marcuse's terms — or, a violent confrontation, much like a "general strike." Action — praxis — was of utmost importance, even when the theory behind it was uncertain. Violence against the whites — in fact pitting race against race — should take every possible form — political, military, guerrilla war, cultural rejection, individual violence, and assassination. To kill a white man was deemed a liberating act — a revenge for centuries of deprivation, oppression, and rejection — a reaffirmation of black individual worth and a badge of honor and equality. The whites were the enemies. They had lived by the sword and now it was time for them to die by the sword.

Fanon appealed to the poor and the peasants. Organizers and intellectuals, he felt, should reach out to the masses of the peasantry and adapt their slogans and strategy to their "inherent ideology" — their traditional ways and folklore. With the first acts of violence, revolutionary praxis would become a collective effort that would lead to national liberation. Freed from the West, politically and psychologically independent, the African nations would then put their revolution in some kind of order.

Franz Fanon's gospel for a revolution was not always followed; in fact it was sharply criticized by many Marxists, but it left a deep imprint and infused many anti-colonial and national liberation movements "with passion." In Kenya, in Zaire, in Algeria, in the Portuguese colonies of Mozambique and in Angola, violence often became an end in itself. It had a powerful organizing effect. Emphasis on praxis led to the exaltation of individual action — the liberation and the reaffirmation of one's ego. Fanon gave a powerful impulse to colonial uprisings and to the mobilization of the poor and the "wretched."

But whatever the justification of violence and murder, they do not represent standards on the basis of which a new society can be built. If Fanon was justifying acts of violence against the white colonizers because they had perpetrated them first against the native blacks, he was building a philosophy of revolt on what was just as uncertain, unjust, and morally as reprehensible as the rule of violence by the whites that he rejected. Fanon represents more a philosophy of revenge than a praxis of revolution. He sought in individual and mass violence the psychic liberation of those who commit it. He ignored, like so many other revolutionaries, Goethe's words: "The evil which you fear becomes a certainty by what you do!"

Revolutionary Guerrillas

Guerrilla warfare has been one of the major instruments of revolutions in much of the colonial world. These revolutions have been directed against a colonial power and against the native rulers — landowners or a bourgeoisie — that act on behalf of the interests or in a manner congruent with the interests of a colonial power (and, as in the case of Latin America, of a dominant, even if not a formally colonial power). The themes invariably are: national independence and the radical overhaul of social and economic relations in the direction of socialism. El Salvador, Guatemala, Nicaragua, Colombia (and possibly other countries of Central and South America) appear to be following in the steps of Algeria, China, Vietnam, and many of the former African and Asian colonies.

Today, Latin America is one of the last remaining areas of the world where guerrilla revolutions are taking place to undermine the dominant elites and their major arsenal of support — the United States. They all are inspired, informed, and, as some point out with considerable justice, are supported by the Cuban revolutionary experience of the 1950s and by direct Cuban military, financial, and technical support. Cuba has become a model for Latin America revolutionaries as the Soviet Union was for European Communists after 1917. The ideology of the various guerrilla movements remains in name "Marxism-Leninism."

Guerrilla revolutionary warfare depends, above all, on the organization of a small avant-garde that will lead the masses — mostly the peasantry — into an insurrectional struggle. It is synonymous with praxis. There is a great deal of discussion about the existing conditions — are they "ripe" for a revolution or not? But many believe that even if they are not, the proper action — military and political — will create these conditions. Ché Guevara, considered one of the foremost theoreticians of guerrilla warfare for Latin

Moving in small groups amidst friendly peasants, the guerrillas gradually undermine the will and organization of the government and its armed force. (*Photo: Wide World Photos*)

America, has stated unequivocally that revolutionary and insurrectional struggle will create the conditions.

Ché Guevara wrote the catechism — or at least what has been taken as such in Latin America — for guerrilla revolutionary warfare.[16] There are three basic precepts and three phases to a successful guerrilla revolution.

The three precepts are:

1. Popular forces can win a war against an army.
2. It is not always necessary to wait until the conditions for making revolution exist; the "insurrectional focus" can create them.
3. In underdeveloped America, the countryside is the basic area for the armed fighting.

The three phases correspond to:

1. The establishment and the consolidation of the "insurrectional focus"
2. Guerrilla warfare against the armed forces of the enemy and the gradual conquest of the hearts and minds of the people, particularly the peasantry
3. The weakening of the governmental forces and, with it, the final assault on them and the takeover of political and economic power by the leadership of guerrilla forces

16. Ché Guevara, *Guerrilla Warfare*, New York: MR Press, 1961.

In a guerrilla warfare there are many ups and downs. What counts, above all, is the development of an awareness on the part of the people that their deliverance is possible. A guerrilla war may fail, but the awareness will remain to spark future guerrilla warlike efforts. Praxis shapes the revolutionary even if the revolution fails.

According to the Ché Guevara, the starting point in the guerrilla revolutionary war is the establishment of what has been called an "insurrectional focus" ("foco" in Spanish means a hearth, a home, a base in broad terms). It is where the guerrillas find shelter, rest, food, and ammunitions, and where they plan their moves. The "home," in order to be secure, must be located in a hospitable environment — among friendly peasants — and, ideally, should be immune from enemy detection and direct threats. The establishment of such an insurrectional base is the first step in a long political and military struggle, but it is an irreversible step as it commits the leadership to the revolution.

In the strategy of guerrilla warfare the proper balance between military and political organization remains uncertain. Many claimed that Ché, and also Regis Debray — a French intellectual and activist who spent many years among Latin American guerrillas and in Latin American jails — unduly stressed military action without the proper political preparation. By excluding the towns from the revolutionary effort, they disassociated the guerrillas from the urban proletariat which in some Latin American countries — Bolivia, Peru, Chile, Venezuela, and so on — is strong and can develop a revolutionary consciousness. Also, by insisting on will and organization they underestimated the significance of the specific circumstances, history, culture, and the political situation that distinguish one Latin American country from another.[17]

Some pertinent questions have also been raised about the emphasis placed on the "insurrectional focus." Even if it is not a military basis, it has been thought of in military terms. The "focus" may prove vulnerable unless it finds itself in a particularly hospitable terrain. This requires advance political preparation long before the insurrection. The inhabitants of the area in which it is situated must become friendly and supportive.

Ché, less than twenty years ago, with a small band of twenty revolutionaries undertook to establish an "insurrectional focus" in Bolivia in order to make the revolution in Bolivia and to ignite it throughout the whole of Latin America. He failed. The peasantry, mostly Indians, was not ready; the revolutionary ideology he attempted to spread fell upon deaf ears. The President of Bolivia, at the time, was an active and popular man who had undertaken many liberal and even socialist reforms including land reform. Ché and his band, after some successful skirmishes with the governmental forces, found themselves isolated like fish out of water. They were destroyed, but they also created a legend for themselves and for the revolution.

---

17. Generally most Latin American Communist parties disassociated themselves from Castro and Ché Guevara. They stressed a "nonviolent" revolutionary strategy asserting that conditions for a revolutionary takeover were not ripe.

Today, in parts of Central America, guerrilla warfare and insurrectional uprisings are still evident. A committed avant-garde continues to seek the support of the peasantry, the poor and underprivileged, in order to oust from power the political and economic elites that have dominated them for so long. What accounts for the revolutionary efforts and their successes, against governments supported by the United States, is that the people have been mobilized, by the will and the organization of a few, in terms of an ideology that promises so much to the many. Guerrillas, in the words of Ché Guevara, are "the Jesuits of warfare," committed to spreading the revolutionary faith far and wide.

Populism and Revolutions

At the beginning of this chapter we distinguished between "inherent" and "derived" ideologies. The first are well-structured propositions about social and political change in terms of well-formulated goals. "Inherent ideology" consists of beliefs and attitudes, widely shared by the people and expressed in folkways and traditions that often separate them from the elite. Populism as a political movement attempts to bring together the various elements of the "inherent ideology" into focus. Depending upon the characteristics of the "inherent ideology" — let us call it the tradition and culture — the substance of the populist ideology and movement varies from one society to another. Yet, the manifestations of populism are generally similar. First, an attack against privilege and the privileged classes and a rejection of the various elites — financial, intellectual, and governmental; second, an emphasis on communitarian and egalitarian themes; and third, a demand for a return to national and nationalist traditional values. Most populist movements are generally a reaction against modernization.

The groups to which populism appeals and from which it seeks supports vary. Frequently it is the peasantry; occasionally it is the workers (as with Peron's Argentina), or the lower-middle classes who have moved from the village and the countryside into the urban centers and who are insecure and uncertain of their position in the society. Or it may be ethnic groups mobilized against certain minorities (as with the pronounced "populist" appeal of the Nazis). But populism may also arouse the middle classes, especially if their status and income are threatened by rapid technological changes that make them feel obsolete (the case of some American populist movements and their appeal to "middle-America"). National values are always evoked in all populist movements — they are inward-looking and fear everything from the outside.

Personal leadership, stressing the charisma of one man or woman who embodies the popular traditions and beliefs, is indispensable in all populist movements. Peron, Khomeini, Nasser, and Khadafy, all major leaders of populist movements, have welded popular and nationalist myths together. As a result, a populist movement may not outlast the leaders and the prophet. It has little structure and organization and relies upon the emotional springs that give rise to it and the emotional attachments it creates. It is like a powerful windstorm that obliterates all shapes and forms until it dies down and once again reveals the contours of the landscape.

But sometimes a powerful populist movement may have lasting effects upon the body politic. The "inherent ideology" may be successfully blended with the "derived ideology" — notably this is the case with populist movements exploited by Marxist leaders. Populism then may give rise to a strong radical political party. More often, populism leads to the rule of a military dictatorship, to a right-wing authoritarianism, or to an authoritarian system that allows for a return to power of the previous social classes. But in all cases, populism is a destabilizing political movement that rarely leads to democracy.

The Iranian "Revolution"

The Iranian "revolution" had all the earmarks of populism as we have described it. It appealed to the traditionalist forces which were, in this instance, the religious masses. Appeal was strong especially among the fanatically religious Iranian lower-middle classes that were organized and mobilized by their religious leaders. There are some two hundred thousand clergymen, called the *mullahs,* who are mostly of peasant and lower-middle class origin; they are recruited from villages for religious training in the holy city of Quam and then sent back to their native villages. They were the backbone and the instrument of the "revolution." In the late 1970s they exploited — like most populist movements — the aversion of the average Iranian for the modernization of the country under the Shah. The modernization did not provide for an equitable distribution of wealth and did not make room for social mobility and political participation. The system remained despotic, with a small privileged class and the army controlling not only the government but also the major share of the rising wealth, and often quarreling about the division of the spoils.

Another element of the Iranian revolution, again common to populism, was nationalism — directed this time against the West and especially against the United States' position and influence in the affairs of Iran. Nationalism was manifested by an appeal to Iranian traditional values — that is, the religious values of the Islamic faith that were endangered by modernization. For others — a minority consisting of the left-wing intellectuals and communists — the revolution was primarily a way to combat "foreign intervention" and "imperialism." As a matter of tactics, they joined the traditionalists in order to destabilize the regime and ultimately bring down the Shah of Iran and the divided oligarchy that ruled them.

All that was needed was a leader. One who could incorporate for some the religious values of the past and at the same time serve as a symbol to rally the people against the regime. The religious values that were stressed rested on the five pillars of Islam — an affirmation of faith, daily prayers, a month of fasting, pilgrimage to Mecca, and the law of the Koran. Ayatollah Khomeini, who had been imprisoned by the Shah and later escaped to Paris, appeared as the leader. His anathemas and exhortations for violence and revolution were disseminated by the chain of the organization that the mul-

Demonstrators outside the U.S. embassy where hostages were held
for several weeks. One holds a banner portraying America as a war-
monger, while another holds a mystic-style portrait of Ayatollah
Khomeini. (*Photo: Wide World Photos*)

lahs had developed to incite the masses into what amounted to guerrilla uprisings against the Iranian army. The officer corps resisted, but the enlisted men and the noncommissioned officers that came from the peasantry and the lower-middle classes quickly crumbled; the army became paralyzed, the Shah fled the country, and Khomeini returned to take charge of the various people's committees that enforced the true faith and Islamic law.

The ideology that emerged to sustain the New Prophet was a combination of nationalism, anti-Westernism, and anti-Americanism. It was an attack against the privileged groups, as well as the intellectuals, and a return to the traditional values of the faith. The "party" that kept the government going was the same old traditionalist network of the religious leaders — leaders who appealed to the same values of Islam that they had always supported and that had been threatened. The tactical alliance between them and the leftist groups, including the Communists, quickly broke down. The mullahs were able to gain power and to impose the religious values and traditions under which they had lived. Conformity required quick reprisals not only against the previous elites but against all dissenters, and the mobilization of the masses for the administration of Islamic justice through committees and revolutionary courts.

What is ahead for Iran? As with all other populist movements, the Iranian revolution, since the prophet and leader, Ayatollah Khomeini is over eighty, will soon attempt to reach a compromise with economic needs and realities and to reach some kind of political institutionalization. It may lead to an accommodation side by side with a strong military dictatorship, but it may also lead to the upswing of the leftist forces and the development of a strong secular and radical party that will supplant the mullahs. The Iranian revolution — like all other populist movements — may move in the direction of left- or right-wing authoritarianism to reconcile in some form or another the traditional values and religion with the requirements of secular government and modernization.

Populist revolutions live dangerous and intense — but short — lives!

Bibliography

Aron, Raymond. *The Elusive Revolution*. London: Pall Mall, 1969.

Bakunin. *The Political Philosophy of Bakunin* (edited and compiled by G. P. Maximoff, New York: Free Press, 1953).

Brinton, Crane. *Anatomy of Revolution*. New Jersey: Prentice-Hall, 1939.

Carr, E. H. *Michael Bakunin*. New York: Vintage, 1937.

Carter, A. *The Political Theory of Anarchism*. New York: Harper & Row, 1971.

Cohn-Bendit, Daniel and Gabriel. *Obsolete Communism: The Left-Wing Alternative*. London: André Deutsch, 1968.

Davies, James C. (ed.). *When Men Revolt and Why*. New York: Free Press, 1971.

Debray, Regis. "Revolution in the Revolution? Armed Struggle and Political Struggle in Latin America," *Monthly Review*, July–August, 1967.

Draper, Hal. *Berkeley: The New Student Revolt.* New York: Grove Press, 1965.

Erikson, Erik H. (ed.). *The Challenge of Youth.* New York: Anchor, 1965.

Fanon, Franz. *The Wretched of the Earth.* New York: Grove Press, 1963.

Fischer, Michael M. J. *Iran: From Religious Dispute to Revolution.* Cambridge, Mass.: Harvard University Press, 1980.

Goodman, Paul. *Growing Up Absurd.* New York: Vintage, 1956.

Guevara, Ché. *Guerrilla Warfare.* New York: MR Press, 1961.

Gurr, Ted Robert. *Why Men Rebel.* Princeton, N.J.: Princeton University Press, 1970.

Gusfield, Joseph R. *Protest, Reform and Revolt: A Reader in Social Movements.* New York: John Wiley & Sons, 1970.

Jacobs, Paul, and Landau, Saul. *The New Radicals.* New York: Vintage, 1966.

James, Daniel (ed.) *The Complete Bolivian Diary of Che Guevara* (with an introduction by Daniel James). New York: Stein Day Publishers, 1968.

Jansen, C. H. *Militant Islam.* New York: Harper & Row, 1980.

Kaplan, Lawrence. *Revolutions: A Comparative Study From Cromwell to Castro.* New York: Vintage Books, 1973.

Lamb, Robert, et al. *Political Alienation.* New York: St. Martin, 1975.

Lipset, Seymour Martin, and Altbach, Philip G. (eds.). *Students in Revolt.* Boston: Houghton Mifflin, 1969.

Long, Priscilla (ed.). *The New Left: A Collection of Essays.* Boston: Porter Sargent, 1970.

Marcuse, Herbert. *One-Dimensional Man.* Boston: Beacon Press, 1968.

Murchland, Bernard. *The Age of Alienation.* New York: Random House, 1971.

Olman, B. *Alienation.* New York: Cambridge U.P., 1977.

Orwell, George. *1984.* A Signet Classic. New York: New American Library, 1949.

Reich, Charles. *The Greening of America.* New York: Bantam, 1971.

Roszak, Theodore. *The Making of a Counter-Culture.* New York: Doubleday, 1969.

Rudi, George. *Ideology and Popular Protest.* New York: Pantheon Books, 1980.

Sale, Kirkpatrick. *SDS.* New York: Vintage, 1973.

Smith, Donald E. *Religion, Politics and Social Change in the Third World.* New York: The Free Press, 1971.

Teodori, Massimo (ed.). *The New Left: A Documentary History.* New York: Bobbs-Merrill, 1969.

Tolstoy, Leo. *The Law of Love and the Law of Violence.* New York: Holt, Rinehart & Winston, 1970.

Touraine, Alain. *The May Movement.* New York: Random House, 1971.

von der Mehden, Fred R. *Comparative Political Violence.* New Jersey: Prentice-Hall, 1973.

Woodcock, George, and Avakumovic, Ivan. *The Anarchist Prince.* New York: Kraus Reprint, 1970.

12 | *Nationalism*

All those who live within the borders of the Roman empire are Roman citizens.
EDICT OF EMPEROR CARACALLA, 212 A.D.

Without a country . . . you are the bastards of humanity. Soldiers without banner . . . you will find neither faith nor protection.
MAZZINI "The Duties of Man"
To the Italians in the mid-nineteenth century.

People who watch the Olympics once every four years or who occasionally tune their TV to United Nations debates cannot help but marvel at the number of nation-states with their delegates, their flags, their athletes or diplomats, and their national anthems backed by armies and navies stressing the same themes — those of pride and strength, and unity and loyalty to the fatherland or the motherland. "Our fight for our land will never cease; it was ours and it will be ours forever and ever" (Uganda); "We will live crowned with glory or we swear with glory we will die" (Argentina); "Fatherland, fatherland . . . thy sons swear to breathe their last on thine altar" (Mexico); "Onward sons of *la patrie* . . . The day of glory is before you" (France); "Germany, Germany above all others" (West Germany); "My country 'tis of thee . . . ", and so on.

Ours is a world of nation-states. Nationalism has become one of the most tenacious ideological bonds binding human beings together into separate political communities. Its values may vary, its particular content may change, but fundamentally the nationalist feeling is described in terms of a common feeling of togetherness that identifies the "we" against the "they." Nations are invariably defined in terms of a *community* and in terms of the *loyalty* of the individual to the community. It is a community of values, a common heritage, a common history, a common character, a common race, a corporate will, a common soul. Loyalty is invariably described in terms of dedication, sacrifice, subordination, love, and affection. Nations are either a

267

motherland or a fatherland, evoking the obedience and affection that children owe to their parents.

Even if taken for granted, nationalism is a relatively recent ideology. It is a political ideology that developed in Europe in the latter part of the eighteenth century and throughout the nineteenth; it spread, after the end of World War II, to the Third World (the then colonies in Africa, Asia, and the Middle East).

Like all political ideologies, nationalism is an instrument for the acquisition of political power by certain groups, and the organization of political power on the basis of new principles — notably popular participation. Hugh Seton-Watson, in his book *Nations and States*, properly defines nationalism to be an ideology that "creates national consciousness within a politically unconscious population"[1] and he notes that its purpose was precisely the mobilization of a population behind new leaders and new leadership groups.

Nationalism was, and remains, a unifying and an integrative ideology manufacturing consent on the basis of strong common symbols and identification. It generates emotional supports, creates a state of exaltation and sacrifice, and provides for loyalty to new political elites. Nationalism solidifies a community, creates allegiance, establishes uniformities, and attempts to absorb the citizen into the purpose and the life of the nation-state. In the last analysis, nationalism tends to be a totalitarian ideology.

Nationality, Nation-States, and Nationalism

Some clarifications are needed in order to better understand the dynamics of nationalism.

Nationality denotes an ethnic and cultural identity. A *state,* on the other hand, is a political organization holding supreme power and exercising it through its various agencies over a given people within a given territory. A state may include a number of "nationalities" and the most outstanding example of such a state was the Austro-Hungarian Empire which until 1918 was a political and administrative organization governing Slavs, Slovenes, Croatians, Italians, Montenegrins, Hungarians, Poles, Austrians, Czechs, and quite a few others. A state, in other words, may be "multinational." The best examples today are the Soviet Union and Yugoslavia.

A *nation-state* exists when we have *both* a state and a nationality. Political power stems from and applies to a given national group within a given territory, so there may be nationalities without their own state, and there may also be states that do not derive their legitimacy and identity from a nationality. Catalonia is an example of the first and the Soviet Union an example of the latter.

Nationalism is the ideology that asserts the right of a given nationality to form a state and becomes a movement to attain it. Nationalism is an ideology that rationalizes such a demand; it becomes a powerful political movement

---

1. Seton-Watson. *Nations and States.* p. 449.

mobilizing all nationals to form their state. This was the case with the Greeks throughout the centuries of occupation by Turkey, with Poland as it attempted to reaffirm its nationhood by creating a Polish State; and it has notably been the case with most of the erstwhile colonies after World War II. Nationalism then, is the ideology that has led to the mushrooming of nation-states and continues to be an ideological force which propels every single nationality — no matter how small — to become a nation-state.

Objective Criteria of Nationality

The most common bases of nationality remain (a) religion; (b) language; (c) race; (d) a consciousness of common traditions and history and a will to maintain them; and (e) a common territory. But sometimes, as has been the case with the Jews and, occasionally, the Greeks, it is the *memory* of a territory occupied sometime in the past, and a desire to recover it, that has been the motivating influence. Different authors of nationalist movements have stressed, at different times, one or another of the various factors.

Religion was particularly important in the period of the formation of national consciousness and the assertion of political independence of nation-states in the sixteenth and seventeenth centuries. Religious wars were fought both to emancipate the State from the Papacy and also to create internal unity that was endangered both by Papal control from outside and by the existence of religious minorities inside. People were expected to hold, or were coerced into holding, the religion of their King.

Language is an important criterion for a number of authors, especially German. It was a common and distinct vehicle that bound people together creating a special bond among its users.

Race was used primarily in the twentieth century by the Nazis in order to "prove" the unique character of the German nation. It is supposed to refer to specific biological traits that are not always clearly perceived or agreed upon. *Ethnicity* is a broader term that may or may not include race but usually refers to a number of the common cultural attributes that we find in the term nationality.

The *common past* has been constantly invoked and when one could not easily be found, every effort was made to manufacture it by rewriting history.

Geography — a common territorial basis — is invariably invoked. Nations, like individuals, had to have a "home," a space under the sun.

Subjective Factors: Nationalism and Self-Determination

All the objective traits we have outlined — religion, language, common history, and so on — may exist, and may be commonly shared by a given "nationality." Nationalism becomes an ideology when this self-consciousness is translated into a political movement seeking statehood. The subjective element is an element of will and of purpose. It asserts the validity of the objective factors of nationality for *certain* political purposes; it affirms their uniqueness and often their exclusiveness. It is not only the will to live together but to have a government. It is the assertion that such a purpose has an inherent claim to be heard and to realize itself.

The nation-state may be viewed, therefore, as the creature of the individuals who make it up; it exists and derives its existence from the support and consent the individuals give to it. It is the result of a contract or of "a daily referendum."[2]

Nothing better exemplifies the differences between those who stress objective factors and those who rely upon subjective ones in defining a nation — the first relying upon history and tradition and the second upon individual will and consent — than the conflict between Germany and France over the provinces of Alsace and Lorraine. Renan, the French publicist, in his famous essay *What Is a Nation?* (1882), was willing to accept the verdict of the peoples of the area given through a referendum. German writers, on the other hand, asserted their claims in terms of historical right: "These provinces are ours by the right of the sword," wrote a German nationalist, "and we shall rule them by virtue of a higher right. . . . *We desire even against their will to restore them to themselves.*"[3]

Self-determination refers to the right of those who constitute a nationality with common religious, linguistic, and ethnic characteristics to form their own state. It became a doctrine when it was expressly stipulated in the famous Fourteen Points that President Woodrow Wilson issued to serve as the guidelines for building a new political order in Europe after World War I.

"Self-determination," Woodrow Wilson declared, "is an imperative principle of action, which statesmen will . . . ignore at their peril." He claimed that World War I "had its roots in the disregard of the rights of small nations and of nationalities which lacked the union and the force to make good their claim to determine their own allegiance and their own form of political life." He suggested among other things, in the form of guidelines for the Peace Conference that was to follow the end of the hostilities, "a readjustment of the frontiers of Italy . . . along clearly recognizable lines"; "the freest opportunity of autonomous development" for the peoples of Austria-Hungary; the redrawing of some of the frontiers in the Balkans "along historically established lines of allegiance and nationality"; "an absolutely unmolested opportunity of autonomous development" for the national minorities within Turkey; "an independent Polish state . . . inhabited by indisputably Polish populations."[4]

The French Revolution and the Nineteenth Century

It was the French Revolution of 1789 that, in line with some of Rousseau's theories, asserted the sovereignty of the people *and* the nation. But it was also the French Revolution in its various stages that highlighted the integrative

2. Ernest Renan. "What is a Nation?" in Hans Kohn (ed.). *Nationalism: Its Meaning and History.* Rev. ed., New York: Van Nostrand, 1965, pp. 135–40.
3. Cited by Karl W. Deutsch. *Nationalism and Social Communication.* New York: Wiley, 1953, p. 11.
4. Cited by Alan P. Grimes and Robert H. Horwitz. *Modern Political Ideologies.* New York: Oxford U.P., 1959, pp. 501–3.

and totalitarian dimensions of nationalism. The revolution began as an assertion of individual freedoms and popular sovereignty. It finished with an absolutist ruler and an expansionist nationalism that changed the map of Europe.

With the destruction of feudal privileges and the overthrow of the monarchy in 1792, the French Revolution quickly established patriotism as the highest ideal. Rituals, national festivals, symbolisms, and national songs were all used to create solidarity among the French. A system of national education was instituted to propagate patriotic values. Every attempt was made to wipe out regional and linguistic particularisms in favor of cultural unity, territorial integration, and centralization. The republic was to be "one and indivisible." Compliance with the revolution and its policies was promoted everywhere, requiring coercive measures that gradually were transformed into an outright tyranny. A revolutionary leader spoke of "the tyranny of liberty against despotism."

The last phase of the revolution produced an expansionist nationalism and a desire to conquer and subdue other peoples in the name of liberty *and* France. French men and women were made to conform to the nationalist

The Romantic painter Delacroix (1798–1863) painted "Mother-France" and her children flocking behind the flag and mounting the barricades in the name of Freedom. (*Photo: The Bettman Archive, Inc.*)

ideology: "The citizen is born, lives, and dies for the fatherland," was the inscription in every French municipality. "Oh sublime people! Accept the sacrifices of my whole being. Happy is the man who is born in your midst; happier is he who can die for your happiness," exclaimed the revolutionary leader, Robespierre. The citizen-patriot gradually became transformed into the citizen-soldier, ready to die for his country. A national army — the people in arms — was the inevitable corollary of nationalism.

Throughout nineteenth-century Europe, nationalism played the same important role in forging tightly integrated communities. It was strongly related to the rise of the middle classes and the destruction of feudal structures. Politically speaking, it became a vehicle for the acquisition of power by the middle classes by mobilizing the masses as they had never been mobilized before. Controlling "their minds and souls" was a source of far greater power than any ruler or class appealing to status, tradition, authority, or divine will had ever claimed or possessed before. No cosmopolitan idea, no internationalist efforts of any significance appeared to mitigate nationalisms. What is more, internationalist movements, developed in the name of liberalism and socialism and in the form of various international organizations, were ineffective in curbing nationalisms.

Traditional Nationalism

The French nationalism that came with and after the revolution of 1789 was an intensely ideological movement that broke with tradition and the past. It formulated a new way of life and shaped a new community integrated on the basis of common loyalties. This was not the case with traditional nationalism as it grew in response to French nationalism, especially in Germany. French nationalism was man-made and future-oriented. Traditional nationalism, on the other hand, sought its symbols of loyalty in the past — it was portrayed as a natural phenomenon, not an act of political will; it was to be found in the interstices of history.

German nationalists, influenced by Rousseau, naturally picked and chose from his writings what suited them best. Herder (1744–1803) sought the German national spirit in the people — the *Volk* — as it had developed from the time of the Germanic tribes. Herder also "legitimized" nations and nation-states by claiming that they were "willed" by God and that the diversity of nations represented His will. Men and women could best fulfill themselves within nations.

Traditional nationalism was reinforced not only by biological and racial arguments but also by cultural ones. The purity of the German language indicated, among other things, its cultural superiority. A German writer, Fichte (1762–1814), called upon Germany to assert its "cultural" supremacy. Some asked that all those speaking the German language be united into one fatherland. Others, long before the Nazis, asserted the racial purity of the Germans. Unification and independence was in the air and German philosophers extolled the state as the embodiment of the purest ideals of the Germans. It was the Prussian state that ultimately was to become the vehicle of German national unification in 1871.

What characterized German nationalism, therefore, was its conservative emphasis. It looked to the past; it appealed to the establishment groups; unlike the nationalism of the French Revolution, it was to be imposed by the ruling classes. The same was true with other nationalisms, notably the Russian one, stressing religion as one of its primary forces and only indirectly stressing race and language.

British and American Nationalisms

The early awakening of nationalism in England in the eighteenth century and in America in the decades before and after the Declaration of Independence were closely associated with individual freedoms and toleration. Pride in the Constitution and individual liberties, including religious freedom, characterized this early Anglo-Saxon form of nationalism. It derived from an individualistic ethic; it reflected the proclamation of the virtues and initiative of the individual, not of the collectivity. Even a conservative like Burke, who admired the British institutions, never subordinated religion and tradition to the State. He remained a committed patriot only as long as the nation-state served them well. One must love one's country only if it is "lovely."

As for the United States, the main assertion of nationalism lay in the creation of a constitution stressing individual liberties. The country remained wide open to immigration and, as succeeding waves of immigrants came from England, Scandinavia, Germany, Ireland, Italy, Poland, and elsewhere, it lost whatever particular ethnic, cultural, or religious characteristics it might have claimed. Past history — the Boston Tea Party, the battle of Lexington and Bunker Hill, and so on — retold in school lessons and in literature, strengthened and maintained the political symbolism of individual freedoms and constitutional government. American "nationalism" remained political in character: it meant an attachment to the Constitution and to the individual rights spelled out. It was civic loyalty that counted.

Both in England and in the United States, of course, the assertions that the fatherland is above the individual were made, but not as often and not as convincingly as in Europe. No nationalist ethic developed that subordinated the individual to the collectivity; no religious, historical, or cultural bonds were imposed upon the individuals in the name of the nation; no uniformities of thought and action were shaped in the name of an overriding national reality and goals.

Of course, such views about American and British nationalisms must be taken with a grain of salt. There were frequent assertions of national superiority in both countries — especially vis-à-vis other nationalities and people. In England, Rudyard Kipling — a poet — along with many others, spoke of the "white man's burden": the self-appointed duty for the British to civilize and educate the masses of the colonial peoples — "the lesser breeds," that were under their control. Both cultural and racist considerations entered into the formulation of English nationalism. In the United States, by the end of the nineteenth century, there was a strong nationalist ideology and vocabulary — there was a "manifest destiny" for Anglo-Saxon nations like the United States to play an important role in world affairs, and to assume its own share of domination and tutelage. Considerations that were religious, political, economic, and not infrequently racist entered into it. The effort to exact civic conformity and loyalty around national symbols was and remains ever present. Deviations from the national and political ethos of American liberalism have often been branded as "un-American" and at times became almost synonymous with treason.

Nationalism and the New Nations

Nation-states mushroomed in Europe throughout the nineteenth century and after World War I. But the rest of the world remained relatively immune to nationalism. Colonial empires — British, French, Dutch, Belgian, Portuguese — covered the whole of Asia (except for China and Japan), the Middle East, and Africa. In Africa, on the eve of World War II there were no independent states other than South Africa and Liberia. Today there are some thirty-five independent states in Africa, some sixteen in Asia, and nine in the Middle East, including Cyprus — about sixty new states in Africa, Asia, and the Middle East alone!

A number of factors that had been at work converged after World War II to bring forth the nationalist independence movements. One of the most important was the weakening of the European colonial powers and the emergence of two non-European powers, the United States, and the Soviet Union, both favoring, for different reasons, colonial emancipation and independence. Other major factors, however, can be traced into the past. The impact of Leninism was more recent; and still others related to special circumstances as they developed during and after World War II. Underlying all these independence movements was a political phenomenon: the growth of native elites aspiring to political power. As with European nationalisms, colonial nationalism became an ideology for mobilizing and organizing the quiescent masses. It proved to be a potent force, just as it had been in Europe ever since the French Revolution.

Long-range Factors: Assimilation to Rejection

In discussing long-range factors we must always keep in mind that nationalism is a mobilizing ideology. It incites people to action and calls for conformity and discipline. The strength of its appeal will depend, therefore, on the state of mind, the psychology and the level of awareness and of consciousness of the people involved. The catalyst that welds together various factors is a sense of moral indignation stemming from direct personal threat and humiliation: the history of the colonial independence movements shows that this was present after World War II.

The intrusion of the colonizers during the nineteenth century into Africa and Indochina, and much earlier in India and other Asiatic countries, undermined the organization, lifestyles, authority structures, and the economy of native societies. Traditional societies were opened up; the village life was disrupted; new forms of economic organization and production were introduced; and there was a massive exposure to new types of goods for consumption purposes. The traditional values of authority and deference and the group life that many tribal societies had practiced from time immemorial were seriously weakened. The child of European liberalism and capitalism, the individual, was fostered also in the colonial world.

For some the exposure to western influence was welcome. It was a chance to learn new ways. Indigenous elites sent their children abroad — to London, Paris, and elsewhere — to learn the new ways better. Some became assimilated, as was the case with French colonial natives, and some married French women. Assimilation of European ways and learning of European culture might have been one way to overcome colonial status. However, it was limited, as might be expected, to only a handful.

Whatever this minority sought to accomplish, however, in alliance with the colonial powers and their leaders, was thwarted for two reasons. First, the European elites — army, financiers, businesspeople, investors, administrators — were not willing to relinquish their roles, positions, and profits. The indigenous elites could play only a subordinate role. Second, there was the inevitable phenomenon of discrimination and inequality. The Europeans lived in their own world, with their own clubs, servants, schools, and hospitals, eating their own food and drinking their own water and liquor. They lived in a separate world that was equated with status. Natives could not penetrate it, even if they had studied at Oxford or the Sorbonne.

Together with the impenetrability of status went the difference in color, making the separation even more blatant. Gradually, therefore, it became clear that assimilation was not possible. "We could assimilate mathematics or the French language," wrote Leopold Senghor, a Senegalese leader and intellectual who had received his doctorate at the Sorbonne, "but we could never strip off our black skins or root out our black souls."[5]

The alternative to the unattainable goal of assimilation was rejection. The feeling of being discriminated against bred deep resentment against the colonial master and created the moral indignation which brings out the prophet and the saint. The destruction of the traditional patterns of existence produced a large population which had lost its attachments to authority and traditional lifestyles — one that began to discern, even in a confused way, the discrimination to which it was subjected, but even more, the deprivation to which it was condemned. Without structured and patterned relationships, moving from the countryside into the urban slums, isolated from each other, the indigenous populations became the *Wretched of the Earth*. Their color symbolized their lowly status, and sealed their fate. But they were easy to mobilize and organize, and they became the base of subsequent nationalist liberation movements.

5. In Sigmund. *The Ideologies of Developing Nations.* p. 248.

It was at this juncture that two of the most powerful European ideologies we have studied joined forces. Nationalism and Leninism combined to fashion the national independence movements in the colonial world. The ideological aspirations of these movements went even beyond what communism and nationalism could promise. There was, Kedourie claims,[6] a powerful millenialist spirit in the colonial world, something like the religious vision of the Second Coming. It promised a new heaven and a new earth. For the poor and the downtrodden a new vision of paradise also became a call for action.

It was a call for action that knew no limits. Nationalist guerrillas in Kenya, the Mau Mau, took the following chilling oath:

I speak the truth and vow before our God
That if I am called to go to fight the enemy
Or to kill the enemy — I shall go
Even if the enemy is my father and my mother, my brother or
    sister[7]

Nationalism

Colonial assertion of national independence borrowed directly from European nationalism: the same assertion of a natural right to be a nation; the same search in the past for tradition and culture in terms of which the claims could be justified, the same emphasis upon the basic factors of religion or language or ethnicity, as the occasion suited, and, finally, the same liberal vocabulary about equality, individual rights, and self-determination.

Where is the "Past"?   The Germans found their past in the Germanic tribes. The modern Greeks similarly had no difficulty: in their solemn declaration of independence on January 27, 1821, they asserted their glorious past to be the cornerstone of their future as a nation. "We, descendants of the wise and noble people of Hellas . . . believing it to be unlawful for us . . . to live henceforth in a state of slavery suitable to unreasoning animals than to rational beings . . ."[8]

In Africa, however, the search took many nations to a mythical past. Ethiopians found it in the Bible: "Ethiopia shall soon stretch out her hands unto God." Why not unto Eritrea and Somaliland as well? The Israelis, as Jews, claim valid historical credentials to most of the land they now have, including Jerusalem. African nations looked for past African empires such as existed in Mali and Ghana, and Arab nationalisms invariably found past glories in the days when Islam controlled most of North Africa and had moved deep into Spain. Pakistan also sought its own past in its Moslem heritage, as opposed to India's Hinduism, claiming to be the historically "oldest" of the ten nations that had existed in the Indian subcontinent.

6. Kedourie's *Nationalism in Asia and Africa* is an excellent anthology with a penetrating introduction by the author to whom I am indebted for both.
7. Cited in Kedourie, op. cit., pp. 466–68.
8. Cited in Kohn. *The Idea of Nationalism*, pp. 116–17.

What Language? The search for the past often meant the search for a language. Again, the example of the modern Greeks trying to resurrect the ancient Greek language illuminated the way for the new nations. "Every word in our language, with the exception of scientific terms must be in Turkish, if possible, and if not possible at least Turkified. . . ."[9] But language proved to be a serious problem for India and many of the African nations where tribal dialects could in no way coincide with national boundaries. English or French continue to be widely used.

Race Race began to play a prominent role and became a powerful motive in the rejection of the European colonialists. No other than Marcus Garvey, president general of the Universal Negro Improvement Association in the United States, had proclaimed the purity of the Negro race and the purity of the white race: he was against intermarriage. In his search for "ethnicity" for the blacks in Africa — what he called "negritude" — Leopold Senghor spoke of an "antiracial racialism." Negritude was the "whole complex of . . . values — cultural, economic, social and political — that characterize . . . the Negro African world."[10] God was declared by many black nationalists to be black. He was the "glorious Father of the blacks." One of the leaders of the Congo declared himself to be "the banner of the dominion of the black race." Race leads to the exaltation of its characteristics and suggests that every effort should be made to maintain its purity. Algerian and African leaders fell into disgrace because they had married European women.

Sometimes the search for identity in the past, in religion, in language, took on absurd manifestations. For instance, European-trained African doctors began to use magic and witchcraft for cures; and there were desperate efforts made to find and imitate primitive African art. But emphasis upon race was not exclusively anti-European and antiwhite. In East Africa and Southeast Asia race was used against diverse minorities, especially Chinese and Indians.

Irrespective of the many extreme manifestations, the independence movements had a genuine claim which could not be denied: self-determination and self-government. Its logic, since it had been advanced and practiced by the Europeans, was irresistible. Even pan-African movements failed to gain momentum in the face of claims for the national independence of specific populations in given areas. Thus, colonial nationalisms followed the footsteps of European nationalisms.

Leninism

Marxism appealed to many of the colonial elites seeking independence. It rejected liberal capitalism, which was taken to be synonymous with the capitalist exploitation of the colonial world, and it provided a vision of a new

9. Cited in Kedourie, op. cit., pp. 207–15.
10. Cited in Sigmund, op. cit., pp. 248–50.

world of equality and prosperity. But it was Leninism that had a far more profound impact, both because of its analysis and explicit condemnation of imperialism, and because it provided a theory and an organizational tool for revolution.

From a tactical point of view, as we saw earlier, Lenin considered colonies to be the "weakest link" in the capitalistic chain and pledged Soviet support to colonial national revolutionary movements. The second congress of the Third International in 1920 provided a number of "theses" on "national" and "colonial" questions.

> With regard to those states and nationalities where a backward, mainly feudal, patriarchal, or patriarchal-agrarian regime prevails, the following must be borne in mind: (1) All Communist Parties must give active support to the revolutionary movements of liberation. . . . (4) It is of special importance to support the peasant movements in backward countries against the landowners and all feudal survivals; above all, we must strive as far as possible to give the peasant movement a revolutionary character, to organize the peasants and all the exploited classes into the Soviets, and thus bring about the closest possible union between the Communist proletariat of Western Europe and the revolutionary peasant movement of the East and of the colonial and subject countries; . . . (5) It is the duty of the Communist International to support the revolutionary movement in the colonies and in the backward countries. . . .[11]

The Third International under the leadership of the Soviet Communist Party stressed, therefore, three basic elements in the struggle for colonial emancipation and independence: first, nationalism; second, an outright appeal to the peasantry (since both the middle classes and the proletariat were virtually nonexistent); and third, the role of a well-organized party to provide for leadership and direction, and to bring the people to the appropriate level of mobilization and militancy. It was to consist of trained revolutionaries.

National Independence Movements

The double impact of Leninism and nationalism, and particularly the adoption of political organization that was inspired by Lenin, accounted for the authoritarian and paramilitary characteristics of the national independence movements in many colonies. They purported to be "mass movements," including everybody who favored independence from the colonial power, but the leadership was carefully selected, trained and disciplined. Thus the base was as broadly popular as possible, but the leadership was exclusive. All liberation movements developed their own special armies to wage war against the colonial power — a war that could range from acts of sabotage and terrorism to full-fledged military ecounters. The party was the political arm

11. Cited in Kedourie, op. cit., "Theses of the Second Congress of the Communist International on the National and Colonial Questions," pp. 540–51.

acting on behalf of and organizing the people; the guerrillas were the military arm operating under the direction of the party but with the support of the people. Gradually national liberation movements became like states with their own army, tax collectors, tribunals, and political leaders and warriors.

As in Europe more than a century before, nationalism proved to be a very powerful ideological force in the colonial world. For the first time apathetic and indifferent populations became genuinely mobilized; they were gradually given a political consciousness and a cause. The national movements became vehicles for the acquisition of power by native elites while the native populations found in the independence wars an identity and a sublimation of anonymity and past miseries. Above all, they were given hope about their future. Thus, nationalism, skillfully manipulated by a small group of leaders, gradually asserted itself to lead virtually all colonies to independence and statehood.

The Nation-State and Ethnonationalisms: Current Trends

Nation-states, it appears, are beginning to get an unpleasant taste of the heady medicine of nationalism which first brought them into being. It is what has been referred to as *ethnonationalism* — the search for and expression *within* the nation-state of particular ethnic, cultural, regional, religious, or linguistic autonomies. These separatist movements range from demands for outright independence and the assumption of statehood to claims for "self-government."

Such manifestations sometimes have a clear-cut territorial base — linguistic, ethnic, religious, racial, or cultural groupings are easily identifiable within a given region of the nation-state. For instance, the French-speaking minority in Canada, which is also predominantly Catholic, lives in Quebec — one province of the Canadian federation. So do the Georgians or Uzbecks or Ukranians in the Soviet Union; the Corsicans and the Bretons in France; the Scots and the Welsh in the United Kingdom; Sicilians in Italy; some native American tribes in the United States; the Ibos in Nigeria — all these ethnic groups are located in certain regions of the respective states in which they live.

But not infrequently a territorial identification of an ethnic minority is difficult. The particular people that share the specific ethnic attributes may be spread throughout the nation-state. This is the case, for instance, with the blacks in the United States, with the Protestants in France, the Catholics in England, the Armenians in the Soviet Union. It is not easy to draw a clear territorial line to separate the Walloons from the Flamands in Belgium.

In addition to ethnonationalism, and at times paralleling it, there are manifestations which, for lack of a better term, may be called *loconationalisms*. The assertion of local autonomy in these cases is based explicitly and uniquely on *political considerations*, that is, on the demands made by people in regions, localities, and at times even neighborhoods, to govern themselves and control their own affairs.

Ethnonationalist and Loconationalist Ideologies

Ethnonationalist movements have become so widespread that it is just as difficult to generalize about them as it is to undertake a detailed study of all of them. There is virtually no modern nation-state where the phenomenon is not present. In each and every case they have generated ideological movements of varying degrees of intensity which assume the following patterns: (a) they are downright *nationalist,* borrowing from the nineteenth-century ideology of nationalism; (b) they are *reformist,* calling for administration reforms of the nation-state in the direction of increased federalism and decentralization; (c) despite their professed attachment to local, communal, and regional values they project, at the same time, a vision that is *transnational.* These are revolutionary ethnonationalist movements; (d) some attempt to reformulate a theory of democracy by stressing *direct participation as well as loyalty and control* by the citizens within local or small units, very much along the lines suggested by the advocates of the New Left.

Many explanations have been advanced for the phenomenon of ethnonationalism and loconationalism. They range from self-determination to assertions of individul spontaneity and freedom. Economic theories have also stressed the discrepancies in wealth between regions and localities within one and the same state, stemming from the exploitation of the poorer areas by the wealthier ones. Arguments about efficiency have also been advanced; they claim that the centralized bureaucracy of the nation-state tends to be wasteful, while small local services could handle more efficiently and less expensively the unique local problems.

One response to separatist demands stemming from ethnonationalist movements is administrative: "decentralization," so that a given ethnic group living in a given region may assume many of the powers of the nation-state — without seceding from it. Such a decentralization may take a number of forms that generally amount to "regional government" or "local government," but decentralization may reach a point where the regional units assume powers that are virtually coequal with the powers of the nation-state within which they exist. They may not be bound by decisions made by the national organs unless they consent to them. This is an extreme form of confederalism, in which a long and careful process of negotiations and agreements by all units is required before a decision is made. If it fails to provide for an agreement no decision can be made.

In all these cases the authority of the nation-state is gutted and it is the ethnic territorial entities that assume the power to decide. The nation-state simply tries to reconcile itself and some of its institutions to internal national, ethnic, religious, and group forces that it can no longer control because they have shed their loyalties to it. Larger nationalisms give place to smaller ones.

Large or small nationalisms seem to have become the most pervasive force and ideology of our times. Nationalism shapes the minds and the attachments of all of us in a world that is witnessing a constant proliferation of nation-states. It provided a moment of exaltation to the Argentines when they sent their navy and army into the Falkland Islands (the Malvinas as they call them) miscalculating the immediate and profound nationalist response on the part of the British. A bitter war went on for three months over these remote and inhospitable islands that involved emotionally both British and Argentines. Nothing could show better how seductive the old time religion of nationalism remains. Like Rupert Brooke, a young British poet buried on a small Greek island after dying in combat in World War I, many of the British soldiers whose burial place will be in the Falklands will continue to whisper to the generations to come:

> Think only this of me:
> That there is a corner of a foreign field
> That is forever England . . .
> A dust whom England bore, shaped, made aware.

If nationalism is, as it has been alleged, "the last refuge of scoundrels," most of us continue to remain scoundrels in our hearts and minds!

Bibliography

Betts, Raymond F. *Assimilation and Association in French Colonial Theory 1890–1914*. New York: TMS Press, 1970.

Emerson, Rupert: *From Empire to Nation: The Rise of Self-Assertion of Asian and African Peoples*. Cambridge, Mass.: Harvard U.P., 1960.

Gerassi, John. *The Coming of the New International*. New York: World Publishing, 1971.

Hinsley, F. H. *Nationalism and the International System*. London: Hodder and Stoughton, 1973.

Hobson, John A. *Imperialism*. Ann Arbor: University of Michigan Press, 1965.

Kedourie, Elie. *Nationalism*. Rev. ed., London: Hutchinson, 1961.

———. *Nationalism in Asia and Africa*. London: World Publishing, 1970.

Kilson, Martin (ed.). *New States in the Modern World*. Cambridge, Mass.: Harvard U.P., 1975.

Kohn, Hans. *Nationalism: Its Meaning and History*. Rev. ed., New York: Van Nostrand, 1965.

———. *The Idea of Nationalism*. New York: Collier, 1967.

Schuster, Derek. *Bad Blood Among Brothers: An Inside View Behind Today's Separatist Movement*. New York: Vantage, 1962.

Seton-Watson, H. *Nations and States*. Boulder, Colo.: Westview, 1977.

Sigmund, Paul E. (ed.). *The Ideologies of the Developing Nations*. 2nd rev. ed. New York: Praeger, 1972.

Smith, Anthony. *Theories of Nationalism*. London: Duckworth, 1971.

Von Der Mehden, Fred R. *Politics of the Developing Nations*. 2nd ed. Englewood Cliffs, N.J.: Prentice-Hall, 1969.

Waltz, Kenneth W. *Man, The State at War: A Theoretical Analysis*. New York: Columbia U.P., 1954.

Index

Change: British conservatives' opposition to, 78, 80–81; Chinese commitment to, 158–161

Chartism, 49–50

Chiang Kai-shek, 153, 154, 155, 156, 157

Chinese Communist Party, 133, 151–153, 155, 156, 157–158, 160. *See also* Maoism

Church: reaction to Nazi Party, 195–196; resistance of Italian fascism, 205–207

Civil liberty, 24–25

Civil service, response to Nazism, 195

Class struggle: in Eurocommunist theory, 162–163; in Marxist theory, 106–107; Nazi Party rejection of, 188–189

Collectivism: and anarchy, 242; communists' commitment to, 95, 109, 144, 160; socialists' commitment to, 52–53

Colonial independence movements, 165–167; and assertion of identity, 276–277; assimilation to rejection, 274–276; leadership of, 278; and Leninism, 114–120, 277–278; and revolution, 257, 259. *See also* Nationalism

Cominform, 131–132, 133

Common law, and British conservatism, 78

Communism, 92–93; American extremists' opposition to, 225, 226–228; crisis of, 167–168; defined, 94–97; Eurocommunism, 68, 162–165, Nazi Party's opposition to, 183, 190; New Left opposition to, 243; in Third World, 165–167; and totalitarianism, 92–93. *See also* Communist revolution, dynamics of; Leninism; Maoism; Marxism; Soviet communism; Stalinism; Titoism

Communist Information Bureau, 131–132, 133

Communist Manifesto, The (Marx), 46, 95, 110

Communist revolution, dynamics of: philosophy of history, 103–105; theory of class struggle, 106–107; theory of revolution, 108; theory of State, 107–108; utopian communism, 108–110. *See also* Capitalism; Communism; Marxism

Communitarianism, in Nazi ideology, 192, 193

Competition, conservatives' attitudes toward, 80, 88

Congress of Paris, 257

Consent, individual, in liberalism, 32, 36

Conservatism, 73–74. *See also* American conservatism; British conservatism

Constitution, American, 24, 35–36; and conservatives, 83–85

Constitution, British, 75–76, 78

Constitutionalism, 35–36, 43

Contracts, in liberal economy, 26, 32; conservatives' aversion to, 76

Corporatism: of fascist Italy, 208–209; of Franquismo, 220, 222

Coughlin, Father Charles, 225–226

Counterculture, of New Left, 253–255; anarchism, 252, 255; participation and quality of life, 255–256. *See also* New Left movement

Cuba, 259

Cultural Revolution, Chinese, 159, 160–161. *See also* Maoism

Custom, British conservatives' belief in, 75–76, 81

Darwin, Charles, 175

Debray, Regis, 261

Debs, Eugene, 111

Decentralization, economic: communist, 167; of Maoism, 156; of Titoism, 145–147

Declaration of the Rights of Man, 24

Democracy: crisis of, 62–65; defined, 19–21; and Eurocommunism, 163–164; and fascism, 198–200, 202; and Leninism, 117–118; in Marxism, 108; and Nazism, 189, 194; prospects of, 63; in Stalinism, 124, 125; in Third World, 69–71, 166–167; and Titoism, 147–149. *See also* Conservatism; Democratic socialism; Liberal democracy; Radical democrats

Democratic centralism: in Eurocommunism, 164; of Lenin's Communist Party, 117–118, 120, 129; in Maoism, 157–158; Stalin's abolishment of, 124

Democratic dictatorship, 69–70

Democratic party convention, and New Left, 245

Democratic socialism: in America, 59–61; defined, 53–54; and democrat-socialist synthesis, 58–61; and European revisionism, 56–58; Fabians, 54–56. *See also* Liberal democracy; Socialism

Denitch, Bogdan, 148

Depression, of 1929. *See* Great Depression

DePugh, Robert, 228

Deutscher, Isaac, 127

Dialectic idealism, 104

Dialectic materialism, 105, 112. *See also* Marxism

Dictatorship: democratic, 69–70; of proletariat, 109, 112, 116, 121, 125, 135, 151

Disraeli, Benjamin, 44, 81

Djilas, Milovan, 128, 137

DuBois, W. E. B., 257

Economic core, of liberalism, 25–26; and democrat-socialist synthesis, 58–61; radical democrats' opposition to, 49–50, 51; socialist opposition to, 52, 54, 58, 59

Economic democracy: in France, 68; in Titoism, 145–146

Economic determinism, 107–108, 113

Economic individualism, 22–23, 26–28; conservatives' attitudes toward, 81, 85, 86–89

Economic policy: in Communist China, 159–160; in fascist Italy, 208–209; liberal, 44–45; in Nazi Germany, 197; of New Left, 257–264; in Soviet Union, 125–126, 135, 167; in Yugoslavia, 144–147, 150

Elitism: in conservatism, 74, 79–80; of Soviet Communist Party, 116–118, 124; of totalitarianism, 173

Engels, Friedrich, 97, 98, 108, 109–110

England. *See* Britain

Enlightened self-interest, 30–32. *See also* Utilitarianism.

Escape from Freedom (Fromm), 177, 212

Ethnonationalism, 279–281. *See also* Nationalism

Eurocommunism, 133, 138, 162–165; class struggle and revolution, 162–163; democratic centralism of, 164; foreign policy of, 164–165; nationalism of, 164; and parliamentary democracy, 165. *See also* Communism

European revisionism, 56–58

Evolutionary Socialism (Bernstein), 57

Expansionism: of Italian fascists, 198; in Nazi ideology, 191–192

Explosion, of New Left movement, 252–253

Extremism, American, 223–230

Fabian Essays, The, 54

Fabians, 54–56

Falangists, 220, 221–222

Falkland Islands, 281

Fanon, Franz, 258–259

Farmers, reaction to Nazi Party, 187, 188, 196

Fascism, Italian, 92, 198–200; corporatism of, 208–209; development of party, 204–205; historical background for, 178–181; ideology of, 202–203, 210; intellectual roots of, 173–178; leadership in, 203–204; resistance to, 205–208; rise of, 200–201; theories on causes of, 210–214. *See also* Nazism; Totalitarianism

Fascist Party, Italian, 198–201, 204–205

Federalist papers, 83, 84

Felicific calculus, 28, 29

Fichte, Johann G., 272

Foreign policy: of communist Yugoslavia, 149–150; of Eurocommunism, 164–165

France: communism in, 163–165; emergence of political parties in, 44; liberal reform of, 42–43, 44, 50; New Left movement in, 243–245; radical democrats in, 50–51; socialism in, 53, 59, 67–69, 110–111

Franco, General Francisco, 219–223

Franquismo authoritarianism, 219–223

French Revolution, 106, 191, 270–272

French Socialist Party, 67–69, 110–111

Friedman, Milton and Rose, 89

Fromm, Erich, 177, 212

Gambetta, Jules, 50–51

Gandhi, Mahatma Mahandas, 235

Garvey, Marcus, 277

German Social Democratic Party, 66, 111

Germany: emergence of political parties in, 44; nationalism in, 112, 191, 194, 272–273; rise of totalitarianism in, 178–181, 183–185; socialism in, 53, 59, 66, 67, 68

Goethe, Johann von, 259

Gompers, Samuel, 83

Gramsci, Antonio, 163, 237

Great Depression, 85, 179–180

Great Leap Forward, 159, 160

Greece, 19, 68

Group mind, in political ideology, 173

Guerrilla warfare, 65; Mao's theory of, 153, 156–157; of Minutemen, 228; revolutionary, 259–262

Guevara, Ché, 165, 260–262

Gulag Archipelago (Solzhenitsyn), 133

Handlin, Oscar, 247

Hedonistic orientation, of utilitarianism, 28–30

Hegel, G. W. F. 97, 104–105, 107, 236, 241

Herder, Johann von, 272

Herr, Richard, 222

History, Marxist philosophy of, 103–105

Hitler, Adolph, 171, 174, 185, 200. *See also* Nazism

Hitler Student League, 186

Hitler Youth, 186, 187

Holland, socialism in, 53, 59, 111

Hoover, Herbert, 85

Hundred Flowers campaign, Chinese, 159, 160

Huxley, Aldous, 92

Idealism, 104, 241–242

Ideology: criteria for, 15–16; defined, 2–4; inherent and derived, 236–237, 262–263; major themes of, 4–9; for the New Left, 250–252; and revolution, 236–237; types of, 13–15; uses of, 9–13

Imagination, revolution of, 252–253. *See also* New Left movement

Imperialism, the Highest Stage of Capitalism (Lenin), 114, 119

Individualism: of British conservatives, 81; in Italian fascism, 202–203; of liberalism, 22–23; in Nazism, 192; in New Left movement, 248–250. *See also* Liberal democracy

Individual rights, in liberalism, 38–40

Industrialization: and alienation of individual, 247–248; of Communist China, 159–160; of Soviet Union, 125–126; of Yugoslavia, 144. *See also* Capitalism; Economic policy

International communism, 133

International Working Men's Association (First International), 110

Iranian revolution, 263–265

Irrationalism, of totalitarianism, 174

Italy: communism in, 132, 163–165; rise of totalitarianism in, 81–85; socialism in, 59, 66–67, 68, 111. *See also* Fascism, Italian

Jews. *See* Anti-Semitism

John Birch Society, 227–228

Kautsky, Karl, 67

Kedourie, Elie, 276

Kennedy, John F., 86

Kenyatta, Jomo, 70

Khomeini, Ayatollah Ruhollah, 263–265

Wallas, Graham, 55
Wealth of Nations, The (Smith), 20, 26–28
Webb, Sidney and Beatrice, 55
Welfare State, 20, 39; and conservatism, 80–81, 87
What is to be Done? (Lenin), 114
What is a Nation? (Renan), 270
Wilson, Woodrow, 270
Workers: alienation of, 248; and anarchism, 242; in
  Frantz Fanon, 258; and the French New Left, 245;
  and Italian fascism, 200, 208; in Marxism, 106–107,
  116–117, 120; and Nazism, 187, 188, 196–197

Worker's Councils, Yugoslavian, 146–147, 148
World War One, 179, 183
World as Will and Idea, The (Schopenhauer), 174

Youth International Party (Yippies), 245
Youth organizations: Italian fascist, 205, 207; Nazi, 186,
  187
Yugoslav Communist Party, 132, 133, 141–144. *See also*
  Titoism